The United States and the Americas

Lester D. Langley, General Editor

This series is dedicated to a broader understanding of the political, economic, and especially cultural forces and issues that have shaped the Western hemispheric experience — its governments and its peoples. Individual volumes assess relations between the United States and its neighbors to the south and north: Mexico, Central America, Cuba, the Dominican Republic, Haiti, Panama, Colombia, Venezuela, Peru, Ecuador, Bolivia, Brazil, Paraguay, Argentina, Chile, and Canada.

The United States and the Americas

Brazil and the United States

Joseph Smith

Brazil and the United States: Convergence and Divergence

The University of Georgia Press
Athens & London

Material from *Unequal Giants: Diplomatic Relations between the United States and Brazil, 1889–1930*, by Joseph Smith © 1991. Reprinted by permission of the University of Pittsburgh Press.

Printed digitally in the United States of America

Library of Congress Cataloging-in-Publication Data

Smith, Joseph, 1945–
Brazil and the United States : convergence and divergence / Joseph Smith.
    p.   cm. — (The United States and the Americas)
Includes bibliographical references and index.
ISBN-13: 978-0-8203-2769-3 (hardcover : alk. paper)
ISBN-10: 0-8203-2769-7 (hardcover : alk. paper)
ISBN-13: 978-0-8203-2770-9 (pbk. : alk. paper)
ISBN-10: 0-8203-2770-0 (pbk. : alk. paper)
1. United States — Foreign relations — Brazil.
2. Brazil — Foreign relations — United States. I. Title.
E183.8.B7S54 2010
327.73081 — dc22   2010005964

British Library Cataloging-in-Publication Data available

Contents

Acknowledgments

I wish first to thank Lester Langley for inviting me to do this book and be a contributor to his much acclaimed series. It has certainly been a hard assignment, but completion was greatly assisted by Lester's guidance and encouragement. I am also grateful to Mike Conniff, who read the manuscript and gave me his expert advice. I wish also to thank Luiz Alberto Moniz Bandeira for his kindness in keeping me abreast of his published works. As always, however, my greatest personal debt is to Rachael for her enduring support and understanding.

The United States and the Americas

Brazil and the United States

Introduction

To the people of the United States, Brazil has historically been regarded as a distant and virtually unknown country — stereotypically a tropical
land of palms, coffee, and carnival and whose racially mixed society has more
in common with Africa than the Americas. Contact between the two countries
has long been made difficult by geographical remoteness, adverse trade winds,
and different languages, history, and culture. In addition, there is no shared
common border as Americans have with Canada and Mexico, or no relatively
easy access by sea as with Cuba, or strategic significance as with Panama. Brazil
has, therefore, rarely impinged on American consciousness. While it is known
to be a huge country — as big as the United States with a large and expanding
population, vast natural resources and marvelous economic potential — it has
never posed a military threat to U.S. national security or presented an ideological challenge to the American way of life.

Moreover, in terms of diplomatic relations, the United States has historically found Brazil to be very receptive and generally willing to cooperate
on hemispheric and international issues. This friendly feeling has provided
Washington with a welcome relief and counterweight to the antagonistic relationship that has often existed between the United States and several of the
Spanish-American countries. In fact, historians have referred to an "unwritten alliance" in which the national interests of the United States and Brazil
have converged so that Brazilian diplomacy has acted as a bridge in helping
to facilitate many of the policy initiatives undertaken by the United States in
hemispheric affairs.

For the people of Brazil, the conventional image of the United States has
been of the "colossus of the north," an economic powerhouse where people are
devoted to the Protestant ethic of working hard and making money. Despite
admiration for its political stability and economic success, Brazilians have also
perceived American society as marked by racial discrimination and segrega-
tion and contrasting unfavorably with Brazil's more humane and tolerant idea
of "racial democracy." Until the advent of the airplane and mass media, travel

1

and cultural exchange between the two countries were greatly restricted by geographical distance, different languages, and disparate levels of educational attainment and discretionary income. The main contact has been through business and especially the trade in coffee that made the United States the largest single market for Brazilian exports.

Brazil was aware of U.S. territorial expansionism in the nineteenth century and, on occasion, has expressed suspicion of alleged American imperialist designs on the Northeast and the Amazon region. The distant geographical location of the United States, however, meant that it has not been regarded as a serious military danger to Brazilian national security. This has contrasted with the long-standing Brazilian sense of continental isolation and concern over the threat to its borders posed by Spanish-American neighbors. As a former colony of Portugal, Brazilians considered themselves to be culturally apart and historically different from the Spanish-American countries of Latin America. These nations traditionally observed Brazil's seemingly relentless exploration and settlement of the interior of the South American continent with suspicion. In particular, Brazil felt challenged by the rise of its powerful neighbor, Argentina. Looking for external support, Brazil has turned to the United States as a natural ally because that nation not only was powerful but also represented an Anglo-Saxon rather than a Spanish historical and cultural background. Moreover, fearful of racial violence in the nineteenth century and revolutionary disorder for much of the twentieth century, the Brazilian elite has viewed the United States as a force for maintaining political, financial, and social stability.

The high point of diplomatic collaboration between Brazil and the United States was the period of "approximation" associated with the Baron of Rio Branco and Joaquim Nabuco at the beginning of the twentieth century. In return for supporting U.S. foreign policy aims, Brazil expected to be the beneficiary of a privileged relationship. This materialized in the form of U.S. help to settle border disputes and also encouragement for Brazil's aspiration to be the leading power in South America and to play an active role in extra-hemispheric affairs. A similar strategy motivated the Brazilian decisions to join the side of the United States in World War I in 1917 and World War II in 1942. Both instances pleased the United States because they provided moral and material support, especially access to valuable Brazilian strategic materials.

Moreover, Brazil's cooperative policy notably contrasted with Argentina and was rewarded with economic and military benefits, especially in World War II when substantial U.S. Lend-Lease aid enabled Brazil to surpass Argentina and become the leading military power in South America.

But U.S.-Brazilian relations did not always run smoothly. Quite simply, U.S. officials from their vantage point in Washington usually regarded Brazil and the rest of South America as peripheral to the foreign policy interests of the United States. Much closer attention was directed to the affairs of neighboring Mexico and the "backyard" nations of Central America and the Caribbean, especially Cuba. After 1945 the United States became a superpower with global interests beyond the Western Hemisphere. Except for the 1906 Rio Pan-American Conference and the period of wartime cooperation during World War II, the United States took Brazil's friendship for granted and did not give it any special significance. Even while Rio Branco was serving as foreign minister and Nabuco was ambassador in Washington, the fragility of approximation was demonstrated by the refusal of the U.S. government to side with Brazil against Argentina over the naval arms race. Brazil's expectations of receiving preferential U.S. economic assistance after the end of World War II were given short shrift in Washington even though considerable sums were allocated to European reconstruction. During the 1950s Brazilians became irritated by constant U.S. lecturing and preaching on the virtues of free enterprise and private investment, while U.S. officials arrogantly regarded Brazilian governments as incorrigibly spendthrift and profligate. At the end of the twentieth century and into the twenty-first century divergent interests clearly emerged, and there has been persistent friction over commercial issues relating to tariffs, surcharges, and blacklists.

Most of all, Brazilians resented what they perceived as unacceptable interference in their domestic affairs and slights to national honor. In 1864 an official apology was demanded from the U.S. government for the seizure of the Confederate cruiser *Florida* at Salvador da Bahia. In 1902 the Amazon River was closed to foreign shipping to demonstrate Brazil's concern over U.S.-sponsored business activities in the disputed Acre region. Despite the widespread popular belief that the U.S. embassy ran political affairs in Brazil and was responsible for the 1964 coup that overthrew João Goulart, there was little that U.S. officials could do to moderate the repressive policies imposed by the subsequent military governments. When the U.S. Congress criticized Brazil's record on human rights in 1977, the Brazilian government was so incensed that it retaliated by unilaterally canceling the existing 1952 military agreement. Brazil's response to U.S. pressure in these instances reflected national pride and a determination to assert sovereign rights. This did not necessarily imply a sustained state of serious conflict or even divergence with Washington because Brazil's sense of national identity and purpose was not by definition anti-American. Moreover, the historical record from Emperor Pedro I to President Lula da Silva demonstrated that so long as the two countries shared common aims in seeking political order, economic prosperity, and hemispheric security, the diplomatic relationship would remain friendly and cooperative.

Chapter 1 of this book examines the establishment and development of bilateral relations during the nineteenth century. With the exception of a brief flurry of activity over U.S. recognition of the Brazilian empire in 1824, both countries had little diplomatic contact with each other. A modest but profitable commercial relationship was started and notably included the coffee trade that established the United States as the largest single market for Brazilian exports. In terms of overall commercial relations, however, Brazil was much closer to Great Britain than to the United States.

Chapter 2 covers the emergence of "Pan-Americanism" at the close of the nineteenth century, a period when the United States actively sought to expand its political and commercial contact with Latin America. The timing was opportune for improving U.S.-Brazilian relations because the newly created Brazilian republic was eager to secure U.S. diplomatic endorsement. Brazil contrasted with most Spanish-American nations in feeling less threatened by the more assertive role assumed by the United States in hemispheric affairs.

Chapter 3 considers the convergence of national interests during the first decade of the twentieth century and how this was exemplified in Brazil's strategy of "approximating" its foreign policy to that pursued by the United States. The inherent weakness of approximation was revealed by Washington's unwillingness to support Brazil against Argentina. The outbreak of World War I, however, accelerated closer economic contact between the United States and Brazil. One of the main reasons for Brazil joining the war in 1917 was the calculation that close association with the United States would not only result in economic gains but also assist its ambition to be the leading power in South America.

Chapter 4 examines Brazil's attempt to play an active role in world affairs during the 1920s, culminating in the failure to secure a permanent seat on the Council of the League of Nations. As Brazil turned inward, it also experienced growing economic and political crises. U.S. officials were surprised by the military rising in 1930 and hesitated to recognize the new regime of Getúlio Vargas. Relations improved when Vargas responded favorably to the "Good Neighbor" policy advocated by President Franklin D. Roosevelt.

Chapter 5 explains why U.S. officials were disturbed by the perceived fascist sympathies of Vargas and the establishment of the Estado Novo in 1937. A particular concern was the flourishing economic relationship between Brazil and Nazi Germany. World War II, however, ended the German economic challenge and brought close links between the United States and Brazil just as in the previous war. The reward was substantial U.S. financial and material assistance that enabled Brazil to surpass Argentina as the leading military power in South America. In addition, the participation of the Brazilian Expeditionary Force (FEB) in the Italian campaign encouraged Brazil once again to aspire to the status of a world power.

Chapter 6 stresses that throughout the 1950s Brazilian diplomacy sought U.S. loans to fund large-scale projects for industrial development and economic modernization. In 1958 President Juscelino Kubitschek proposed "Operation Pan America," but a negative response was forthcoming from Washington. U.S. complacency toward Latin America markedly changed as a result of growing anxiety over the perceived inroads of International Communism in the Western Hemisphere. In Brazil, this took the form of American irritation at the "independent" foreign policy proclaimed by Presidents Jânio Quadros and João Goulart. Covert U.S. financial assistance was given to Goulart's political opponents in the 1962 elections, while close personal relations were cultivated with the senior military officers who launched the coup that overthrew Goulart in 1964.

Chapter 7 shows that U.S. officials wished for the restoration of democracy and proved unable to moderate the repressive policy of a succession of Brazilian military governments. Moreover, Brazilian diplomacy began to emphasize a "nationalist" approach that resulted in tension with the United States especially over respect for human rights and the proliferation of nuclear power. During the 1980s economic factors brought about a return to closer cooperation because Brazil needed U.S. diplomatic and financial assistance in order to negotiate satisfactory terms for a resolution of the Debt Crisis. The United States, however, diverged from Brazil by forming NAFTA (North American Free Trade Agreement), while Brazil opted instead for a separate customs union known as Mercosur.

The epilogue covers the period of the presidencies of Fernando Henrique Cardoso and Luis Inácio "Lula" da Silva and concludes that despite disagreements over trade and certain foreign policy issues, both countries share common national interests and agree that these are best served and promoted by maintaining a friendly and cooperative relationship.

1 The South American Empire

"Brazil is, next to ourselves, the great power on the American continent," remarked the U.S. minister to Brazil, James Watson Webb, in 1867.[1] That observation, however, did not reflect the special historical relationship between the two giants of the Western Hemisphere. During the colonial period when Brazil was under Portugal's control and the North American colonies were ruled by Britain, geographical distance and restrictive mercantilist policies limited contact between the people of the two regions. At the end of the eighteenth century, political differences were accentuated as the United States became a republic with a pronounced disdain for Old World diplomatic practice. U.S. leaders, however, took a pragmatic approach by establishing diplomatic relations with Portugal. More than three decades later in 1824, the Monroe administration demonstrated a similar realism and sought to gain short-term political and economic advantages by recognizing the newly independent Brazilian empire before Great Britain.

The flurry of diplomatic activity in 1824 was brief and atypical. For the next half century both Brazil and the United States pursued expansive territorial policies, but they were so geographically remote from each other that their national interests rarely converged. The notable exception was trade. Despite initial U.S. optimism, commercial activity proved relatively modest. In fact, the balance of trade was invariably in Brazil's favor, a trend that was increased by the growing U.S. demand for coffee, which made it the largest single market for Brazilian exports. In terms of overall commercial relations, however, Brazil was much closer to Europe than to the United States. During the nineteenth century the nation most admired by the Brazilian elite was Great Britain, which "ruled the waves" and was "the workshop of the world." By comparison, the Brazilians regarded the United States as a much less significant power and cultural role model. In fact, diplomatic relations were often strained by the superior and overbearing attitude of U.S. diplomats serving in Brazil. The Americans might have likened the South American empire to their own coun-

7

try in terms of geographical size and economic potential, but they were not prepared to grant it equal status.

Diplomatic Relations with the Portuguese Court

When the United States became an independent nation in the 1780s, Brazil was still a colony of Portugal, a status that had lasted almost three centuries. After putting aside its moral misgivings about the aristocratic Old World's diplomatic malpractices, the new republic's government established formal relations with all the European powers, including Portugal. David Humphreys of Connecticut presented his credentials as U.S. minister resident at the Portuguese court in Lisbon on May 13, 1791. Humphreys served until 1797 and was replaced by South Carolina's William Smith, who stayed at his post until September 1801. From the very beginning the two countries formed a correct but distant relationship because they were geographically so far apart and had little in common beyond modest commercial dealings. No U.S. minister was in Lisbon when a French invasion of Portugal prompted the unexpected departure of the Portuguese royal family and its court to Brazil in November 1807.

In marked contrast to the detached attitude of the United States, the British government had maintained an attentive interest and long-standing influence in Portuguese political and commercial affairs. It was British diplomacy that characteristically played a vital role in persuading the Portuguese royal family to escape from imminent French imprisonment and leave Lisbon for Rio de Janeiro under the protection of the British navy. As a result of the move, Brazil became the administrative center of the Portuguese empire, and Portugal was spared the crisis of local political authority that initiated the violent movements for independence from colonial rule in the neighboring Spanish-American colonies. Moreover, the close historic ties and dependence between Portugal and Great Britain were highlighted when the prince regent, Dom João, arrived in Brazil and issued a decree in January 1808 for the first time opening Brazilian ports to trade with all friendly foreign nations. As Dom João intended, British merchants were the main beneficiaries of this action. Their hold over Brazilian trade became a position of economic preeminence when it was further strengthened by an 1810 commercial treaty between Britain and

Portugal that gave a tariff advantage of 15 percent on British goods imported into Brazil.

North American merchants had already taken advantage of a similar relaxation of commercial restrictions in Spain's American colonies made in 1797. American ships from ports such as Boston, New York, and Baltimore became actively involved in trading in the Caribbean, the Atlantic, and the Pacific. After 1808 American traders sought to exploit the equally attractive opportunities presented by the opening of Brazilian ports. To assist this trade Thomas Sumter Jr., a former cotton planter from South Carolina, was appointed U.S. minister to Rio de Janeiro in 1809. When he presented his credentials in June 1810, Sumter became the first resident diplomatic agent of the United States in Latin America. Sumter's instructions from Washington included negotiating a commercial treaty that would give American goods the same preferential terms as those from Britain. Although the treaty never materialized, trade developed reasonably well in that Brazil purchased American goods to the value of almost one million dollars in 1809. On their return voyages American ships carried Brazilian agricultural products including coffee, the first shipment of which was landed at Philadelphia on September 18, 1809. Trade between the two countries doubled within two years but then declined sharply because of the severe dislocation of transatlantic commerce during the War of 1812 between the United States and Great Britain.

Sumter could make little material progress to promote U.S. commercial aims as conflicting interpretations over the exact meaning of maritime neutrality during time of war increasingly strained diplomatic relations. Despite the royal family's move to the New World and the subsequent elevation of Brazil to "kingdom" status, the Portuguese court always believed its stay in Rio was temporary. Thus, officials neglected local affairs and remained preoccupied with observing the political and dynastic developments in Europe. Dom João adopted a European perspective on the War of 1812. He was sympathetic to Portugal's long-standing ally Britain, and there was even a report that he intended to join the conflict on Britain's side. The fact that British shipping was able to take refuge in Brazilian ports annoyed the United States and led to protests over Portugal's alleged failure to act as a neutral nation. In turn, the Portuguese government condemned the U.S. government's inability to prevent South American privateers from using U.S. ports as bases for operations against Portuguese shipping in the Atlantic. These activities, which included the visible employment of American seamen and of ships built in the United States, continued after the end of the War of 1812 and provoked the Portuguese minister in Washington, José Correa da Serra, to complain about "depredations and unwarrantable outrages."[2]

Relations were further damaged by evidence of strong antimonarchical sentiment in the United States. While President Thomas Jefferson had courteously welcomed Dom João's move to the New World, he remained a staunch advocate of the superiority of the republican form of government.[3] It was axiomatic for Americans that the Brazilian monarchy was an anomaly in the New World, especially at a time when revolts for independence from Spanish monarchical rule were occurring throughout the Spanish-American colonies. Indeed, Americans displayed overt sympathy for the 1817 uprising in Pernambuco, whose separatist leaders claimed to be inspired by constitutional developments in the United States. The American press approved the struggle to establish a federal republic and described the rebels as "patriots" who were "entirely in favor of the United States."[4]

Despite making some private gestures of sympathy with the aims of the revolt, the Monroe administration publicly declared its intention to maintain neutrality and refused to officially recognize the rebel provisional government. As expected, in Pernambuco itself imperial forces quickly suppressed the revolt. Nevertheless, the Portuguese government suspected the existence of American filibustering designed to seize Brazilian territory in the Northeast and closely watched the movement of American visitors and ships in the region. The U.S. consul in Pernambuco reported that the local authorities "have since the late Revolution looked on the Americans as suspicious persons who came here for the sole purpose of aiding the patriotic cause in this country."[5]

Meanwhile in Rio, Sumter had caused considerable offense by refusing to dismount from his horse when he encountered members of the royal family in the street. The minister's insistence on an equal social status with royalty was interpreted locally as typical American insensitivity and arrogance. The deliberate breach of etiquette not only provoked considerable ill-feeling at the royal court but was compounded by Sumter's strongly worded protests against the actions of the Portuguese navy, especially the impressment of American seamen and the stopping and searching of U.S. merchant ships for contraband goods. The result was growing diplomatic isolation for the U.S. minister and his eventual recall to the United States in 1818. Secretary of State John Quincy Adams later admitted that diplomatic relations between the two countries had "festered into all but open hostility."[6]

Recognition of Independence

During the period of the Portuguese court's residency in Rio from 1808 to 1821, the court had little reason to cultivate the political favor of the United States. In fact, where diplomatic relations intersected, as in the case of maritime neutrality, they were marked more often by conflict than by cooperation or understanding. A clear convergence of national interests occurred, however, after Dom João, who had become King João VI in 1816, returned to Lisbon in July 1821, and the Portuguese Côrtes subsequently demanded that Brazil be reduced to its former colonial status. Attitudes in Brazil toward the United States markedly changed, if only briefly, as a result of the declaration of independence from Portugal in September 1822 and, one month later, the crowning of Dom João's son, Pedro, as Emperor Pedro I. A priority of the new ruler of Brazil was to secure his formal diplomatic recognition from the great European powers. Such recognition was necessary because it would not only confer legitimacy upon the new regime but also lessen the likelihood of any future attempt by Portugal at military reconquest of its former colony. However, the outright refusal of the Portuguese king to recognize Brazil's independence initially prevented the other European monarchs from establishing formal diplomatic relations with the new country because it would mean breaking ranks with their fellow monarch.

By default, Pedro I and his leading adviser, José Bonifácio de Andrada e Silva, looked for diplomatic support from neighboring states and especially the United States. Cordial relations were now cultivated with American officials in Rio. In conversations in 1822 with the U.S. consul, P. Sartoris, José Bonifácio indicated his awareness of the importance of American friendship and diplomatic endorsement. "He appeared," noted Sartoris, "very desirous of knowing how the Brazils might rely upon some support from the U. States in case Portugal and England in virtue of its treaties with Portugal, should attempt to force them to submission to the Cortes of Lisbon." The successor to Sartoris, Condy Raguet, reported an extremely friendly welcome on his arrival at Rio in September 1822 and added that "this Government is desirous of cultivating the most friendly relations with the United States." In his subsequent dispatches Raguet referred to the imperial government's constant fear of an imminent Portuguese military invasion and its anxiety over the likelihood of civil war breaking out. It was against this background of insecurity that he noted the timely arrival in January 1824 of copies of President James Monroe's special message to the U.S. Congress in December 1823. Raguet remarked that the speech had "excited great interest" and was interpreted locally "as a pledge to stand by this country in the event of any interference on the part of the Holy Alliance."[7]

The receipt of news of the president's message coincided with the decision of the imperial government to send a diplomat, José Silvestre Rebelo, to Washington to secure U.S. diplomatic recognition of the new Brazilian empire. The Brazilian minister was aware of the recent difficulties in diplomatic relations between Brazil and the United States. He also knew that the U.S. government and public were strongly anti-monarchical. On the other hand, there were encouraging signs pointing to success for his mission in that the Monroe administration had recently established diplomatic relations with several Spanish-American states including the monarchical regime set up by Emperor Augustín Iturbide in Mexico. It was also evident that the United States was strongly motivated by economic calculation and wished to improve relations in order to grasp the attractive commercial opportunities that were perceived to exist in Brazil. Indeed, Rebelo had no need to take any positive action because his presence in Washington prompted the convening of a meeting of Monroe's cabinet on April 6, 1824, which debated the issue of the recognition of Brazil and, with the sole exception of Attorney General William Wirt, decided in favor. While Wirt had made known his opposition to recognizing a monarchy as a matter of principle, John Quincy Adams noted that the rest of the cabinet favored a pragmatic approach that would benefit the United States by promoting peace, stability, and trade. "The form of government was not our concern," the secretary of state disarmingly summed up.[8]

Formal recognition came a month later. Fearful about the prospect of an attack from Portugal, the imperial Brazilian government had also instructed

Rebelo to propose a defensive military alliance with the United States. Though phrased in very vague terms, the proposal received a polite but clearly discouraging response from Monroe and Adams. Undeterred, Rebelo made a formal written proposal in January 1825 to which Secretary of State Henry Clay responded that a defensive alliance was not needed because a military expedition from Portugal against Brazil was an "improbable contingency." Such an alliance would be "inconsistent" with the policy of neutrality that the United States had pursued throughout the period of the wars for Latin American independence. Rebelo replied that he thought the logic of President Monroe's special message in December 1823 pointed to the formation of a military alliance because it advocated that action be taken against European aggression. But Rebelo's argument went unanswered. Although the message had raised Latin American hopes of assistance, it had been a unilateral statement of U.S. policy and did not envisage a collective hemispheric response. Brazilian officials glossed over the negative outcome in Washington by implying that it was not unexpected. "The impression has no doubt always existed here," Raguet wrote earlier from Rio, "that our feelings towards South America were grounded in a community of interests, and that we cared no further for her emancipation, than so far as she embraced our political doctrines."[9]

The convergence of Brazilian and U.S. national interests in 1824 was temporary. While the Monroe administration was conscious of the size and potential of the Brazilian empire, it viewed Brazil as just one of several turbulent Latin American countries seeking to establish diplomatic relations and promote commercial activities. Brazil regarded diplomatic recognition by the United States as pleasing and useful but not a matter of great political, strategic, or financial consequence. In fact, most Brazilian diplomatic effort was still directed at cultivating close relations with Great Britain, a country that had considerably more to offer than the United States. The British government was actually pleased that Brazil would remain a monarchy and was prepared to use its considerable influence to secure Portuguese formal acquiescence to the fact of Brazilian independence. Moreover, the British foreign secretary, George Canning, wished to maintain the commercial privileges contained in the 1810 treaty and was aware that the treaty expired at the end of 1825 and would shortly come up for renewal. He was also conscious of growing diplomatic and economic rivalry with the United States, a threat that was underlined by the timing of the U.S. recognition of Brazil and of other Latin American nations ahead of similar British action. Clearly, the Brazilians knew where their best interests lay. As a Brazilian diplomat reported from London in July 1823, "With England's friendship we can snap our fingers at the rest of the world."[10]

Britain was invited to assume a mediatory role that proved to be the decisive factor in persuading Portugal to abandon its intransigent attitude and agree to a treaty recognizing Brazilian independence. The treaty was celebrated at the imperial court on September 7, 1825. Raguet, however, did not attend the event, explaining that his absence was due to his failure to receive diplomatic credentials from Washington raising his post from the rank of consul to that of minister. Their late arrival attracted negative local comment and even some irritation. By contrast, British prestige was at a high point. In return for diplomatic assistance in securing the greatly desired Portuguese recognition, Brazil negotiated with Britain a separate commercial arrangement that was ratified in 1827 and renewed the preferential tariff enjoyed by British goods contained in the 1810 treaty. In the meantime, Britain officially recognized the independence of Brazil in January 1826. Similar action was soon forthcoming from the other leading European powers, including Austria, France, and Prussia.

A system to regulate foreign commerce emerged in which the 1827 commercial treaty with Britain provided a model for similar agreements that the imperial government subsequently concluded with several nations including France, Austria, Prussia, Denmark, Holland, and the United States. The latter treaty was negotiated by the U.S. minister, William Tudor, and signed in Rio in December 1828. It was scheduled to be in force for an initial period of twelve years after which it could be terminated by either government. Each of the commercial treaties negotiated by Brazil was similar in containing a most-favored-nation clause that not only granted tariff reductions on imported goods but also gave special legal privileges to foreign nationals. Despite local criticism that the treaties represented political humiliation and economic subordination for Brazil, the emperor and his ministers justified the concessions as necessary to secure diplomatic recognition from the European powers and to assist the country's economic development.

A particularly controversial issue relating to treaty arrangements with Great Britain was Brazil's undertaking to abolish the transatlantic slave trade from 1830 onward. Convinced that the continued importation of slaves from Africa was necessary for national economic prosperity, successive Brazilian governments flouted the treaty arrangement. The United States proved to be an unexpected ally. Although the foreign slave trade had been made illegal in the United States in 1808, U.S. governments refused to cooperate with Britain in the suppression of the trade from Africa to Brazil. Conscious of the War of 1812, the United States once again resisted British naval attempts to institute a right of search policy that involved detaining U.S. ships sailing in international waters. This resulted in Brazilian slave merchants using American-built and registered schooners to continue the slave trade. "It is fact not to be disguised or denied," U.S. minister George Proffitt wrote from Rio in 1844, "that the slave trade is almost entirely carried on under our flag and in American built vessels sold here, chartered for the coast of Africa and to slave traders."[11]

Rivalry in the Plate River

From the beginning of their independence, Brazilians fondly believed that their nation was the leading power in the South American continent. In marked contrast to the views of U.S. political leaders, the very fact that Brazil was still a monarchy and had rejected republicanism was regarded as not only a positive advantage but also an affirmation of Brazilian superiority over its neighbors. "What a picture unhappy [Spanish] America shows us!" commented José Bonifácio in 1823. He proudly, if somewhat arrogantly, added: "For fourteen years its peoples have torn themselves to pieces, because, after having known a monarchical government, they aspire to establish a licentious liberty. And, after having swum in blood, they are no more than victims of disorder, poverty, and misery."[12]

The outbreak of the movements for independence in Spanish America presented tempting opportunities for Brazilian territorial expansion in South America. Taking advantage of the political instability to the south in Buenos Aires, Dom João sought to extend Portuguese control over the Banda Oriental and gain direct access to the Plate River. In 1821 the Banda Oriental was officially incorporated into Brazil as the Cisplatine Province. The newly independent Argentine nation, however, was intent on restoring the former boundaries of the Spanish viceroyalty of the Plate to include not only the Banda Oriental but also Paraguay and Upper Peru (Bolivia). Consequently, a battle for regional hegemony began between Brazil and Argentina that would last throughout the nineteenth century. The long anticipated hostilities in the Banda Oriental eventually erupted in April 1825 when a group of rebels known as "the Thirty-Three" declared war on Brazil and advocated union with Argentina. In October Argentina proclaimed the annexation of the Banda Oriental. Emperor Pedro I replied by formally declaring war on Argentina in December 1825.

In the case of the Cisplatine War, Argentina saw the United States as a useful aid against Brazilian territorial expansion. Prior to the outbreak of fighting, the Argentine minister in Washington, Carlos de Alvear, sought to persuade the U.S. government to put diplomatic pressure on Brazil to vacate the Banda Oriental. For the Monroe administration, the conflict in the South Atlantic was regarded as geographically remote and lacking in strategic significance for the United States. The president was known to be critical of what he regarded as Brazil's act of territorial aggression, but he refused Argentine requests to invoke the Monroe Doctrine. The same detached policy was pursued by President John Quincy Adams, who became president in 1825. While carefully avoiding any direct involvement in the war, the United States allowed Argentine ships to use U.S. ports. In Washington, Ambassador Rebelo protested that the U.S. government was not observing neutrality. He singled out what he described as the one-sided attitude of the U.S. press, which he claimed reflected "Republican intolerance" and an "unfriendly disposition" against Brazil. He was particularly incensed over "the insults, ridiculous and sarcastic ideas in this country against the August Person of H.M. the Emperor of Brazil."[13]

Like the War of 1812, the conflict in the South Atlantic resulted in interference with U.S. shipping, leading to numerous complaints and claims by American merchants against the actions of the Brazilian government in attempting to enforce a naval blockade of Argentine ports. The U.S. minister in Rio, Condy Raguet, stated that it was not sufficient for the Brazilian government simply to declare that it had established a naval blockade along the whole of the Argentine coastline. He insisted that the Brazilian navy should not interfere with neutral shipping unless it was clearly able to enforce and maintain an effective blockade. Raguet acted in a similar manner to Sumter in pressing American claims for damages so vigorously that he provoked the personal resentment of Brazilian officials. As Sumter had done before him,

Raguet also incurred the displeasure of John Quincy Adams, who remarked on his minister's "temper and want of judgment."[14]

The United States played no direct part in the Cisplatine War. In the war Brazilian forces experienced a series of setbacks both at sea and on land. But Argentina failed to achieve a decisive military victory. Consequently, both sides became war weary and eventually accepted Great Britain's offer to help broker an end to the conflict. With the assistance of British diplomatic mediation, the two countries reached a compromise in August 1828 that ended the fighting and resulted in the Banda Oriental becoming the new independent state of (the Oriental Republic of) Uruguay in 1830.

Midcentury Relations

After the first decade of Brazilian independence, diplomatic relations between Brazil and the United States were mostly concerned with transacting routine commercial and consular business. A large majority of the population in Brazil were illiterate and engaged in subsistence agriculture. For the elite, who dominated Brazilian politics, economy, and society, the United States had minimal appeal. Their diplomatic and cultural world revolved around contact with the aristocratic courts and societies of Europe, especially Great Britain, France, and Portugal. There was no Brazilian equivalent of the French political scientist Alexis de Tocqueville or the Argentine diplomat Domingo Sarmiento, both of whom visited the United States and later published widely read accounts of their experiences and opinions. News about the northern republic was sparse and usually reached Brazil from biased European sources. Among the Brazilian elite, there was little knowledge of the English language. The works of U.S. literature that attracted considerable popularity, notably the novels of James Fenimore Cooper, were invariably read in a French translation.[15]

For the people of the United States, Brazil was a distant country that lacked political and strategic significance. While U.S. writings on Brazil were scanty, they invariably contained a positive image of the one Latin American country whose huge territorial extent and reputedly abundant natural resources and economic potential invited direct comparison with the United States. After his visit to South America as a member of an official U.S. commission in 1817–18,

Henry Brackenridge enthused: "The only empires that can be compared to the Brazil, in point of magnitude, are those of China, Russia and the United States." In the opinion of Secretary of State John C. Calhoun in 1844: "Next to the United States, Brazil is the most wealthy, the greatest and most firmly established of all the American powers." Even more admiring was the comment in a best-selling travel account published in 1857 by the Protestant clergymen Daniel P. Kidder and James C. Fletcher that Brazil "embraces a greater territorial dominion than any other country of the New World, together with natural advantages second to none on the globe."[16]

The U.S. public was also informed by the contemporary travel literature that Brazil was politically "different" from the Spanish-American nations in that the country had retained the monarchical system of government. One feature that particularly impressed American travelers in the mid-nineteenth century was that, in marked contrast to its unruly Spanish-American neighbors, Brazil was evidently a model of political stability and respectability. Kidder and Fletcher attributed this to the considerable personal skills of Emperor Pedro II, who ruled as a constitutional monarch since his coronation in 1841 and became greatly admired not just in Brazil but throughout the Western world. It was most unusual for American citizens to praise a monarchical system, but they readily acknowledged the success of the "South American empire." In 1866 Professor Louis Agassiz of Harvard University visited the country and concluded that Brazilians were fortunate to be ruled by "a sovereign as enlightened as he is humane."[17]

Agassiz had been drawn to Brazil by his professional interest in exotic flora and fauna. The travel account compiled by his wife and published in 1868 confirmed the popular image of Brazil as a tropical paradise. Another contemporary American traveler, Thomas Ewbank, engagingly described the country as "the land of the cocoa and the palm" and the inhabitants as gentle, courteous, and hospitable. Such attractive portraits of Brazil were undermined, however, by reports of negative personal experiences. In their diplomatic and commercial transactions in the United States, Americans generally encountered Brazilians who were white or fair skinned. On their first arrival in Brazil, however, they were often dismayed to discover that the country was very similar to Africa in that a large majority of the Brazilian population were either black or of mixed race, a fact that was readily interpreted by white Anglo-Saxon

Americans as representing national degeneracy and backwardness. On his visit to Rio Henry Brackenridge remarked that "the number of Negroes and of the mixed race was such, as to give a different caste in the general appearance of the population, from that of any town I have ever seen." According to the U.S. consul at Rio, Henry Hill, the social tolerance of miscegenation "had caused an admixture of blood and color in the Brazilians that defies all description, as it does all example." The results were very visible because in contrast to the United States, people of color were not confined in residence to a particular section of the country. Ewbank observed: "In the maritime cities and provinces the mixture of blood is obvious, but in the interior the preponderance of color is awful." He added with a note of disgust that one city in Minas Gerais was said to contain "only five pure white families among twelve thousand inhabitants."[18]

Among the black population in Brazil were more than one million slaves in 1822, and this number doubled to over two million by the middle of the nineteenth century. Some American visitors were particularly disturbed by the holding of auctions of enslaved Africans and to witness the brutal treatment often meted out in public to slaves by their white masters. Slaves were sometimes compelled to wear iron masks, a practice considered degrading and inhuman and virtually unknown in the United States. In the opinion of John Codman, however, Brazilians were "generally kind and indulgent masters."[19] While American travelers to Brazil had different opinions on how slaves were treated, they agreed that there were relatively large numbers of free blacks in the Brazilian population and that this resulted in social conventions between the races being notably less restrictive than in the United States. "The prejudice with respect to complexion, did not appear to me as strong as in the United States," remarked Brackenridge.[20] At a restaurant in Rio, Ewbank was surprised to observe the evident absence of a color line: "Young colored men came in, sat down without hesitation at the same table with whites, and, on a perfect equality, took part in the conversation."[21] While they acknowledged that "insurmountable" obstacles were placed in the way of blacks in the United States, Kidder and Fletcher remarked that, in Brazil, "if a man has freedom, money and merit, no matter how black may be his skin, no place in society is refused him."[22] Frederick Douglass referred to the fanciful idea of Brazil as a unique racial paradise in his campaign for civil rights in the United States. Brazil was the "only country where the Negro could rise to a high position in society, even to that of a judge or major general, if he were possessed of character and talent."[23]

Another link that travelers made between Brazil and Africa was the country's reputedly unhealthy tropical climate and the prevalence of infectious diseases such as malaria, smallpox, typhus, cholera, and especially yellow fever. The latter was first transmitted from Africa in 1849, and epidemics became a regular occurrence. In Rio alone it was estimated that the scourge of yellow fever had claimed more than fifty thousand lives by the end of the century. Visitors from the United States often attributed the spread of disease to low standards of hygiene. A typically derogatory impression was recorded by William E. Curtis, who briefly visited Rio in 1885 as the secretary of the U.S. Latin American Trade Commission. Approaching Rio by sea, he viewed the city at a distance as "a fragment of fairyland," but "the illusion is instantly dispelled upon landing, for the streets are narrow, damp, dirty, reeking with repulsive odors, and filled with vermin-covered beggars and wolfish-looking dogs."[24]

In terms of travel and communications, the sheer size of Brazil was considered to be a liability rather than an advantage. Beyond the capital city of Rio de Janeiro, the rest of the country was perceived as an enormous and intimidating wilderness. Large areas were still unmapped and virtually inaccessible. In fact, relatively few Americans traveled to Brazil during the nineteenth century. These included mainly individual explorers, geographers, entrepreneurs, and Protestant missionaries attracted to the tropics by scientific curiosity, an appetite for exotic adventure, and a desire to spread the Gospel. With the exception of a few thousand Confederate exiles who mostly settled in São Paulo immediately after the American Civil War, organized emigration from the United States was rare. The Confederates wished to relocate "to nearly the last place on the globe where they can hold slaves."[25]

The scheme began auspiciously, but the Anglo-Saxon Protestant newcomers found it hard to relate to a society with a pronounced Latin and Catholic culture and in which free blacks were treated on a level of social equality with whites. Moreover, whereas Brazilians were hospitable to travelers, they generally manifested a suspicion and unfriendly attitude toward foreign settlers, especially Protestants. One Confederate settler, George Barnsley, enumerated the difficulties as "dissimilarity of language and customs; difficulties of transportation; low price for skilled labour; differences in religion; inability to vote and be sovereign; disgust for the Brazilian idea that a man who sweats from work is not a gentleman; and finally — the most potent of all, that this country offers and gives nothing for the American, which he cannot get in his own country — nothing worth the sacrifices of exile from his native soil and kindred."[26] Consequently, the Confederate settlements soon fragmented, and their well-publicized failure virtually terminated popular interest in the United States in pursuing schemes for organized emigration to Brazil.

Commercial Relations

The most frequent and ultimately enduring contact between Americans and Brazilians was through trade. Despite initial U.S. optimism when Brazilian ports were first opened to foreign merchants in 1808, the resulting trade between the United States and Brazil turned out to be disappointingly modest. The economic reality was that both countries were primarily agrarian economies that produced very similar products and had therefore little to sell to each other. From the beginning of the nineteenth century the actual balance of trade was invariably in Brazil's favor. Merchants from the United States imported sugar, cocoa, tobacco, and rubber from northeastern Brazil, coffee from Rio and especially São Paulo, and hides from the Plate region. In return Brazilians bought dairy products from New England and flour milled from the winter wheat of Maryland and Virginia and shipped via Baltimore. During the 1830s annual trade amounted to less than $10 million and had risen to $25 million by 1860. These figures, however, represented no more than 3 to 4 percent of total U.S. foreign trade. Nevertheless, a reasonably profitable commercial relationship was established in which Brazil ranked along with Cuba and Mexico as one of the largest trading partners of the United States in Latin America.

Commerce, however, was mainly conducted in a triangular fashion that allowed European countries to dominate the export trade to Brazil. European ships carried their own goods to Brazil and then loaded Brazilian cargoes for their return trip home or, just as frequently, for carriage onward to the United States. A relatively small number of American sailing ships plied the same waters but made only a small dent in what amounted to a virtual European monopoly.[27] American merchants were particularly envious and critical of the powerful influence exercised by Great Britain in all aspects of Brazilian commercial activity. For most of the nineteenth century, however, they could do little to upset British economic preeminence, which rested not so much on Britain's presumed capacity to extract unfair commercial advantages but on the ability of "the workshop of the world" to supply, transport, and offer credit facilities for the purchase of the manufactured goods Brazilians wanted. A Brazilian diplomat observed that "the commerce between the two countries is carried on with English capital, on English ships, by English companies" and added that "everything goes into the pockets of Englishmen."[28]

U.S. businessmen and companies were notoriously deficient in providing adequate shipping services and credit to finance trade. In the earlier age of sail power, "Yankee" clippers had been more than a match for any European rivals, but Americans were generally reluctant to adapt to the introduction of steam power. The resulting lack of direct steamship lines between the United States and Brazil meant that both passengers and freight usually had to travel on European ships going between the two countries via at least one stop at a European port. Kidder and Fletcher described communications with Brazil as "exceedingly difficult" and complained that Britain "is reaping golden harvests" while "our Government and our merchants, notwithstanding their boasted enterprise, have done next to nothing to foster trade with Brazil."[29]

Poor communications were exacerbated by internal commercial rivalries in the United States. New Orleans and Newport News, Virginia, sought to compete with Baltimore and New York for the Brazilian trade, but these ports were unable to provide adequate return cargoes and lacked access to the extensive internal railroad communications within the United States that were enjoyed by their rivals in the North. From the Civil War through the 1880s New York controlled more than 60 percent of the import trade from Brazil. By contrast, Baltimore's share was just over 20 percent. Nevertheless, the merchants of Baltimore attempted to resist the trend of economic events. Their early primacy in the trade with Brazil during the first half of the nineteenth century had been based upon the fact that the sailing time from Baltimore was forty-eight hours less than from New York. Dismayed by the development of steam power, they successfully lobbied the U.S. Congress to reject pleas from entrepreneurs for financial subsidies to operate a line of steamships from New York to Brazil.

Kidder and Fletcher urged American businessmen to seize the immense commercial opportunities presented by Brazil. The first edition of their book in 1857 included a statistical appendix emphasizing that Brazil had not only become the most prosperous country in South America but also represented "the largest and the last undeveloped field of trade now left open to the industry and enterprise of man." Although Kidder and Fletcher thought primarily in terms of seeking business in the established and rapidly growing cities of Rio de Janeiro and São Paulo, the most exciting economic "frontier," and potentially a "new Texas," was farther away to the north in the vast Amazon region. The marvels of the Amazon River had been revealed to the U.S. public in 1853 by the report of an exploratory geographical survey undertaken on behalf of the Department of the Navy by Lieutenants William L. Herndon and Lardner Gibbon. The findings endorsed the promotional activities of Herndon's brother-in-law, Lieutenant Matthew Fontaine Maury, who was energetically engaged in writing articles and organizing public meetings in the southern United States designed to arouse U.S. commercial interest in the Amazonian region. Maury glowingly predicted that the area was so fertile that it was "capable of supporting with its produce the population of the whole world."[30]

Conducting business in Brazil, however, was not so easy or straightforward as the travel literature implied. For the small number of American merchants who were willing to try, there were many practical difficulties. A pertinent example was provided in 1866 by John Codman, who took his steamer to ply the coastal trade of southern Brazil. Not only was the market many times smaller than Codman had been led to expect, but he was also constantly infuriated by the obstructive attitude of local customs officials. In attempting to transport a cargo, his goods would be subject to numerous official inspections, and he might be required to fill out several documents — in one transaction he completed ninety-six separate forms in one day! The "vexatious impediments" to trade quickly persuaded Codman to abandon his Brazilian enterprise and to conclude that the accepted standard reference work on Brazil by Kidder and Fletcher had been written "through glasses of couleur de rose."[31]

Although American merchants complained of frustrating difficulties in exporting to Brazil, Brazilian sales to the United States encountered far fewer obstacles. Quite simply, the people of the United States were becoming a nation of coffee drinkers, who showed a clear preference for the good quality and mild flavors of Brazilian coffee and in so doing provided Brazil with its largest single and most profitable export market. In 1872 the U.S. Congress removed the duty on imports of coffee. The resulting boost to coffee exports from Brazil was extremely significant in making the two nations more conscious of each other's existence. Up to the American Civil War, Americans had bought their coffee in the form of unroasted green beans. After 1865 the market expanded considerably as a result of developments in roasting and packaging. In 1873 Arbuckles and Co. took advantage of the elimination of duty and introduced "Ariosa," the first successful national brand of packaged coffee. Selling roasted coffee "in little paper packages like peanuts" initially aroused ridicule, but it soon formed the basis of one of the world's great commercial enterprises.

From the middle of the nineteenth century onward shipments of coffee steadily increased from Brazil to the United States. However, the pattern of trade in the other direction was markedly different as there was no similar lucrative item that Brazilians desired in return. The result was a further widening of the trade balance in Brazil's favor to more than $20 million annually during the 1860s and 1870s. The discrepancy did not go unnoticed. Business leaders and their political allies in the U.S. Congress argued that Brazil should take steps to redress the imbalance by granting reciprocal tariff concessions to U.S. goods. "We are her best customer and friend," affirmed Lieutenant Maury in 1853, and he called upon Brazil to show "her appreciation of this patronage and friendship by some sign or token at least that she too would be liberal in her policy."[32]

In matters relating to foreign customs duties and commercial regulations, U.S. merchants frequently looked to the diplomatic and consular officials of the State Department for assistance. The trade treaty negotiated with Brazil in 1828 had defined the rights of U.S. merchants, but its provisions had lapsed in 1841. It was official U.S. policy to negotiate a new commercial agreement, but the Brazilian government was unwilling to comply. This did not signify any particular hostility toward the United States because a similar attitude was shown by Brazil toward Great Britain, whose commercial advantages gained by treaties in 1810 and 1827 were not renewed in 1844. From that year onward a wide range of foreign imports were subject to rates of duty, rising to as much as 60 percent. In fact, higher tariffs reflected official government policy that was deliberately designed not just to protect local industries from foreign competition but also to raise additional and much needed financial revenue. As a result, the Brazilian government was resistant to concluding new trade treaties containing tariff reductions. Although this was irritating to U.S. officials, it was not discriminatory because American goods were placed on an equal footing with those of Britain and other nations competing in the Brazilian market.

Nevertheless, a succession of U.S. ministers in Rio continued to point out that the United States was Brazil's best customer and to argue that this entitled U.S. goods to special preferential tariff treatment. The appeal to Brazil's sense of commercial justice was often accompanied by hints of the imminent imposition of an increase in the U.S. tariff on coffee. A duty on imports of coffee had been originally introduced in 1862 as part of an emergency measure to raise revenue for the Union during the American Civil War. After 1865 there was domestic political pressure to reduce if not abolish the duty in order to lower the price of coffee for consumers. U.S. diplomatic officials, however, saw the ability to alter the rate of duty as a valuable bargaining tool in their negotiations to secure a new trade treaty with Brazil. This strategy, however, was crucially undermined by the decision taken unilaterally by the U.S. Congress in 1872 to make coffee imports free of duty without requiring anything in return. It would not be the first time during the "gilded age" that diplomatic considerations would be subordinated to the political complexities of the tariff question. "We acted with undue liberality," regretfully summed up the U.S. minister, James Partridge, in what would prove to be a classic understatement.[33]

Diplomatic Controversies

Continuing the examples set earlier by Thomas Sumter and Condy Raguet, U.S. diplomatic officials in imperial Brazil often hindered rather than helped the promotion of trade by assuming a superior and insensitive approach in their personal dealings with the officials of the Brazilian Ministry of Foreign Affairs. Although the existence of the imperial court gave Brazil a higher standing than other Latin American countries, Brazil was scarcely a significant or prestigious posting. Invariably appointed for purely political reasons in accordance with the dictates of "spoils politics," U.S. ministers generally lacked diplomatic or consular experience and rarely possessed any knowledge of the Portuguese language or an acquaintance with Brazilian affairs. The most notorious example during the second half of the nineteenth century was James Watson Webb, who did not disguise his personal disappointment at being offered a posting to Brazil in 1861. On his arrival at Rio, Webb freely admitted that he had no knowledge of Portuguese and had no desire to learn. It was a foretaste of the insensitive and controversial style that would characterize his stay in Brazil.

The Brazilian government demonstrated, however, that it could resist and, if required, retaliate against foreign diplomatic pressure. For example, Brazil steadfastly refused U.S. requests to open the Amazon River to foreign trade. Although Lieutenant Maury emphasized that he advocated a "policy of commerce" and not "the policy of conquest," his lobbying coincided with the period of "manifest destiny" during which the United States acquired large amounts of territory after fighting a war with Mexico and when American filibustering expeditions were notoriously active in the Caribbean and Central America. Consequently, Maury's activities aroused concern in Brazil that a filibustering expedition to seize the Amazon region was being secretly prepared in the United States. In a series of well-publicized letters Maury roundly condemned what he described as Brazil's "Japanese spirit." He warned: "It may well be imagined that the miserable policy by which Brazil has kept shut up, and is continuing to keep shut up, from man's — from Christian, civilized, enlightened man's use the fairest portion of God's earth, will be considered by the American people as a nuisance, not to say an outrage."[34]

Ironically the activities of Maury, Herndon, and Gibbon had stimulated Brazilian awareness of the commercial possibilities of the Amazon region. But nationalist sensitivity prevailed over financial consideration. Any immediate prospect of the river being opened to foreign shipping was effectively eliminated by what Kidder and Fletcher described as Maury's "offensive language."[35] Indeed, the tactic of issuing threats invariably proved counterproductive in relations between the two countries and only stirred latent Brazilian fears of what became known as "Yankee imperialism." The result was a vigorous declaration of Brazil's sovereignty over the Amazon region, resulting in the closure of the river to foreign shipping until 1867. Moreover, the political furor created by Maury adversely affected U.S. commercial interests in Brazil for some years. Kidder and Fletcher believed that it was responsible for Brazilian reluctance to discuss the negotiation of a new commercial agreement with the United States.

Brazil's independent spirit and wide latitude of diplomatic maneuver were further illustrated in 1861 by its declaration of neutrality in the American Civil War. Following the example of the European governments but not that of the Spanish-American nations, Brazil granted belligerent rights to the Confederate States. Consequently, Confederate warships were able to enter Brazilian ports to refit and take on supplies. The Lincoln administration was annoyed but did not regard the Brazilian government as unfriendly. In fact, Emperor Pedro II privately expressed his wish that the Union would ultimately be victorious in the war. Therefore, U.S. diplomacy was more concerned with European infractions of maritime neutrality and paid relatively little attention to Brazil. The appropriate diplomatic protests, however, were made by the State Department whenever it was reported that Confederate ships had entered Brazilian ports. In one instance in October 1864, Brazil's sovereign rights were directly infringed when a U.S. warship, the U.S.S. *Wachusett*, captured the Confederate cruiser *Florida* at dock in Salvador da Bahia and towed the vessel from the port. The incident was a sobering demonstration to Brazilians of how the United States could project its superior naval power with virtual impunity in Latin American waters. Nevertheless, the Brazilian government resolutely declared that the national flag had been insulted and demanded that the U.S. government make an official apology. Secretary of State William H. Seward was conciliatory and explained that the naval action had been unauthorized. But Brazilians were unhappy that the *Florida* had been sunk en route to Hampton Roads, Virginia, and could not therefore be returned. Anti-American feeling was also aroused over the long delay in firing a naval gun salute to honor the Brazilian flag at Salvador da Bahia. This was promised by Seward at the beginning of 1865, but was not carried out until July 1866.

The limited interest of the U.S. government in South American affairs was also demonstrated by its policy toward the Paraguayan War. Conflict had returned to the Plate River region during the 1840s when the Argentine dictator, Juan Manuel Rosas, attempted to expand his authority into Uruguay and Paraguay. Brazil would not allow Argentina to dominate the region and supported Uruguay in its military action against Rosas. Despite the overthrow of Rosas in 1852, Brazil remained actively involved in the internal politics of Uruguay. A new factor, however, entered the strategic balance when the Paraguayan dictator, Francisco Solano López, sent troops to Uruguay in 1864. Paraguayan forces also invaded and occupied a small portion of Brazilian territory in Mato Grosso. Brazil responded to the threat to its regional influence by joining with Uruguay and Argentina to form the Triple Alliance against Paraguay. In the resulting Paraguayan War from 1865 to 1870, Brazil contributed most to the victory of the allies in terms of money and military resources and thereby demonstrated that it had become the major military power in the region. Instead of promoting regional peace, however, the defeat of Paraguay only stimulated rivalry between Brazil and Argentina. This was evident in their disagreement over the postwar settlement especially concerning the transfer of the former Paraguayan territories of the Chaco and the Misiones. Tensions were also increased by Argentina's proclaimed determination to redress its perceived military imbalance with Brazil that had developed during the war.

Just like Henry Clay during the earlier Cisplatine War, Secretary of State Seward sought to avoid diplomatic entanglement in distant South American conflicts. Moreover, Seward was preoccupied with other more pressing hemispheric issues relating to European military intervention in Mexico and his own schemes to purchase Alaska and to conclude an isthmian canal treaty with Colombia. Despite his "expansionist" image, Seward carefully avoided involvement in the Paraguayan War. This contrasted with his minister-on-the-spot, James Watson Webb, who was suspicious of European diplomatic meddling in the war and proposed U.S. mediation to bring the belligerents together to discuss peace. But Seward was more circumspect. He believed that the United States should not interfere unless formally requested to do so by the belligerents. "It is not within the province of the U.S.," he informed Webb, "to pronounce an opinion upon either the original merits of the war, or upon the wisdom or necessity of its longer continuance."[36]

Seward's cautious and correct diplomacy indicated the fact that Brazilian affairs possessed marginal strategic significance for the United States. At the same time Brazil was able to pursue its own regional foreign policy aims without any need to consider Washington's opinion. Although Brazilian concern was occasionally expressed over rumored American filibustering schemes, diplomatic relations were friendly. Trade was the strongest link. During the half century after the achievement of Brazilian independence, a profitable but modest commercial relationship developed between the South American empire and the northern republic. The barriers of language and geographical distance, however, ensured that the people of both nations were culturally and physically kept apart from each other. Nevertheless, as communications improved throughout the second half of the nineteenth century, a convergence occurred as Americans and Brazilians became more conscious of each other's existence. A significant turning point was the visit of Emperor Pedro II to the United States in 1876.

2   From Empire to Republic

"Altogether, it seems to me," noted the U.S. consul-general at Rio in 1888, "that we now have an opportunity such as seldom occurs for extending our trade."[1] The vigorous promotion of commercial relations with Latin America was a salient feature of U.S. diplomacy at the close of the nineteenth century. It was exemplified in the initiative to hold the Washington Pan-American Conference and the policy of commercial reciprocity. The timing was propitious for U.S.-Brazilian relations because the new Brazilian republic, which came into being as the result of a military coup in 1889, wanted U.S. diplomatic endorsement. The Brazilian government therefore responded positively to U.S. proposals to negotiate the first reciprocity treaty. Brazil's co-operative attitude was appreciated by Washington because it enabled the Harrison administration to put pressure on other countries to conclude similar treaties. When the United States negotiated a treaty with Spain that gave Cuban products the same preferential tariff duty, the Brazilian government privately complained of double dealing but to no avail.

Brazil was different than most Spanish-American nations in feeling less directly threatened by the more assertive military role assumed by the United States in hemispheric affairs. Although Brazilian nationalist sensitivities were aroused by U.S. naval intervention in the Naval Revolt, the action turned out to be helpful to the government in power. In fact, the leaders of the new Brazilian republic regarded the United States as an important countervailing force against the perceived threat posed by Spanish-American neighbors, especially Argentina. They were delighted with President Grover Cleveland's arbitration of the boundary dispute with Argentina over the Misiones territory in 1895. Unlike the Spanish-American nations, the Brazilian government showed a sympathetic attitude to the United States during the Spanish-American War. A few years later in the Acre question, U.S. officials helped Rio Branco gain his first major diplomatic success as foreign minister.

Improved Communications

The arrival of the emperor Pedro II at New York in 1876 stimulated an unusual amount of popular interest by Americans both in the person himself and the country that he represented. Although the emperor traveled to Washington where he was officially received at the White House by President Ulysses S. Grant, he displayed disarming personal modesty by requesting that state formalities be reduced to an absolute minimum. The purpose of his eight-week visit was to travel by railroad across the length and breadth of the United States and to attend the 1876 centennial exhibition at Philadelphia. Unaccustomed to Brazilian visitors and even more so to royal heads of state, the American public was intrigued and impressed by the tall, fair-complexioned and blue-eyed Dom Pedro, who appeared in a plain black suit rather than ornate imperial regalia. He could also speak and understand English and was clearly genuinely delighted to be visiting the United States. Although bemused by his unexpected personal appearance and characteristics, Americans resolved the puzzle by calling him "Our Yankee Emperor" and considering him to be a white Anglo-Saxon just like themselves. As Professor Louis Agassiz had remarked a decade earlier, Brazilians were regarded as fortunate to have such an enlightened and dignified ruler who, even better, looked and acted just like an American.[2]

Dom Pedro came to the United States primarily to indulge his personal passion for scientific discovery and foreign travel. But he also reflected a growing Brazilian interest in a country that had successfully abolished the institution of slavery and was achieving impressive industrial progress. While the visit lacked political motivation, the emperor did publicly allude to the desirability of developing closer commercial ties between the two countries. A meeting was arranged with John Roach, a leading advocate of the establishment of regular steamship service between New York and Rio. Roach sought to take advantage of the favorable publicity arising from Dom Pedro's visit by lobbying the U.S. Congress for financial subsidies to carry the U.S. mail to Brazil. After considerable debate in Congress, Roach's proposals were eventually defeated in 1879. The most determined opposition arose from the merchants of Baltimore who feared the loss of further Brazilian business to their rivals in New York. In addition, the fact that Roach received Republican backing prompted Democrats to seize upon the issue for partisan political advantage. The desire to improve shipping links with Brazil was denounced as a ruse to plunder the public purse. "The American people," remarked James Blount, the Democratic congressman from Georgia, "have been cheated and deceived and millions have been taken out of the treasury under the false delusion of aid to American commerce."[3]

Roach argued that American exports would benefit from regular steamship communication with Brazil because "trade follows the flag" and that this would significantly help to reverse the long-standing imbalance of trade between the two countries. But Roach did not adequately address the question of what exactly would Americans sell to Brazil. Furthermore, his optimism could not hide the fact that the same economic fundamentals that had long restricted trade were still firmly in place during the 1880s. The U.S. consul-general in Rio, Christopher Andrews, explained that the Brazilian market might possess great potential, but in the short term it remained as limited as ever: "[Brazil] has not the capacity for that rapid commercial development which her resources would at first seem to indicate. . . . With a population of some 13 million scattered over a region nearly as large as the United States, her territorial extent is a source of weakness. Her resources, though undoubtedly imposing and calculated to ensure for her an important future, are yet inferior to what is commonly supposed."[4]

The dispatch in 1884 of an official trade commission to tour Latin America indicated that the United States was attaching a new importance to developing commercial links with its hemispheric neighbors. The policy, which became popularly known as "Pan-Americanism," was particularly associated with Republican politicians, notably James G. Blaine, and became increasingly a subject of American domestic political debate during the 1880s. Most attention was initially directed to Mexico and the nations of Central America and the Caribbean. From 1887 onward, however, Brazil became an integral element of U.S. commercial diplomacy. Surprisingly, the actual initiative came from Democrats rather than Republicans. As part of his political strategy to win reelection in 1888, President Grover Cleveland decided to stress the promotion of American overseas commerce. The inclusion of Brazil in his plans was revealed in a private interview with the Brazilian consul-general at New York,

Salvador de Mendonça. After praising Brazil as the most important nation of South America, Cleveland suggested the formation of a customs union between the two countries on the lines of the German zollverein.[5] The president's proposal was studiously vague, but he wished it to be communicated to the imperial government in Rio.

For more than thirty years the U.S. legation at Rio had frequently raised the question of concluding a new commercial treaty between the two countries to replace the 1828 treaty that had lapsed in 1841. The Brazilian government had steadfastly resisted entering into substantive discussions for a variety of reasons ranging from reluctance to give up valuable customs revenue to concern over the reaction of local merchants and foreign interests to preferential advantages being granted to their U.S. competitors. In 1887 the whole question acquired a new significance, however, as a result of the unexpected intervention of the U.S. president and his apparent singling out of Brazil for special consideration. Brazilian officials also viewed Cleveland's initiative as a reflection of the growing economic power of the United States. Cultivating closer links was not only sensible but would also offset Brazil's traditional but often humiliating dependence on the great European powers. Moreover, greater access to the growing U.S. consumer market offered a welcome opportunity to boost sugar exports and thereby reverse the worrying decline of the Brazilian sugar industry. A convergence of national interests was taking place. For the first time since the signing of the original trade treaty in 1828, both governments wanted to conclude a formal commercial treaty.

That opportunity came with the First International Conference of American States, commonly known as the Pan-American Conference, held in Washington from October 1889 to April 1890. The Brazilian government saw the conference as a convenient opportunity to send a delegation empowered to enter into formal discussions leading to a bilateral commercial treaty. For the second time, James G. Blaine was secretary of state and had an opportunity to fashion the hemispheric economic union that he had proposed in his brief tenure in the department in 1881. His appointment was considered advantageous to Brazil because he had been an active supporter of John Roach and had once written that "Brazil holds in the South much the same relationship to the other countries that the United States does in the North."[6]

Recognition of the Brazilian Republic

The conferees convened briefly in Washington at the beginning of October 1889 and then adjourned to allow delegates to be taken on a deluxe railroad tour of the United States. Just before the resumption of the conference, the sensational news arrived that a military coup had overthrown the Brazilian empire on November 15. After his visit to Philadelphia, both the power and the image of Dom Pedro II had steadily declined in Brazil. The monarchical system was challenged by a growing republican movement that argued that monarchy was obsolete and hampered Brazil's development as a modern nation. Republicans also advocated the end of slavery, not violently, as in the United States, but gradually. In another contrast with the U.S. example, the Brazilian military became directly involved in political activity and thereby initiated its role as national arbiter. After the Paraguayan War a new generation of junior officers emerged who differed from their predecessors in their professionalism and in showing less attachment to the monarchy. They felt particularly frustrated by the failure of the imperial government to improve military pay and conditions, especially after the substantial sacrifices that the army had made during the war. A desire for radical reform of the political system evolved and was stimulated by the teaching of officers who had visited France and returned to Brazil imbued with the ideas of positivism expressed in the writings of the French philosopher Auguste Comte. In the 1880s, as the emperor's health deteriorated, his popular appeal as national unifier and leader diminished. Brazilians increasingly began to doubt the institution of empire. During a political crisis in November 1889, a group of junior officers persuaded Marshal Manoel Deodoro da Fonseca to lead a military coup. The hapless Pedro readily accepted the takeover and departed the country.

For once Brazil was front-page news in the United States, and press attention focused on the question of when the United States would recognize the provisional government of the new republic. Diplomatic recognition was quickly forthcoming from Uruguay and Argentina, and most of the other Latin American countries followed suit in December. Just like 1824, however, the United States adopted a cautious and legalistic response that reflected more the diplomatic style of the Old World rather than the New World. Officials in Washington had slight personal knowledge of the country and lacked up-to-date information on political conditions. Even experienced diplomats were genuinely astounded by the course of events of November 1889. Although the U.S. minister at Rio, Robert Adams, viewed the coup as "the most remarkable ever recorded in history," he recommended prompt recognition of the new government.[7]

Blaine declined. His delay was puzzling because U.S. politicians and press opinion clearly welcomed what was regarded as a signal victory for republicanism in the New World. But the prospect of the emergence of "a new Brazil" was moderated by the existence of genuine sympathy and sadness for the much admired Dom Pedro, who had peacefully and graciously yielded to the ultimatum that the imperial family leave immediately for exile in France. A few U.S. politicians were alarmed at the overthrow of a respected symbol of authority and stability by the military, in effect a palace coup carried out by army officers. Their leader, Marshal Deodoro da Fonseca, became head of the provisional government. Senator Henry M. Teller of Colorado critically observed: "We have had in the past some experience with republics in South America that were republics only in name, unworthy even of the name of republic, and that brought disgrace upon republican government the world over. We do not want to make that mistake. Whenever the people of Brazil say that there is a republican government in that country, then we are for Brazil."[8]

Like the imperial government in 1822, the attitude of the United States was a matter of importance to the new provisional government in Brazil because it regarded U.S. diplomatic recognition as an aid in strengthening its domestic authority. Moreover, Foreign Minister Quintino Bocaiúva knew the United States from personal experience and was particularly eager to cultivate friendly relations with the northern republic.[9] The policy was ably supported and facilitated by the newly appointed Brazilian minister at Washington, Salvador de Mendonça, who had served for almost fifteen years as Brazil's consul-general in New York. Salvador was married to an American and was already a well-established and popular figure in Washington society. In addition, his personal access to U.S. political leaders was most unusual for a Latin American diplomat, many of whom tended to be either ignored or treated with condescension. Most notably, Salvador was able to cultivate a close working relationship with Secretary of State Blaine.

One weekend toward the close of January 1890, Blaine called Salvador to the State Department to tell him that U.S. recognition was approved. The exact reasons for Blaine's action are unknown, but the whole episode was characteristic in that it reflected his habitual swings of behavior between vacillation and impulsiveness. In fact, the formal decision to recognize Brazil attracted little notice in the United States, and the U.S. Congress gave its approval without dissent in February. By that time it was considered that a sufficient interval had elapsed as a mark of respect to Dom Pedro, and if the United States had acted ahead of the European governments, so much the better. Some apprehension still lingered that a military dictatorship was being imposed upon Brazil. This concern greatly diminished during the summer of 1890 when it was reported that a new Brazilian constitution had been drafted. Moreover, Americans were flattered to discover that it rejected the European parliamentary system and proposed a federal government openly modeled on the political system of the United States. The *New York Daily Tribune* accordingly called it "the best possible augury for the future of the country," while the *New York Times* predicted that "the future of the republic is regarded as most encouraging."[10]

Commercial Reciprocity

These references, however, were merely minor items of political news. After the drama of the 1889 coup, Americans quickly lost interest in Brazilian political affairs. At the official diplomatic level, however, discussions were in progress to expand the commercial relationship between the two countries. They were suspended in February 1890 when the question became entangled with domestic political controversy over the progress in the U.S. Congress of the McKinley tariff bill, especially the establishment of a "free list" of products that would be exempt from customs duty. In October an amendment was added to the bill allowing President Benjamin Harrison the discretionary authority to manipulate the "free list" in order to secure the negotiation of commercial arrangements with foreign countries. These countries would enjoy the provisions of the free list, which included sugar and coffee, only if they "reciprocated" by granting tariff reductions on their imports of American goods.

Talks quickly resumed between the United States and Brazil. For John W. Foster, the principal State Department negotiator, the conclusion of a treaty with Brazil "was to be the test case of success or failure and we awaited the result not without some misgivings."[11] This anxiety did not result in a weak bargaining position on the American side because Salvador de Mendonça wanted a treaty even more than Foster. By responding positively he hoped to gain for Brazil a virtual monopoly of American sugar imports. A treaty also possessed significant short-term political and diplomatic benefits because it would highlight U.S. support for the new republic and demonstrate to the other South American countries that Brazil enjoyed a privileged relationship with Washington.

The treaty was formally signed on January 31, 1891. In return for the provisions of the free list, Brazil removed duties on various American goods including wheat, flour, and certain manufactured items such as tools and machinery. The new U.S. minister at Rio, Edwin Conger, sent his congratulations to Blaine and predicted enthusiastically that the "successful reciprocity negotiations have opened the doors of Brazilian trade to wonderful opportunities for our people." But only a few weeks later, he was writing that public reaction was "by no means as cordial as we had a right to expect," and there was even the prospect that the Brazilian Congress would vote to repeal the treaty.[12]

The hostile response was most unexpected. Unfortunately, the reciprocity question coincided with a period of acute political controversy in Brazil arising from President Deodoro da Fonseca's arbitrary style of leadership. When Deodoro threatened to enforce the reciprocity agreement by executive decree, his critics accused him of high-handedness and insisted that it was a treaty that required congressional consultation and approval. The controversy was intensified in May 1891 when it was learned that the United States had concluded an identical arrangement with Spain on behalf of Cuba. The fact that Cuban sugar would now also have free entry into the United States effectively destroyed Brazilian expectations of capturing a monopoly of the American sugar market. In June the Brazilian government instructed Salvador to express officially its misgivings and state that Brazilian public opinion "requires good ground to sustain the agreement before the country." But a sympathetic response was not forthcoming from Washington. Foster answered that Harrison was "taken greatly by surprise by attitude of Brazilian government." Any insinuation that the U.S. government had not acted in good faith was curtly dismissed by the assertion that the arrangement with Brazil had never precluded the United

States from negotiating similar agreements with other countries. Moreover, Foster ominously declared that failure of Brazil to ratify the treaty "will be interpreted as an unfriendly act to the United States" and that the "consequences to the future relations of the two countries cannot fail to be most unfortunate and dangerous."[13]

A sense of grievance existed in Rio that Salvador had been tricked by the promise of "free sugar," but in the light of the unyielding attitude of the Harrison administration, Brazil could hardly do otherwise than stand by the arrangement. In fact, the Brazilian government felt firmly committed to ratifying the treaty and proceeded to mobilize all its resources of persuasion and patronage to win congressional ratification by a close vote in September 1891. Conger praised Deodoro's leadership and described him as "a true friend of the policy of reciprocity."[14] But Conger's delight was short-lived. A military coup occurred in November 1891 when a naval squadron commanded by Admiral Custódio José de Melo threatened to bombard Rio. Fearful of unleashing civil bloodshed, Deodoro resigned.

Alarmed by Deodoro's fall from power, Conger was relieved that the new regime headed by Vice-President Floriano Vieira Peixoto made no overt move to denounce the reciprocity treaty. But government support could not be taken for granted. British dispatches suggested that the Brazilian government found the arrangement "very unpalatable" and that abrogation could not be ruled out.[15] An open breach with the U.S. government, however, was craftily avoided by Brazilian resourcefulness. Floriano adopted an argument already employed to secure congressional ratification — that if Brazilian goods were adversely affected by preferential reductions given to U.S. products, then the Brazilian tariff should be raised to restore the original price differential. Floriano increased import duties by up to 60 percent, thus restoring the competitive advantage of the home producer. Although the action was clearly against the spirit of the treaty, American merchants could hardly complain because the margin of their preferential privilege over foreign imported goods remained intact. The critics of reciprocity in Brazil were therefore effectively disarmed, and the issue became much less politically controversial.

For the Harrison administration, Brazil's consent to a treaty had been crucial to the further success of the reciprocity policy. A British official summed up that Brazil's "surrender" had "crippled" the other Latin American governments.[16] However, the treaty failed to revive the Brazilian sugar industry and therefore upset one of Brazil's main purposes in signing the arrangement. To make matters worse, Brazilian protests to Washington were treated in an unsympathetic manner. Nevertheless, despite the bruised feelings of Brazilian diplomats, the arrangement proved advantageous for Brazil because it gave a boost to coffee exports and thereby assisted the development of the fastest-growing sector of the Brazilian economy.

The conclusion of the reciprocity arrangement in January 1891 marked the high point of diplomatic convergence between the United States and Brazil during the second half of the nineteenth century. By 1893, however, both Blaine and Harrison, the leading architects of the reciprocity policy, had departed from office. In keeping with the politics of the "gilded age," the incoming Grover Cleveland administration carefully considered lists of "deserving" Democrats for jobs in the foreign service, including Brazil. Consequently, Brazilian affairs were relegated to a state of virtual limbo until the newly appointed U.S. minister, Thomas L. Thompson, took up his post. Only a few days after Thompson's arrival in Rio in August 1893, a major political disturbance erupted and, if only temporarily, made Brazil newsworthy once again in the United States.

The Brazilian Naval Revolt

Despite Deodoro's resignation in November 1891, political peace had not materialized in Brazil. Vice-President Floriano Peixoto succeeded to the presidency, but his hold on power was precarious. A serious split emerged within the military as naval officers grew resentful of the political prominence and privileges accorded to the army since the fall of Dom Pedro. On September 6, 1893, Admiral Custódio de Melo took command of the fleet in the harbor of Rio and demanded Floriano's resignation. Contrary to Custódio's expectation, Floriano refused to surrender power as Deodoro had done in almost identical circumstances only two years previously. The result was a military stalemate in which Custódio commanded all the Brazilian warships in Guanabara Bay, while Floriano controlled the artillery batteries on shore. What had been originally intended as no more than a demonstration of naval power leading to a swift change of government personnel became transformed into a prolonged siege lasting from September 1893 to March 1894.

The Naval Revolt attracted international attention on account of its damaging effect upon foreign trade within the harbor. The governments of the United States and the European powers were confronted with the delicate questions of how to protect their commerce and whether belligerent rights to stop and search foreign merchant shipping should be granted to the insurgents. For U.S. officials there was the additional consideration that the revolt might represent ulterior motives adverse to U.S. commercial interests. Allegations that foreign nations, especially Great Britain, were secretly supporting the insurgents in order to restore the monarchy and terminate the reciprocity treaty were assiduously propagated in Washington by Salvador de Mendonça, who called almost daily at Secretary of State Walter Q. Gresham's home during the revolt. U.S. officials were naturally concerned over reports of European intrigues in the New World, but State Department policy toward the revolt was pragmatic and stressed legalistic rather than commercial or ideological considerations.

The wily Floriano also sought foreign assistance in various ways. Although it would take many weeks before they could arrive, he placed orders for warships with private companies in the United States.[17] In the meantime, he attempted to compensate for his lack of a navy by calling on the foreign powers to use their warships in the harbor against the insurgents. At the beginning of the revolt he requested that all the foreign diplomats at the capital come to the presidential palace and discuss measures to safeguard merchant shipping. But the diplomatic corps were not so easily manipulated. Thompson joined with his European colleagues to refuse the invitation on the ground that compliance would be viewed as a departure from his instructions to observe strict neutrality.

The foreign representatives and their naval commanders did not give serious consideration to the idea of simply withdrawing from the scene of conflict and leaving the Brazilians to fight among themselves. Instead, they decided to present a series of notes to both Floriano and Custódio stating that merchant ships flying foreign flags should continue to go about their legitimate business in the bay under the protection of their respective national warships. The policy was legally correct although its enforcement would tend to restrict Custódio's operations and consequently favor the established government. Approval came from Gresham, who instructed Thompson that American goods should continue to be landed at Rio, with naval assistance if necessary, provided that this did not interfere with military operations in the bay.

The actual implementation of the guideline was the responsibility not of Thompson but the commander of the U.S. naval squadron. No American warships were actually present at Rio when Custódio declared his revolt. Two cruisers, the U.S.S. *Newark* and U.S.S. *Charleston*, arrived in October. On entering the bay, Commodore Oscar Stanton followed normal naval protocol and ordered an exchange of salutes and visits with Custódio. This provoked a diplomatic furor in which Floriano accused the U.S. commander of collusion with the insurgents. Stanton had not sought to interfere in the revolt, but he had acted unwisely. He was recalled by the Navy Department, and the next ranking officer, Captain Henry Picking, assumed temporary command.

Placed in the middle of two warring factions, Picking confronted an unenviable task. Although Custódio refrained from bombarding the city, the frequent outbreak of sporadic firing between the insurgents and the harbor artillery batteries made commercial operations hazardous and at times impossible. Despite their earlier declaration that they would support their own merchant ships, all the foreign naval commanders adopted a passive role. In answer to complaints about lack of protection, Picking stated that forceful action on his part must inevitably assist one side against the other and would be construed as a departure from the policy of maintaining strict neutrality in the domestic affairs of Brazil. No doubt the example of Stanton's recall also persuaded the U.S. commander to avoid taking any controversial initiative.

The continued uncertainty as to the exact legal status of the insurgents added to the difficulties of the foreign officials on the spot. When Custódio realized that the revolt would be prolonged, he sought to strengthen his position by forming an alliance with separatist political forces already active in southern Brazil. On October 24 Custódio announced the formation of a provisional government with its headquarters in Santa Catarina. The foreign powers declined, however, to confer the desired recognition. Thompson's dispatches were particularly dismissive of the insurgents. Two days before Custódio's announcement, the U.S. minister telegraphed Gresham that the position of the insurgents in the harbor at Rio was "becoming desperate." On October 24 he reported that the Uruguayan government had refused to receive a deputation sent by the insurgents. On the basis of this information, Gresham judged that U.S. recognition of the provisional government was not justified.[18]

The morale of the insurgents was given a considerable boost in December when the head of the prestigious naval academy, Admiral Luís Felipe Saldanha da Gama, joined their cause. Saldanha took command of the insurgent fleet in the harbor and declared his determination to institute a more vigorous prosecution of the siege. It now became extremely difficult for the foreign naval commanders to find a safe landing place for their merchant shipping. British merchants complained in particular of the inadequate protection afforded to them by their own naval commander. Saldanha's monarchist sympathies were well known, and the fact that his entry into the struggle coincided with rumors of the withdrawal of naval protection by the British commander revived local suspicions of British complicity in plots to restore the Brazilian monarchy.

The charge made by the Floriano government that the insurgents intended to destroy the republic was designed to win support primarily within Brazil, but it was realized that this might also sway American opinion. Thompson had limited knowledge of Brazilian affairs and was susceptible to official propaganda. As early as October 3 he relayed government statements to Washington that the true aim of the revolt was to bring back the monarchy. Two months later he informed Gresham that the Brazilian foreign minister claimed to possess documented proof that British naval forces were giving material support to the insurgents.

The secretary of state showed little immediate concern. Uppermost in his mind was not the question of monarchist intrigue but how to resolve the practical difficulties posed to American merchant shipping by the naval siege and now made worse by Saldanha's more energetic policy. Conditioned by his legal training and conservative instincts, Gresham could only suggest a continuation of the very same policy that the foreign diplomats and naval commanders had been pursuing since the beginning of the revolt. On January 9, 1894, he instructed Thompson to cooperate with Picking to find a docking place "where neutral vessels may receive and discharge cargoes in safety without interference with military operations." The next day, the minister was informed that unless all foreign shipping suffered common restrictions, "no substantial interference with our vessels, however few, will be acquiesced in."[19]

Coincidental with the dispatch of these instructions, Admiral Andrew

Benham arrived at Rio. The Navy Department had ordered three additional ships to Rio and wished an officer more senior in rank than Captain Picking to be in command. Benham assumed control of a squadron comprising five warships that now represented the most powerful foreign fleet in the harbor. Moreover, the admiral's arrival came just at the time when Saldanha was demanding the right to stop and search all foreign merchant vessels in the bay. After consultation with his foreign naval colleagues, Benham informed Saldanha on January 28 that he would not tolerate interference with American merchant shipping and would employ the force at his command to ensure the safety of American ships. On the following day shots were exchanged between American and insurgent ships as Benham successfully escorted an American merchant vessel to the docks. Benham claimed to be neutral, but his action indicated a refusal to allow Saldanha to establish the very blockade that would secure recognition of the belligerent rights of the insurgents. Moreover, his firing on the insurgent ships undoubtedly assisted Floriano. That this was not the purpose of American diplomacy was evident in the frantically worded telegram sent by Gresham on January 30 instructing Thompson to "report fully and speedily present situation, what has occurred at Rio and in harbor."[20]

While Benham's naval intervention solved the immediate problem of the protection of neutral shipping in the bay, the insurgent fleet still remained in the harbor. Furthermore, reports of military successes by the separatists in southern Brazil suddenly gave the question of recognition new urgency and significance. Thompson once again raised the specter of British plots. But Gresham was dubious. He outlined his views to the U.S. ambassador in London, Thomas Bayard, in January: "I do not believe Great Britain, or any other European Power, will attempt to re-establish the Monarchy in Brazil. The present state of things at Rio can not last much longer and I shall not be surprised at the result whatever it may be. I do not believe the Brazilian people are very patriotic. Perhaps a majority of them are indifferent to what is now going on."[21]

Gresham was typical of Americans who displayed a condescending attitude toward Latin America. In his opinion, the Brazilian republic was in peril not from an external conspiracy wishing to restore the monarchy but from the lack of moral virtue and patriotism among its own citizens. Americans had welcomed the creation of the republic in 1889 but always expressed reservations concerning the undemocratic type of government that had taken power. These doubts were reinforced as Brazil lurched from one political crisis to another. "The Brazilians care very little how or by whom they are ruled," observed the Rio correspondent of the *New York Times*. The Naval Revolt appeared as yet another example of military infighting in which the Brazilian people were reluctant to give support to either faction. In October 1893 Captain Picking described Brazilians as showing "little interest" in the Naval Revolt.[22]

Nevertheless, American independence of action was constantly emphasized. There was no formal attempt to concert policy with the European powers, and when the intervention by Benham took place, it was executed unilaterally. Gresham initially took alarm on receiving reports of fighting involving U.S. warships. His immediate anxiety was that the United States had somehow been drawn directly into the conflict. He was therefore reassured to learn that Benham's objective was not to maintain Floriano in power or to crush the insurgents but to assert the right of American merchant ships to carry out their commercial operations without hindrance. There was no special significance that the intervention had occurred in Brazil. Secretary of the Navy Hilary Herbert put the whole matter in the broader context of the protective and humanitarian role pursued by the U.S. Navy in the world's trouble spots during the late nineteenth century. Commending Benham's action as meeting with "universal approval," Herbert haughtily declared that it would "have a far-reaching and wholesome influence in quite a number of countries where revolutions are so frequent as to almost constantly imperil the rights of American citizens."[23]

Whatever his exact intention Benham effectively demonstrated how the growing military power of the United States could be projected to assert U.S. rights in Latin America. Like the case of U.S.S. *Wachusett* thirty years previously, minimal consideration was given to local feelings. Indeed, the British minister at Rio reported that Benham's action had created "a very bad impression on shore."[24] Brazilian nationalist sensitivities were aroused by the deliberate act of interference by foreigners in their affairs, but little adverse comment surfaced on this occasion because Benham had dealt a severe blow to the cause of the insurgents for which the Floriano government was naturally very appreciative. Thwarted in his attempt to establish a legal blockade, Saldanha's position became untenable, and the insurgent fleet withdrew from Rio in March 1894. Saldanha's death in June 1895 brought an end to the naval rebellion.

Floriano's eventual triumph owed most to his own determination not to give up power. Diplomacy was merely one of a number of instruments he used to gain assistance in his fight against the insurgents. While Floriano valued the material and moral support of the United States, he never directly requested U.S. military intervention nor did he propose any commercial deal between the two governments. From the vantage point of Washington, Gresham was wary of becoming entangled in an internal quarrel for which he had little personal sympathy. He adopted a reactive policy that stressed neutrality. However, by its insistence on upholding the status quo, Gresham's legalistic approach actually assisted the established government and had the fortuitous effect of strengthening diplomatic relations between the two countries. Floriano was so grateful that he ordered July 4, 1894, to be observed as a Brazilian national holiday.

The Troublesome Nineties

The departure of the insurgent fleet led to the resumption of normal commercial activities at Rio, but this was of more immediate benefit to European rather than American merchants. At the end of the siege, Thompson recalled that there were only five ships in the harbor flying the American flag. At the same time, he counted over a hundred British vessels. In a plea reminiscent of those made by Kidder and Fletcher some forty years earlier and Roach more recently, the U.S. minister urged that "something should be done to meet this already dominating and rapidly increasing European influence."[25] But the U.S. Congress had consistently refused to vote financial subsidies to set up American shipping lines. Similar political constraints had also hampered the reciprocity policy with Brazil in 1890 and would do so again with the passage of the Wilson Tariff in August 1894.

When the Cleveland administration came to office in 1893, its declared priority was to reverse the Republican policy of tariff protection. The U.S. Congress prepared a bill that proposed not only tariff reduction but also the abrogation of all the agreements made under the 1890 tariff, including the reciprocity arrangement with Brazil. The threat of congressional interference prompted Salvador de Mendonça to inform the State Department that his government regarded the reciprocity arrangement as a formal treaty and that there were agreed terms of giving three months' notice for its abrogation. Gresham responded by privately devising a formula to allow time to terminate the treaty "in the proper manner." But Democratic congressmen were unsympathetic to diplomatic niceties and refused to accept the proposed compromise. Gresham was therefore compelled to reject Brazil's contention that there was an agreed procedure to terminate what he now chose to describe as a "so-called treaty."[26] It was clear that U.S. diplomacy enjoyed a latitude of maneuver not permitted to Brazil. Three years previously Salvador's hints that his government might not ratify the arrangement had met with a brusque reply. In 1894 Cleveland abrogated the controversial arrangement by the simple statement that the U.S. Congress had passed a law to this effect.

Democratic politicians had no particular ill will toward Brazil; in the main, they were indifferent. Reasons of domestic politics rather than commercial calculation required that a duty be reimposed on imports of sugar. Fortunately for Brazil, no such political significance attached to coffee, which remained on the free list. Prior to the Wilson Tariff more than 99 percent of Brazilian goods entered the United States free of duty. Afterward, the figure decreased only slightly to 95 percent. Consequently, the 1894 tariff had little detrimental effect on the volume of Brazilian exports to the United States. Ironically, American merchants stood to lose most from the action of their own government since the unilateral abrogation of the reciprocity arrangement removed at a stroke the preferential tariff advantages that they had briefly enjoyed. British merchants resident in Brazil were described as "greatly pleased" to learn of the demise of the treaty.[27]

Brazilian diplomats were annoyed at the cavalier manner in which the reciprocity treaty was terminated, but they no doubt welcomed the putting aside of what had long been a controversial matter. Considerably more importance was attached to President Cleveland's arbitration of the Misiones boundary dispute with Argentina. The failure of Brazil and Argentina to agree to a territorial settlement in 1891 had resulted in the question going to the arbitration of the president of the United States. The respective cases were formally submitted to President Cleveland in February 1894. As months passed, the president's delay in coming to a decision aroused growing apprehension in both Argentina and Brazil, but in February 1895 Brazilians were jubilant at the announcement of an award that gave Brazil virtually all of the disputed territory. The result was regarded as a personal triumph for the negotiating skill of the Brazilian diplomat, José Maria da Silva Paranhos Júnior, Barão do Rio Branco, who had presented his country's case in Washington. Any annoyance over the 1894 Tariff was dismissed in the light of what was interpreted as a conclusive demonstration of U.S. friendship for Brazil.

In 1895 the diplomatic controversy between the United States and Great Britain over the arbitration of the Venezuela boundary crisis provided a timely opportunity for Brazil to show its gratitude to Cleveland and also affirm its support for the principle of taking territorial disputes to arbitration. In December 1895 the Brazilian Senate sent a public message of congratulations to the U.S. president for his firm policy that had "so strenuously guarded the dignity, the sovereignty, and the freedom of the American nations."[28]

A few years later Brazil was unusual among the Latin American countries in openly sympathizing with the United States during the Spanish-American War. Despite proclaiming a policy of neutrality, Brazilian officials indirectly helped the American war effort. Two warships that Brazil had currently under construction in British shipyards were sold to the U.S. Navy. American ships were also allowed to take on fuel and to refit in Brazilian ports. The most famous was the first-class battleship U.S.S. *Oregon*, which stopped at Rio and Bahia on its epic voyage lasting sixty-six days from the West Coast of the United States to Key West, Florida, via Cape Horn. The U.S. minister, Charles Page Bryan, noted that Brazilian warships were positioned to protect the battleship while it was in the bay at Rio. "This act of friendliness is only one of many shown our visiting ships," the U.S. minister gratifyingly remarked.[29]

The gestures of friendship toward Washington occurred at a time when Brazil was experiencing internal political difficulties that considerably diminished the country's international prestige and diplomatic activities. No sooner had the Naval Revolt ended than the survival of the republic appeared to be threatened by popular rebellion in the form of a millenarian community established at Canudos in the remote "backlands" (*sertão*) of the Northeast. After two abortive military expeditions in 1896, an overwhelming force equipped with artillery was sent to crush the settlement in 1897. Brazilian political, social, and industrial elites attributed the rebellion to the backwardness and lack of civilization of the mixed race inhabitants of the Northeast. This belief reflected the influence of fashionable theories of social Darwinism and scientific racism that sought to prove the supremacy of the Aryan race and were used in Brazil to advocate a "whitening" (*branqueamento*) of the national population as a vital means of assisting the republic's progress and modernization. At the end of the nineteenth century immigration was actively encouraged from Europe. Although this policy was motivated primarily by a desire to gain cheap labor, it was also intended to import European ideas and influences and especially to increase the number and proportion of "whites" in the national population.

Racist ideas also explained Brazil's supportive attitude for the United States during and after the Spanish-American War. In the same way that the Brazilian elite felt threatened by the rebellion at Canudos, it was disturbed by the occurrence of racial violence in the struggle for Cuban independence. Contrary to the concept of "whitening," the influential writings of the Cuban revolutionary leader José Martí professed the equality of all races and urged that whites, blacks, and mestizos unite and take power through armed revolution in Cuba and Puerto Rico. For Martí, the great danger to the achievement of national liberation was the "monster" represented by U.S. imperialism. The views of the Brazilian elite, however, were more consonant with the interventionist policy of the U.S. government that sought to maintain political and financial stability and, by implication, uphold the prevailing social order in Cuba and the Caribbean region.

Brazil was not actively involved in the implementation of U.S. policy in Cuba. As always, commerce remained the most important link between the two countries and attracted diplomatic attention in 1897 when the Republicans returned to political power and passed the Dingley Tariff. The new law included the reinstatement of the 1890 reciprocity provision giving the president authority to negotiate reciprocal commercial arrangements. The reciprocity policy was aimed at the whole of Latin America, but it was seen as especially applicable to Brazil because the balance of trade with that country still remained notoriously adverse to the United States. In 1897 the difference was estimated at more than $50 million in Brazil's favor and attracted more attention than in the past as a result of a vigorous lobbying campaign undertaken by the merchants of Baltimore. They pointed out that a reduction in the Brazilian tariff on imports of flour was crucial for their city's commercial prosperity because that product made up more than 50 percent of American exports to Brazil.

Section 3 of the Dingley Tariff specifically empowered the president to impose a three-cent duty upon each imported pound of coffee. American policy initially stressed, however, a desire for fair commercial treatment and regarded retaliatory action as a threat only to be implemented after persuasion had failed. A willingness to be reasonable highlighted Secretary of State John Hay's instructions to the U.S. minister at Rio, Charles Page Bryan. Hay pointed out that in 1898 the United States had imported more than $61 million of Brazilian products and that 95 percent of these were admitted free of duty. In return Brazil purchased American goods valued at only $13 million out of which a mere 13 percent was admitted free. These "unequal conditions" greatly discouraged American trade and had led to demands from American merchants for retaliation against Brazilian coffee. "It is due," Hay remarked, "to the cordial friendship of which this Government has given many proofs to Brazil, to inquire whether that Government will not make such reasonably adequate concessions to the exports of the United States as to justify the continuance of our present free market for the important products of Brazil."[30]

After the disagreeable experience of the earlier reciprocity agreement, Brazil's response in 1897 was much less accommodating than in 1890. Prior to the passage of the tariff bill, Salvador de Mendonça candidly informed the State Department that he could not see in the proposed measure "one single word which can attract Brazil."[31] Indeed, there was now a clear reluctance in Brazil to grant commercial concessions to the United States. The protectionist lobby in the Brazilian Congress backed by influential state politicians and industrialists urged a general increase rather than a reduction in tariff levels. This course of action was attractive to the federal government for whom import taxes contributed more than half of total government revenue. Any reduction of duty would inevitably result in a decrease of income at a time when the Brazilian economy was on the verge of bankruptcy.

The hostile attitude of foreign governments was an additional complication. The 1891 agreement had drawn protests from several European countries whose governments were opposed to U.S. goods enjoying preferential tariff treatment once again. The issue also coincided with strong pressure from

Argentina for a bilateral commercial treaty. Argentine merchants sought to increase their exports of flour and were acutely aware that this was the product on which the Americans most wanted Brazilian concessions. In the opinion of the British minister at Rio, Brazilian commercial policy was "in an inextricable tangle in every direction."[32] Any concessions granted to the United States must inevitably provoke Argentine discontent and vice versa.

U.S. officials, however, were naively optimistic that a satisfactory agreement would eventually be reached. The stick of the retaliatory tax on coffee existed but was held in reserve because its use would indicate that diplomacy had failed. On the other hand, Brazilians queried whether the threat of retaliation was actually credible. So well established was the coffee trade that Brazilians were confident that American consumers would continue to purchase substantial quantities no matter what the particular commercial policy pursued by the U.S. government. Indeed, any tax imposed on Brazilian coffee must inevitably lead to a higher price eventually being charged consumers in the United States.

American commercial policy was so unpredictable, however, that Brazilian officials could never be completely certain that the threat would not be carried out. In June 1899 the new Brazilian minister at Washington, Joaquim Francisco de Assis Brasil, noted apprehensively that New York firms were buying up coffee stocks in apparent anticipation of the imminent imposition of a retaliatory tax on the product. Another source of pressure arose from the persistent and forceful presentation of the American case. Hay stressed fairness and reason, but his dispatches talked of the United States "demanding" and "insisting" on reciprocal concessions. On learning that the Brazilian Congress was considering an increase in the import duty on flour, Hay telegraphed the blunt warning that "this Government would regard it as an act directed against our commerce and justifying countervailing action on our part."[33] Charles Page Bryan later revealed that during 1900 he had "urged" Brazil to grant tariff concessions "at nearly every weekly audience" with the Brazilian foreign minister.[34]

It seemed that U.S. diplomacy had finally achieved success in 1900 when the Campos Sales administration undertook to grant tariff concessions on imports of American flour. But the Brazilian Congress would not confer its approval. American retaliation was rumored but did not materialize. A State Department memorandum later disclosed that "we had tried to scare Brazil, but failed to do so, and that was the end of the matter."[35] Unlike 1890, the turn of the century was not a propitious time for the revival of the reciprocity policy. In fact, Brazil's resistance to negotiating a treaty with the United States was not unique and was shared by the rest of the South American nations with the sole exception of Ecuador. U.S. diplomatic pressure on Brazil was considerable, but financial crisis and internal political divisions compelled the Brazilian government to proceed with circumspection. Hay confessed his inability to conclude an arrangement with Brazil, but this was only a temporary setback for American diplomacy. So long as the United States remained Brazil's largest export market, the Brazilian government would be directly affected by any change in American commercial policy.

The Acre Question

While Brazilian officials could be difficult in commercial negotiations, they invariably showed themselves at their most sensitive and awkward whenever the national territory was perceived to be in danger from foreign encroachment. This had been evident during the 1817 Pernambuco revolt and in the response toward Maury's scheme to open the Amazon River to foreign commerce during the 1850s. They showed a similar attitude at the end of the nineteenth century over the "Acre question." A remote area adjoining the state of Amazonas, the Acre Territory acquired prominence during the 1890s as a result of the growing international demand for rubber. Reckoned at the time to be the sole location of natural rubber in the world, its ownership had long been a matter of dispute between the governments of Brazil, Bolivia, and Peru. In 1899 Bolivia attempted to assert its authority over the territory by taxing shipments of rubber. President Manuel Ferraz de Campos Sales retaliated by insisting that the Acre Territory belonged to Brazil.

It was rumored that Bolivia had secretly acquired U.S. diplomatic support in its quest to acquire Acre. Brazilian suspicions of American imperialist designs were later heightened by the unauthorized voyage up the Amazon in 1899 by the American warship U.S.S. *Wilmington*. In Washington Hay explained to Assis Brasil that the voyage was intended to be friendly and had no ulterior motive. However, when Hay complained about reports of "unfriendly feeling" shown locally to the captain and officers, the Brazilian minister quickly reminded him of "the perfect right of Brazil to establish that warships of friendly nations may not navigate the national rivers without special permission, asked for and granted in each case."[36]

In 1902 anti-American sentiment in Brazil was further aroused after it was learned that the Bolivian government had evidently granted not only commercial rights to cultivate rubber but also virtual sovereign powers of administration in the Acre Territory to a syndicate of American capitalists. The latter were reported to be already moving equipment and supplies to the disputed region. Only a few years previously, Brazil had adopted a sympathetic attitude toward U.S. military intervention in Cuba. The emergence of what was now popularly referred to as "the American danger" to Brazil's own territory caused a marked change of opinion. Brazil's displeasure was frankly expressed in July 1902 when Foreign Minister Olinto de Magalhães informed the U.S. minister that he hoped that American capitalists would be "discouraged" from involvement in "an undertaking which was sure to result in financial disaster to themselves and in discord between nations."[37]

Shortly before leaving office in November 1902 Campos Sales ordered the closure of the Amazon River to foreign shipping. The action was intended to highlight his government's serious concern over the Acre question. It also effectively isolated the syndicate from its source of external supplies and underscored how much any exploitation of the rubber trade was dependent on Brazilian consent and assistance. The new Brazilian foreign minister, the Baron do Rio Branco, was determined to avoid any show of weakness and resolved to continue the demonstration of Brazil's sovereign power despite protests from Great Britain, France, Germany, and the United States. The U.S. consul-general at Rio, Eugene Seeger, was incensed. With language reminiscent of Maury some fifty years earlier, he condemned the closure "as a thrust against the United States." He believed himself justified in warning Rio Branco that the U.S. government "has always considered the navigation of the Amazon through Brazil as being free to all nations."[38]

But Seeger's contention could not be sustained either by international law or historical practice. It was rejected by his superiors in Washington, who had no desire to provoke a conflict with Brazil. Moreover, the legal rights of the American members of the syndicate were uncertain, and there was no evidence that they were being infringed. Nor was there any collusion between the State Department and either the Bolivian government or the syndicate. Assis Brasil was informed that the syndicate was regarded as a purely private venture.

The State Department not only acknowledged the validity of Brazil's claim to the disputed territory but also showed that it wanted good working relations with the Brazilian foreign ministry. This was underlined by the expression of pleasure at the news of Rio Branco's appointment as foreign minister in 1902. American officials "agreeably recalled" his residence in Washington at the time of the Misiones arbitration when he had been in charge of presenting Brazil's case. The U.S. minister in Rio, David Thompson, also confirmed that the baron was "most friendly." While he acknowledged that some Brazilians were suspicious of American motives, Thompson stressed that Rio Branco "does not court this feeling, and wants to feel faith in our good intentions."[39]

The mood of mutual goodwill helped Rio Branco to gain his first major diplomatic success as foreign minister. Deprived of outside supplies and any real prospect of diplomatic support from Washington, the syndicate gratefully took up his suggestion that it discuss a financial arrangement with the Brazilian government. With the knowledge and approval of the State Department, negotiations commenced in Washington between Assis Brasil and representatives of the syndicate. In February 1903 the syndicate agreed to renounce its contract in return for an indemnity of $550,000 to be paid by the Brazilian government. The financial arrangement was confirmed during the following month by which time the Amazon River had been reopened to foreign shipping and the draft of an agreement settling the territorial dispute had been concluded between Brazil and Bolivia. By the Treaty of Petrópolis, signed in November 1903, Bolivia formally recognized Brazil's possession of more than 70,000 square miles of the Acre Territory.

The boundary question, however, was not yet completely resolved. The Peruvian government was annoyed at being excluded from the settlement and reaffirmed its own territorial claims to the area. Like Brazil, Peru was well aware of the critical importance of U.S. influence and attempted to win Washington's favor by promptly recognizing the new republic of Panama in December 1903 ahead of similar action by Brazil and other South American countries. But Rio Branco was confident that American opinion was firmly on the side of Brazil.

He responded to Peru's intervention by encouraging the State Department to help bring about a negotiated settlement. The Brazilian foreign minister correctly interpreted the desire of the administration of President Theodore Roosevelt to act as a force for peace and stability in the hemisphere. This was confirmed by Hay's instructions to Thompson to work for an outcome "mutually honorable and advantageous" to both countries.[40] In fact, by deliberately not taking sides, Thompson implicitly reaffirmed the status quo and thereby dashed Peru's strategy of reopening the whole question. The diplomatic victory belonged to Rio Branco because Peru was effectively isolated and soon agreed to recognize Brazil's legal title to the Acre Territory.

The Acre question demonstrated that at the beginning of the twentieth century the U.S. government was no longer a distant and indifferent spectator of South American affairs. Indeed, the interested parties in the dispute saw Washington as the decisive focal point of their diplomatic maneuvers, and each side competed to win American support. Brazilian diplomacy had already, if only fitfully, reflected this development during the late nineteenth century. Emperor Pedro II began the process by visiting the United States in 1876. Salvador de Mendonça stressed the vital importance of securing U.S. recognition of the republic. Floriano Peixoto appreciated the usefulness of American diplomatic support during the Naval Revolt. But it was Rio Branco who would be the person most credited with articulating the strategy of "approximating" Brazil's foreign policy as closely as possible to that pursued by the United States.

3   The New Era

"It is just," commented a Rio newspaper in 1905, "that the United States should receive us from now as equals in the guarding of the destinies of the American continent."[1] A convergence of national interests during the first decade of the twentieth century meant that the diplomatic relationship between Brazil and the United States was visibly strengthened. The Brazilian diplomats, Rio Branco and Joaquim Nabuco, formulated a strategy that sought to "approximate" their country's foreign policy as closely as possible to that currently pursued by the United States. The high point of mutual good feeling was the 1906 Rio Pan-American Conference. For the United States, however, the region of primary strategic concern was still Mexico, Central America, and the islands of the Caribbean. Washington's long-standing desire not to become involved in South American affairs was reaffirmed in its unwillingness to support Brazil against Argentina over naval armaments. Rio Branco and Nabuco were deeply disappointed, and the limitations of their policy of approximation were exposed.

When war broke out in Europe in 1914, both the United States and Brazil responded with declarations of neutrality. Taking advantage of the closure of European markets, U.S. business grasped a signal opportunity for increasing trade with Brazil and displacing the formerly dominant British competition. Brazil's decision to join the war against Germany in October 1917 not only was influenced by the submarine threat but also reflected a desire to revive the strategy of approximation. Brazilian leaders reckoned that close wartime association with the United States would bring material economic benefits and assist their country's ambition to be the leading power in South America. The resulting economic gains were mixed, but Brazil's prestige was boosted by being on the winning side in the war and thereby receiving an invitation to send a delegation to the Versailles Peace Conference. However, in the hierarchical structure that prevailed in world affairs, Brazil was not regarded as a great power like the United States. Far from enjoying a position of influence at the conference, the Brazilian delegation was relegated to a minor role.

Beginning of Approximation

In the early years of the twentieth century, visiting U.S. journalists, business-men, and diplomats exhorted their countrymen to exploit the apparently boundless commercial opportunities offered in Brazil. The most celebrated publicist was Theodore Roosevelt, who took part in a scientific expedition through the Amazon region in 1913–14. "This country and the adjacent regions, forming the high interior of western Brazil," he wrote, "will surely some day support a large industrial population" and "will be a healthy home for a considerable agricultural and pastoral population."[2] The American public, however, still knew very little about Brazil. If anything, the ex-president's travel account, with its descriptions of hacking through jungles and encountering poisonous snakes, swarms of flying insects, bloodthirsty piranhas, jaguars, and native peoples, merely confirmed its stereotypical image as a dangerous place more suited for intrepid adventurers than settlers. During the heyday of mass emigration to Brazil at the beginning of the twentieth century only one-quarter of one percent of immigrants originated from the United States. From 1890 to 1919 fewer than seven thousand Americans were recorded as entering the country as immigrants in comparison to more than a million Italians for the same period.[3]

In Roosevelt's opinion, the Brazilian republic had made "astonishing progress" since its formation in 1889.[4] This was especially evident during the first decade of the twentieth century when a combination of political stability and economic prosperity facilitated the desire of the Brazilian elite to improve the nation's image. Rio was "regenerated" based upon French architectural ideas. Wide publicity was given to the construction of modern dock facilities and the completion in November 1905 of the splendid Avenida Central. Linked to the latter was the Avenida Beira Mar, which provided a picturesque boulevard stretching for several miles along the bay. Even more famous was the successful campaign organized by Dr. Osvaldo Cruz to rid the city of yellow fever. The fear of disease still remained, but visiting foreigners were greatly impressed by the visible changes. "No nation can show a more conspicuous example of modern energy and enterprise than is seen in the new federal capital of Brazil," stated an American traveler.[5]

The rebuilding of the capital was matched by similar reorganization and expansion of the country's foreign policy establishment. A remarkable element of continuity in the conduct of diplomacy was provided by Rio Branco, who served as foreign minister continuously from December 1902 until his death in February 1912. The Ministry of Foreign Affairs, popularly known as "Itamaraty," acquired its celebrated reputation for professionalism and diplomatic skill as Rio Branco masterminded a conspicuous effort to promote a positive image of his country and its people to the wider world. The creation of several new diplomatic missions overseas meant that Brazil was represented in thirty-nine countries. Rio Branco also insisted that the buildings of Itamaraty Palace be extended and modernized so that foreign representatives would be received in a manner and style worthy of an important nation. The new look was particularly evident in the physical appearance and deportment of the young men who were recruited to the foreign service. In line with the idea of promoting the "whitening" of society, Rio Branco preferred that Brazilian diplomats sent to Europe should be "tall, well groomed, and personally attractive," and that their wives should be "if not always beautiful . . . white or near-white in appearance."[6]

Rio Branco's particular regard for European opinion reflected the sense of racial and cultural inferiority that was typical of the Brazilian elite. The desire for the praise and approbation of the Old World was also mixed with fear of falling victim to European imperialism. Large areas of Africa and Asia had recently been subjected to colonial status. Indeed, Rio Branco came to office at a time of heightened Latin American anxiety over the spread of European imperialism arising from the resort to "gunboat diplomacy" of Great Britain, Italy, and Germany in their attempt in 1902–3 to coerce Venezuela to resume payments of its foreign debt. The new foreign minister stressed a policy of diplomatic cooperation rather than conflict with the great European powers. As a result of its adherence to the terms of the 1898 Funding Loan, Brazil was on good terms with its foreign creditors. Nevertheless, rumors persisted of European designs upon Brazilian territory especially relating to German activities in the south of the country.

In Rio Branco's opinion, internal divisions prevented the Latin American nations from effectively uniting against the European danger. Just as the imperial government had grasped in 1824, the obvious counterweight was provided by the perceived power of the United States, whose Monroe Doctrine had checked European territorial ambitions in the Western Hemisphere. "The great service given to the hemisphere by the Monroe Doctrine," affirmed Rio Branco, "is the liberty guaranteed to each nation to develop freely."[7] In marked contrast to most of his Spanish-American diplomatic colleagues, the Brazilian foreign minister regarded the United States as a benevolent guardian, and he even gave tacit approval to the Roosevelt Corollary that justified U.S. military intervention to punish Latin American "wrong-doing." Far from being the danger portrayed by Spanish-American writers such as José Martí, Rubén Darío, and José Enrique Rodó, the rising power of the United States was appreciated in Brazil as a force for peace because it promoted hemispheric political and financial stability and social order, and it served as a restraint upon European aggression.[8]

Rio Branco's views reflected a strong element of Brazilian national self-interest. Traditional Brazilian suspicion of "Yankee imperialism" was allayed by the recent evidence of U.S. diplomatic goodwill that had contributed significantly to the very pleasing resolution of Brazil's boundary dispute with Argentina over the Misiones in 1895 and aided Rio Branco in securing Peruvian recognition of Brazil's legal title to the Acre Territory in 1904. There were also significant economic benefits. "The United States," noted Rio Branco, "are the principal market for our coffee and other products."[9] The extension of commercial relations with the northern colossus would increase Brazil's wealth and thereby help reduce financial dependence upon Europe. Relations with the great European powers would continue to be important and vital, but the friendship and support of the United States was now considered crucial to the achievement of Brazil's own national interests.

Rio Branco reasoned that American assistance would be assured if Brazil aligned its own foreign policy closely to that pursued by the United States. As foreign minister, he was naturally seen as the instigator of this strategy, but it similarly attracted other distinguished advocates including the celebrated politician and orator Joaquim Aurélio Barreto Nabuco de Araujo, who had served as Brazilian consul in New York from 1876 to 1877, and the editor of the influential *Jornal do commércio*, José Carlos Rodrigues, who had also lived for several years in New York.[10] Nor was the concept completely original. Similar ideas had been proposed during the 1890s by Quintino Bocaiúva and Salvador de Mendonça and even earlier by José Silvestre Rebelo in the 1820s. But the baron's talk of shifting the "axis" of Brazil's foreign relations from Europe to the United States sounded different and justified the new popular description of his policy as the strategy of rapprochement or "approximation."

The first tangible evidence that Washington had become as diplomatically important as the capitals of Europe was the upgrading of relations to ambassadorial rank in 1905. The change came about rather casually in December 1904, after Rio Branco proposed that the replacement for the departing Brazilian minister in Washington should assume the higher rank of ambassador. Brazil now acquired a distinct diplomatic advantage over its rivals because the raising of rank gave its representative in Washington seniority over other South American ministers. This practical benefit was soon superseded by broader considerations. Indeed, the special status — what Brazilians called "diplomatic approximation" — accorded by the United States gave a boost to Brazilian ambitions to become the leader of South America.

The choice of Joaquim Nabuco as Brazil's first ambassador to the United States became a matter of no small significance. Despite Nabuco's doubts about the benefits and some misgivings expressed in the Brazilian Congress over the relatively high cost of embassy rank, the elevation of diplomatic status was generally welcomed as adding to Brazil's hemispheric and international prestige. An important adjunct to this was the constructive response of U.S. officials, who were simultaneously reappraising their own attitudes and policies toward Latin America. The result was essentially a reaffirmation of the Pan-Americanism of the 1890s. What was novel was Washington's deliberate emphasis on securing an improved image of the United States throughout the hemisphere.

Despite his reputation for outspoken criticism of the "wrong-doing" of some of the Latin American republics, President Theodore Roosevelt genuinely wished for friendly hemispheric relations. His new secretary of state, Elihu Root, who assumed office in July 1905, urged State Department officials to show Latin American diplomats much more personal attention and consideration than they had experienced in the past. He wrote in December 1905: "The South Americans now hate us, largely because they think we despise them and try to bully them. I really like them and intend to show it. I think their friendship is really important to the United States, and the best way to secure it is by treating them like gentlemen. If you want to make a man your friend, it does not pay to treat him like a yellow dog."[11]

The Rio Conference

The timing of Root's policy recommendations coincided almost exactly with Rio Branco's formulation of the policy of approximation. Moreover, Root's initiative in desiring to improve personal relations was fully reciprocated by Joaquim Nabuco. From his arrival in Washington in early 1905 the Brazilian ambassador worked assiduously to cultivate and charm U.S. officials. One indication that something important was in the offing became apparent during the fall of 1905, when in a private conversation Root suggested to Nabuco that the United States, with the assistance of Mexico and Brazil, would take responsibility for affirming the Monroe Doctrine throughout the hemisphere. A few weeks later Nabuco added that President Roosevelt wished to see Brazil rather than Argentina or Chile exercise the preponderant influence in South America.

These unofficial soundings coincided with the choice of Rio instead of Caracas or Buenos Aires as the location for the 1906 Pan-American Conference and the announcement in December 1905 that Root would personally head the U.S. delegation. This would be the first time that a serving secretary of state had left the United States, and the U.S. chargé d'affaires in Rio remarked that the unprecedented decision emphasized "the predominance of Brazil among the nations of South America" and presented that country "a trump in the diplomatic sphere." Nabuco was excited by what he believed was a "unique opportunity" for Root and Rio Branco to meet and perhaps establish an "entente" that one day might become an "alliance."[12]

Nineteen nations attended the conference. Nabuco was elected as the permanent conference president and set the tone when he told delegates that their aim was "to promote harmony."[13] Pan-American goodwill exuded throughout the ensuing conference sessions, but little of a substantive nature was achieved. The high point of approximation was reached when Root left Brazil in August with the parting words that the two countries "acting together, would form a single and eternal guarantee for the integrity of America."[14] Elated by this apparent selection of Brazil as the preferred partner of the United States, Rio Branco was able to indulge his dreams of Brazilian leadership of the southern continent.

The conference was undoubtedly judged a great triumph for Brazil and also a personal success for Nabuco. But the alliance, for which Nabuco had so much hoped, did not materialize. Certainly, the conference allowed Rio Branco and Root to become personally acquainted and to learn more about each other's policies. Root came away impressed and described the baron as "an exceedingly astute and capable man." Except for various ambiguous public remarks, however, there appears to be no evidence that an alliance was ever discussed. Root's decision to go on from Rio to the other capitals of South America indicated that the visit had taken on a broader perspective in which Brazil became merely one part of an official itinerary. Indeed, the British minister at Rio later reported that "a far more magnificent reception" awaited Root in Buenos Aires, where he could not conceal his admiration for Argentine wealth and progress.[15]

The concept of approximation between Brazil and the United States soon received an extremely critical examination at The Hague Peace Conference in 1907. Rio Branco eagerly grasped the opportunity for Brazil to appear on the world stage as one of the powers contributing to the cause of world peace. Indeed, a prominent role was envisaged because Brazil sent one of the largest delegations, comprising twelve officials. At its head was the distinguished Brazilian jurist and orator Rui Barbosa. Root believed that the conference would successfully confirm the spirit of Pan-American cooperation, but Roosevelt showed a lack of consideration for Latin American sensibilities over contentious issues involving the right to use force to collect debts and the creation of an international court in which only the great powers would have permanent representation.

During the conference Rui Barbosa emerged as the spokesman and champion not only of his own country but also of the whole of Latin America. Rui's initial instructions were to work closely with the U.S. delegation, but a divergence of national viewpoint was soon apparent. As the United States and the European powers sought to dominate the proceedings in their own interest, Rui took special satisfaction in reminding the U.S. delegates of Root's recent remarks made in Rio about the equality of all nations whether large or small.[16]

Rui's oratorical brilliance made him the sensation of the conference. His determined if obstinate defense of the sovereign rights of small nations irritated the U.S. delegation and greatly pleased his Latin American colleagues. Rui was proclaimed "the eagle of The Hague" and regaled with a hero's welcome when he returned to Rio at the close of 1907. Two weeks later a lavish though very much more subdued reception attended the visit to Guanabara Bay of the U.S. fleet en route to the Pacific Ocean. Despite the effusive speeches proclaiming the closeness of U.S.-Brazilian relations, a jarring note was introduced by Rui's refusal to attend the banquet held in honor of the U.S. naval officers. In October 1907 the British minister at Rio concluded that the discord at The Hague had "effaced" the effects of Root's visit.[17]

Brazilian Rivalry with Argentina

At The Hague, the Latin American delegates cheered Rui when he criticized the U.S. delegates and championed the sovereign rights of Latin America. But a suspicion and mistrust of Brazilian motives also existed and particularly applied to Rio Branco. Despite his repeated expressions of desire for friendly relations with all Latin American countries, Spanish-Americans suspected that his real purpose was the extension of Brazil's power and influence at their expense. The U.S. ambassador at Rio, David Thompson, considered that Rio Branco had "no little ill-feeling" for the countries of South America with the possible exception of Chile. On one occasion he reported the private remarks of the foreign minister that "no Spanish speaking country is good, and no person of Spanish blood can be believed."[18]

What Brazilians most resented was the attitude of superiority adopted toward them by Argentines. At the beginning of the twentieth century both countries vied with each other in a battle of statistics. Whenever comparisons were made, Brazil was proud to point out that it was almost three times the size of Argentina in both area and population. The press of Buenos Aires focused, however, on the greater per capita wealth of Argentina. Especially provocative were derogatory references to Brazil's racially mixed population and how this was responsible for Brazilian economic and cultural backwardness. During the 1890s Brazil's internal political disorders muted the traditional rivalry between the two South American giants, but the emergence of a politically stable and economically prosperous Brazil disturbed the regional balance of power at the beginning of the twentieth century. Argentina was alarmed by the expansion of Brazil's boundaries in the Acre Territory and by reports of increased Brazilian diplomatic activity in Uruguay and Paraguay. Argentine sensitivity was further heightened by the talk of approximation between Brazil and the United States. Moreover, the choice of Rio rather than Buenos Aires for the 1906 Pan-American Conference gave Brazilians a signal opportunity to overshadow the Argentines. A year after Root's historic visit, the U.S. minister in Buenos Aires concluded that Argentine-Brazilian relations were "far from satisfactory" and that this unfortunate state of affairs was mainly due to Argentine suspicion of approximation.[19]

The ill feeling was absorbed into what briefly became an arms race. Conscious of its huge territory, vast coastline, and inadequate defenses, Brazil felt increasingly insecure as international crises proliferated at the beginning of the twentieth century. In 1904 the Rodrigues Alves administration commenced a program of increased military spending designed to modernize the army and navy. Particular emphasis was put on replacing antiquated naval ships with purchases of the most modern warships available from Great Britain. The military buildup complemented Rio Branco's plan to promote Brazil's international status, but it also upset the existing regional balance of power in which Argentina possessed naval superiority over both Chile and Brazil. The Argentine press duly denounced Brazil's "warlike preparations." When Argentina threatened to retaliate against Brazil's plans for naval rearmament with its own military buildup, Rio Branco looked to Washington for assistance. Nabuco was instructed to inform Root of Argentina's bellicose attitude. The Brazilian ambassador reported reassuringly in January 1907 that Root had shown "visible sympathy" and had described the Argentines as "crazy" to think of going to war.[20]

Root was genuinely sympathetic to Brazil, but he had no intention of interfering in the quarrel between the two South American neighbors. While Rio Branco sincerely wished to be on friendly terms with Argentina, he also desired to assert his country's leadership in South America. The naval arms race openly flaunted Brazil's continental aspirations and provoked Argentine countermeasures. The personal antipathy between Rio Branco and Argentine foreign minister Estanislau Zeballos was publicly displayed as both accused each other of preparing for war. In fact, Argentine diplomats sought reassurance that the United States would not back Brazil in the event of hostilities. "The Argentines have a strong impression that the U.S. shows a preferential friendship for Brazil," noted the State Department diplomat, Alvey A. Adee, in October 1908. "Is there," he asked Root, "any way of convincing them that we love them just as much as the Brazilians?"[21]

The talk of approximation disturbed the balance of power in South America because it intensified the historic rivalry between Argentina and Brazil. While American flattery was pleasing to Brazilian pride, it conferred only slight if not false benefits. The concept of an alliance or partnership to maintain the Monroe Doctrine lacked any real foundation. The United States was confident of its ascendancy in the Caribbean region and saw no need to become entangled in the political affairs of South America. By its unwillingness to side with Brazil against Argentina, the U.S. government revealed the limitations of approximation and thereby exposed the precariousness of Rio Branco's pretensions to South American leadership.

Local events, especially the resignation of Zeballos as Argentine foreign minister in 1908, were instrumental in leading to a dramatic improvement in relations between Rio and Buenos Aires. In August 1910 the Argentine president-elect, Roque Sáenz Peña, received an "exceptional" welcome at the Brazilian capital on his way home to Buenos Aires from Europe. Enthusiastic applause greeted the Argentine statesman whenever he concluded his speeches with the sentence: "Everything unites us; nothing separates us." Rio Branco confided in the U.S. ambassador that "Brazil now counted with greatest satisfaction upon having a friend during the coming six years in the presidential chair at Buenos Aires."[22]

Dollar Diplomacy

Despite the efforts of Rio Branco and Nabuco, the concept of approximation between Brazil and the United States had never been seriously considered in

Washington. When it came to conducting relations with Brazil, American diplomats were traditionally more concerned about extracting tariff concessions and exploiting commercial opportunities for U.S. business than assisting Brazilian aspirations to be recognized as the leading power in South America.

While Rio Branco preferred to direct his attention to such prestigious matters as his country's role at The Hague or plans for the state visit to Brazil of the king of Portugal in 1908, he could not escape the unrelenting pressure from the U.S. embassy in Rio for increased tariff concessions. Even though a preferential tariff reduction of 20 percent had been given on a small number of American goods in 1904, U.S. officials pointed out that American exports to Brazil were still less than one-third the value of Brazilian sales to the United States. A stream of personal interviews, letters, and memoranda requested that this imbalance be partially rectified by doubling the preference to at least 40 percent. Although the existing 20 percent advantage was maintained, representations for change met with polite refusal. "There is," summed up U.S. ambassador Irving Dudley in 1909, "still a lack on the part of Brazil of reciprocity in her trade relations with the United States."[23]

Roosevelt's successor, William H. Taft, and Secretary of State Philander Knox implemented a structured approach to overseas commercial expansion, especially in Latin America and China. A distinct emphasis was placed on using American capital investment to create bigger overseas markets and to tie them commercially to the United States. This policy became popularly known as "dollar diplomacy," with the intent to use "dollars" rather than "bullets" to achieve order in the protectorates of the Caribbean and Central America. But the frustrations with the policy, ironically, led to more U.S. military intervention in the Caribbean region, notably in Nicaragua. Brazil was never in danger of experiencing U.S. military or political interference, of course, but dollar diplomacy affected diplomatic relations by giving further impetus to what had already been more than a decade of persistent demands from Washington for tariff concessions.

Added to the insistence for an extension of commercial preference was similar diplomatic pressure exerted directly on behalf of American business. The Taft administration strongly supported the expansion of trade with Latin America and was especially desirous of assisting U.S. companies to win big contracts for warships and armaments. Brazil's desire to rebuild its navy was well known and presented a particularly "encouraging" market. In January 1912 Assistant Secretary of State Francis Huntington-Wilson wrote directly to Brazilian Ambassador Domício da Gama on the question of a proposed naval arsenal. Pointing out that the American consumer was a "large purchaser" of Brazilian goods and that American firms "have never in the past figured on the list of foreign concerns to which the Brazilian Government contracts have been awarded," he hoped that Brazil would "give special consideration" to bids placed by American companies for the construction of the arsenal.[24]

Domício sent back a tactful response but privately expressed annoyance at American tactics. The forceful dollar diplomacy of the Taft administration was particularly resented because it undermined Brazil's sovereignty and status. Despite his wish for increased commercial relations with the United States, Rio Branco recognized that Europe and particularly Great Britain still supplied most of Brazil's trade and investment. Contrary to American popular belief, he informed the U.S. chargé that European governments did not request special favors in the awarding of armaments contracts. Furthermore, matters of national defense were kept separate from those of commerce and required "the greatest delicacy and responsibility." In a statement worthy of Rui Barbosa, Rio Branco insisted that "each country has the right to choose freely" and should be guided only by its own national interest.[25]

Demise of Approximation

When Rio Branco died in February 1912, the strategy of approximation with the United States appeared to be in ruins. In his obituary of the baron, the British minister concluded: "His one aim was to place his country at the head of South American states . . . [and] to induce the United States to back Brazil against Argentina, or at least to make the other South American states believe that they would do so. In the latter he succeeded . . . [but at the price of] demands from the United States for preferential customs treatment of so wide a character and pressed in so peremptory a manner that he was compelled to resent them."[26]

Joaquim Nabuco had died two years previously and therefore escaped the unhappy experiences that caused Rio Branco to doubt the feasibility of achieving approximation with the United States. In retrospect, the euphoria of 1906 had been short-lived. Approximation contributed to Brazil's sense of national security, but it also encouraged Brazilian diplomatic ambitions. It soon became painfully apparent, however, that Brazil lacked the stability and resources to lead the southern continent. The hollowness of this pretension was exposed in 1909–10 by what seemed like a return to the political chaos of the early years of the republic. The emergence of Deodoro's nephew, Marshal Hermes da Fonseca, as a leading presidential candidate evoked fears of a revival of "militarism" and persuaded Rui Barbosa to challenge the prevailing political system known as the "politics of the governors." Despite mounting a brilliant campaign, Rui could not prevent Hermes from achieving electoral victory.

Only a few days after Hermes da Fonseca assumed presidential office in November 1910, sailors of the navy's two largest warships *Minas Gerais* and *São Paulo* mutinied at Rio. The city was terrified of bombardment, and the new government felt compelled to grant an amnesty to the mutineers, most of whom were either black or of mixed race and were prominently led by a black sailor, João Cândido. The mutiny of the ships, which were regarded as the pride of the Brazilian navy, followed by the speedy capitulation of the government, represented a humiliating blow to Rio Branco's attempts to portray his country to the world as a model of stability and progress. The U.S. ambassador confirmed that the baron was "very pessimistic" and that the events were "a bitter experience" for the government.[27]

Just as Brazil's prestige was declining, Argentina enjoyed the glory of hosting the Pan-American Conference in 1910, followed shortly afterward by elaborate celebrations to mark the centenary of Argentine independence. The gloom and pessimism of the Brazilian elite was heightened as the world's press praised their rival's achievements and proclaimed Buenos Aires "the Paris of South America."

The fragility of approximation was further demonstrated in the controversy over the "valorization" of coffee. At the beginning of the twentieth century the government of the state of São Paulo responded to the problem of overproduction by devising a scheme to purchase and store coffee in order to withhold surplus supplies from the world market. In this way coffee would be increased in value or "valorized." A financial arrangement was reached in 1908 with the coffee merchant Herman Sielcken, who formed a valorization committee known as the New York Dock Company. In the United States the subsequent sharp rise in the price of coffee stimulated demands for official investigation under the antitrust laws. In May 1912, the Justice Department filed a suit in the New York district court requesting that the New York Dock Company be prevented from disposing of stocks of "valorized" coffee currently held in its possession.

The Brazilian ambassador to Washington, Domício da Gama, was taken aback by what he regarded as unacceptable interference in a contractual agreement made by the government of São Paulo. He was most displeased not to have been forewarned of the legal action and only to have learned of the development from reports in the press. Giving vent to his feelings at a banquet held in New York to celebrate the first meeting of the Pan-American Society, he roundly criticized the U.S. government for "an unthoughtfulness for the consideration due to a friendly state which borders on international discourtesy."[28]

Huntington-Wilson later described Domício's speech as an "outrageous and insulting attack upon this Government."[29] It was uncertain, however, whether Domício's remarks had been delivered with the express approval of his government. Consequently, the Taft administration tactfully chose to take no official notice of them. The State Department's response was confined to telegraphing its new ambassador at Rio, Edwin Morgan, to send information clarifying the exact position of the Brazilian government.[30]

While mindful that Brazilians were extremely sensitive to any action adversely affecting coffee, Morgan was convinced that Foreign Minister Lauro Müller was like Rio Branco in genuinely wishing for friendly relations with the United States. In September Müller informed the ambassador that the government of São Paulo and the valorization committee would meet during January 1913 to dispose of all the existing stocks of coffee and, by doing so, preclude the need for any further legal action in the United States. Morgan recommended that the State Department agree to this. Approval was forthcoming, though Attorney General George W. Wickersham insisted on assurances that the coffee would actually be sold on the open market and not simply apportioned among a group of "insiders."

Governor Francisco de Paula Rodrigues Alves of São Paulo privately complained that his state was the victim of Wickersham's "insolence." During his presidential administration from 1902 to 1906, Rodrigues Alves had endorsed the strategy of approximation with the United States. He now informed Müller that he was "beginning to doubt the wisdom of our direction in international affairs."[31] Even the departure of Taft and Knox from office in March 1913 provided little comfort for Brazil as the declared priority of the incoming administration of Woodrow Wilson was a new tariff bill that provisionally included a tax on coffee to make up for reductions in duty on other products. Well might Müller deplore what he interpreted as the American "crusade" against his country's most important export.[32]

The Wilson administration, however, preferred to rid itself of an awkward inheritance from its Republican predecessor. Consequently, the legal suit was abandoned; in return it was privately understood that the valorization scheme would not be applied to the United States. Wickersham and the Justice Department could claim success insofar as the attempt to "corner" the coffee market had been defeated and the American valorization committee had been disbanded. From the Brazilian point of view, the intervention of the U.S. government was a cause of considerable annoyance. The spirit of approximation withered as Brazilian irritation provoked U.S. leaders into an unsympathetic response. The voice of conciliation came from Edwin Morgan, who constantly reminded both sides of their mutual desire for friendly relations. Finally, the inauguration of a new American administration presented a convenient opportunity to bring the controversy to an end.

The Mexican Crisis

On taking office in March 1913 Woodrow Wilson stated that one of his "chief objects . . . will be to cultivate the friendship and deserve the confidence of our sister republics of Central and South America."[33] The new president, however, had little personal interest in foreign affairs. Nevertheless, contrary to his initial expectations, he became gradually immersed in and sometimes perplexed by a series of diplomatic crises. The first one arose in Mexico only a few weeks before Wilson's presidential inauguration when General Victoriano Huerta staged a military coup that resulted in the murder of President Francisco Madero in February 1913. Wilson was morally outraged. He refused to recognize the new military government and put pressure on Huerta to leave office. This eventually resulted in U.S. military intervention at the Mexican port of Veracruz in April 1914.

Wilson's resort to armed force as an instrument of policy provoked controversy throughout Latin America. In marked contrast to the Spanish-American republics, however, Brazil was traditionally less critical of forceful U.S. diplomacy in Central America and the Caribbean region. This accommodating attitude reflected the strategy of approximation and also the historical fact that Brazil had relatively little political or economic contact with the area. Consequently, the events culminating in the Mexican Revolution had been of minor concern. The Veracruz crisis was accorded greater attention because it took place in the aftermath of the valorization controversy and gave Lauro Müller an opportunity to demonstrate his desire for friendly relations with Washington. Even before the crisis occurred at Veracruz, the U.S. government had requested Brazil to look after its embassy's affairs in Mexico City should diplomatic relations be disrupted. Domício da Gama proudly explained that Brazil was chosen because it was considered the "most important American nation" represented in the Mexican capital.[34] Müller not only complied with the request but also backed Wilson's policy of refusing to grant diplomatic recognition to Huerta. In doing so, the foreign minister provoked adverse comment from sections of the Brazilian Congress and press, who pointed out that his policy could be interpreted as expressing Brazil's approval of armed U.S. intervention in the internal affairs of a Latin American country.

Müller answered his critics by stressing that his sole aim was to assist the peaceful resolution of a potentially grave crisis and that at no time had he consented to Wilson's use of military force against Mexico. In fact, the Brazilian government sought to exert a moderating influence upon both the United States and Mexico by joining with Argentina and Chile to propose a joint mediation of the dispute. The fact that collective diplomatic action implied the abandonment of Brazil's pretensions to a special relationship with the United States was not a cause of concern to Müller. He described the "ABC" initiative as a sincere and necessary attempt to prevent the Veracruz crisis from escalating into a wider conflict that would be dangerous to the security of the whole hemisphere.

The action of the ABC countries was effective in restraining any further extension of hostilities. A peace conference was held at Niagara Falls, Canada, in May–June 1914, and Huerta fell from power in July 1914. Nevertheless, the violent struggle still continued among the various revolutionary factions in Mexico. Wilson's displeasure was now transferred to the new Mexican leader, Venustiano Carranza, and in an attempt to oust the latter from power, a second peace conference was held in New York during the late summer of 1915. In addition to the ABC ambassadors, the State Department extended invitations to the ministers from Bolivia, Uruguay, and Guatemala. Only a year earlier, the U.S. government had chosen Brazil as the nation to look after its affairs in Mexico City. Now Brazil had evidently lost that special status and had become simply one of a large group of Latin American countries. Müller had little option but to continue to support U.S. policy for the sake of maintaining collective agreement. This accommodating approach received a severe jolt between conference sessions when it appeared that Wilson's views had undergone a radical change. Instead of criticizing Carranza, he suddenly began to press for Carranza's de facto recognition.

Like Rui Barbosa at The Hague, Domício da Gama resented what appeared to be a deliberate attempt to turn the conference into a rubber stamp for U.S. policy. The Brazilian ambassador grumbled that the Latin American countries were being treated as "virtual satellites."[35] The prospect of a highly charged debate, however, was avoided by the arrival of news from Mexico that confirmed that Carranza had definitely established his military ascendancy over his rivals. Consequently, Domício felt able to join his colleagues and comply with American wishes to recognize Carranza. The unilateral and manipulative style of U.S. diplomacy that had annoyed Domício did not just apply to the conferences at Niagara Falls and New York. It was also evident in Woodrow Wilson's diplomatic response to the outbreak of war in Europe.

World War I

Woodrow Wilson's proclaimed intention to cultivate closer diplomatic relations with the nations of Latin America was tested by the outbreak of war in Europe in August 1914. Privately, State Department officials were dismissive about Latin American suggestions that the president convene a conference in Washington for the purposes of affirming Pan-American solidarity and to discuss measures of diplomatic cooperation. Increased trade, however, was another matter. In fact, the severe economic dislocation caused by the world war offered an exceptional opportunity for the extension of U.S. commercial influence throughout Latin America. "The South Americans were like the customers of a store that has burned down, they were looking around for a place to spend their money," remarked Secretary of the Treasury William McAdoo.[36]

The sudden "rediscovery" of Latin America was accompanied by a rehashing of all the well-worn commercial arguments, some of which singled out Brazil as a particularly large and enticing market for American goods and capital investment. Ambassador Edwin Morgan viewed the outbreak of war as a "propitious" moment for Americans to increase their exports to Brazil and thereby reduce the long-standing trade imbalance with that country. British economic influence would also be displaced. In April 1915 the British minister in Rio reported that "the United States are making great efforts." He jealously noted the frequent arrival of commercial missions, the opening of an American branch bank in the capital, and the proposal to establish a direct steamship line with New York.[37]

Although the world war stimulated closer commercial contact between the United States and Brazil, the diplomatic consequences were harder to evaluate. In fact, there was minimal diplomatic consultation and cooperation over the policy of neutrality. This lack of interaction was surprising as both nations bordered the Atlantic and had substantial international trading interests. Where Brazil was most different from the United States was in its consciousness of national military weakness and greater vulnerability to possible acts of aggression from the belligerent powers.

Although Brazil had long maintained friendly relations with all the European belligerents, it was evident that Brazil's most popular sympathy lay with the Allied powers of Great Britain and France, especially the latter. The German invasion of Belgium had caused particular outrage. The unprovoked and callous assault upon the sovereignty of a small neutral nation, which was likened in many ways to Brazil, was regarded as indefensible. The image of Germany as a barbaric nation was also underscored by its resort to submarine warfare and the sinking of merchant ships without warning. On the other hand, Brazil had good reason to maintain friendly relations with Germany. Foreign Minister Lauro Müller was a conspicuous example of the political success and influence of the large community of German immigrants who had settled in southern Brazil. Trade between the two countries had also grown to such an extent that in 1914 Hamburg ranked second only to New York in its share of the Brazilian coffee trade.

Brazil was identical to the other nations of Latin America in showing no desire to become embroiled in the European conflict and in looking to the United States to lead the defense of maritime rights for neutral nations during a time of war. President Wilson publicly championed these rights, but he took little account of Latin American views. As the role of the world's peacemaker came to absorb his attention, the various proposals for collective Pan-American action made from time to time by Latin American statesmen were either politely rejected or studiously ignored. In turning down a suggestion emanating from Lauro Müller to hold a conference of hemispheric nations to discuss how to respond collectively to the threat of German submarine warfare, Wilson expressed his opposition to a meeting in which the United States would possess only one vote out of twenty. He condescendingly explained that the other nations would be motivated by "national considerations," but America's vote would be cast "in the interest of mankind." In the president's opinion, "on this side of the water, we are the only nation that has this position of independence of judgment and of interest."[38]

In his diplomatic strategy to mediate an end to the war, Wilson preferred to act unilaterally and deal directly with the leaders of the European powers. Domício summed up that the president's efforts were "sympathetically humane, though still perhaps impracticable."[39] His comment conveyed the detached attitude that most Latin American diplomats had adopted by default toward a peace process from which they were effectively excluded. But any tendency toward complacency was disturbed in January 1917 when the German government declared its intention of enforcing unrestricted submarine warfare and thereby signified the withdrawal of an earlier pledge to allow the safe passage of unarmed merchant ships from all neutral countries. Should the United States be drawn into the war, the economic consequences were likely to be catastrophic. Consequently, the whole of Latin America anxiously awaited Wilson's response to the German ultimatum.

On February 3 Wilson broke off diplomatic relations with Germany. Hoping that the Latin American nations would follow suit, American diplomats suddenly showed an unusual degree of interest in the attitude of their southern neighbors toward taking action supportive of the United States. As one of the most important nations, the views of Brazil were accorded special significance. But Brazil declined to follow Wilson's lead. While Brazil's relative military weakness made prevarication understandable, action could not be deferred indefinitely because the German declaration of unrestricted submarine warfare was not just an economic issue but posed a direct challenge to Brazil's own sovereign rights as an independent nation. This became evident on April 5, 1917, when a German submarine sank the Brazilian freighter *Paraná* without warning off the coast of France.

Meanwhile, Wilson had decided that the continued sinking of American merchant ships by German submarines had left him no alternative but to recommend that the United States go to war. On April 6, while anti-German demonstrations erupted in Brazil over the sinking of the *Paraná*, the U.S. Congress voted for war against Germany. In a mood of panic mixed with opportunism, Brazilian diplomacy actively revived the strategy of approximation with the United States. Economic reasons were uppermost in Brazilian thinking. Particular emphasis was placed on securing from the United States what were considered to be lifeline supplies of coal and wheat. In return, Brazilian officials indicated their willingness to facilitate the export of strategic materials such as manganese. On April 11 Brazil broke off diplomatic relations with Germany. Despite frequent reports in the U.S. press that a declaration of war was imminent, the Brazilian government refrained from taking this step until October 26, 1917.

The actual decision for war was not the result of either persuasion or pressure from Washington. When Brazil broke off diplomatic relations with Germany in April, Morgan pointed out that this was not a mere imitation of the example of the United States. "She did not follow because we led," he stated; "her senses were shocked by German procedure just as ours were." Similarly, the declaration of war in October came three days after a German submarine had sunk the Brazilian steamer *Macao* off the coast of Spain. In his message to the Brazilian Congress, President Venceslau Brás Pereira Gomes declared that Brazil must act "in order to maintain the dignity of the nation."[40] Joining the war was an affirmation of the nation's determination to fight for the traditional principles of respect for the sanctity of international treaties and neutral rights.

The assertion of Brazilian sovereignty was also underscored by the fact that Brazil became a full co-belligerent in the war and not simply an ally of the United States. Brazil's course of action contrasted markedly with that of Argentina, which preferred to maintain normal diplomatic relations with Germany and pursue the idea of hosting a special Latin American peace conference from which belligerent powers such as the United States would be pointedly excluded. Brazil's decision to go to war and break ranks with the other South American countries effectively sabotaged the conference and consequently contributed to the revival of the traditional rivalry between Brazil and Argentina. Since 1908 Rio Branco and Müller had pursued a triangular relationship that sought to accommodate close links with both the United States and Argentina. This particular strategy was now abandoned as U.S. and Brazilian national interests once again converged. With the apparent backing of the United States, Brazil renewed its claim to be the leading power in South America. "It was her proud boast," observed the British minister at Rio, "that she was the first among the Latin American republics to support the United States."[41]

U.S. officials had a wider hemispheric perspective and hoped that Brazil's action would be copied by Argentina and Chile. However, far from promoting regional unity, Brazil's decision to join the war only provoked discord because Brazil subsequently sought to build up its military forces and thereby upset the existing balance of power in South America.[42] For example, the Brazilian government requested military equipment from the United States to counter not only reports of German-inspired plots in southern Brazil but also the movement of Argentine troops to the border area. Secretary of the Navy Josephus Daniels regretted that the emergence of "trouble" between Argentina and Brazil only served "to weaken the very end the United States is working towards."[43]

While the sinking of Brazilian merchant ships by German submarines was the principal reason for the timing of Brazil's entry into the war in October

1917, financial considerations also influenced the decision. The Brazilian government expected that wartime association with the Allies and especially the United States would alleviate the damaging economic effects arising from the war. One priority was to maintain adequate supplies of American coal. Another was to increase sales of coffee, which as a luxury product had recently experienced a substantial fall in world demand. But U.S. officials in charge of allocating resources refused to grant any special commercial favors. They were insulated within Washington; their information on Brazil was limited and suggested that the Brazilian people were only half-heartedly committed to the war. Moreover, there was no compelling reason for the United States to make commercial concessions. According to one U.S. diplomat, the State Department believed it had Brazil "in its pocket."[44]

From 1914 onward American trade and investment made significant inroads into Brazil. Lucrative export markets were developed in coal, petroleum, and automobiles. Substantial investments were also evident in Brazilian cable communications and the new meatpacking industry. Contemporaries, however, found it hard to credit that the United States could really have achieved supremacy over its well-established European rivals in such a relatively short space of time. Morgan was typical of those who pointed out that the United States had gained in trade simply because the war had curtailed trade with Europe. He was fully conscious of the powerful ties that existed with Europe when he wrote in March 1919: "Although Brazil and other South American countries entered the war because the United States did so, the effect of their participation has been to enhance their appreciation of Europe and to tighten rather than weaken the bonds of race, language, habits, and customs, that unite them to the civilization of the old world."[45]

Moreover, the dramatic rise of the United States as a leading world power aroused mounting disquiet among Brazilian nationalists. Echoing the familiar theme of the "American peril," influential writers such as Alberto Tôrres denounced Pan-Americanism as "the creation of imagination." With the lifting of the wartime censorship, Morgan expressed concern that Americans were about to be repaid for their unwillingness to give preferential economic treatment to Brazil during the war. The emerging mood of national assertiveness also extended to diplomatic affairs. Morgan was particularly irritated by the anti-American content of some of the speeches and writings of Rui Barbosa.

The Brazilian statesman eloquently argued: "Let us lay aside the stupid conception which places Brazil under the exclusive seal of the United States of America and which would accustom us to the idea that we depend on them more than on France or Great Britain when the truth is that we require equally the friendship of all these three great nations."[46]

The Versailles Conference

Rui's provocative outbursts were aimed at promoting his own ambitions for presidential office, but they also reflected revival of the view that Brazil should be diplomatically active and ought to make its mark on international affairs. The prevarification that had preceded Brazil's decision to enter the conflict in October 1917 was now forgotten as the Brazilian elite were elated by the Allied victory over Germany and looked forward to Brazil's participation in the forthcoming peace conference to be held at the Palace of Versailles in France.

When he arrived in Europe as head of the U.S. delegation to the conference, Woodrow Wilson was greeted by enormous public interest and enthusiasm. The euphoria also extended to Latin America, where Wilson was acclaimed a hero and a great peacemaker. But Latin American diplomatic opinion was inclined to be more circumspect in their appraisal of the president's wartime diplomacy. In particular, Wilson's image as a peacemaker was tarnished by his several military interventions in Mexico, Central America, and the Caribbean. Despite his grand rhetoric, he had little to say about the role of Latin America at Versailles. Indeed, invitations to the preliminary peace conference were pointedly reserved for the great powers. Although State Department officials made known their support for Latin American representation at the conference, they stressed that this would apply only to those nations that had actually joined the war.

Brazil stood to gain from this particular distinction. As the only South American nation to enter the war, Brazil confidently anticipated a position of some importance at the conference table. This expectation was reinforced by the flattering attentions recently paid to Brazil by European governments, especially the upgrading of diplomatic relations to ambassadorial level in London and Rome. For the Versailles Conference, a delegation of four was appointed, headed by Epitácio da Silva Pessoa. Shortly afterward, however, news was received from Europe that Brazil was designated not as a "belligerent great power" but a "belligerent power with a special interest," on a par with Belgium, Greece, and Portugal. This meant that Brazil would be allowed only one or perhaps two, at the most, representatives.[47]

To avoid the acute embarrassment of having to reduce drastically the size of its delegation, the newly appointed foreign minister, Domício da Gama, appealed for assistance to the State Department. Counselor Frank Polk telegraphed Secretary of State Robert Lansing in Paris, advising that Brazil be given "most favored treatment." If the contents of Polk's telegram had been published, they would surely have brought joy to Brazilian hearts. In contrast to the days of the valorization controversy, Domício was now considered a most friendly and dependable ally, whose return to Rio and elevation to the office of foreign minister were seen as positive developments that considerably strengthened the pro-American element in the Brazilian government. Not only did Polk wish to help Domício avoid damaging his diplomatic reputation, but he was also concerned that any public blow to Brazil's prestige "would be a source of gratification" to Argentina and Chile, who had stayed out of the war. "Brazil," he noted, "has stood loyally by us in practically every question that has come up in South America." Moreover, it was "the only power in South America that readily declared war promptly and also was of material assistance in the war by active cooperation, such as sending ships." Polk was even prepared to acknowledge that "Brazil is the greatest power in South America" and thereby entitled "to a fair representation on account of its geographic position."[48]

Woodrow Wilson had concurred in the original decision to enhance the role of the great powers at the conference. Nevertheless, he was sympathetic to Brazil's case and raised the matter at the first meeting of the Supreme Council. He argued that Brazil, as the largest of the Latin American nations, with a population in excess of thirty million, should be granted three delegates. The proposal appeared modest, but it aroused opposition from the British prime minister, David Lloyd George, who suspected the existence of an ulterior motive to increase the overall voting power of the American nations. Participants therefore lost sight of the particular merits of Brazil's own case as the country became a pawn in the game of great power politics. A compromise solution eventually emerged in which the British Dominions were granted two dele-gates each. It was agreed that Brazil would have three delegates, although the same privilege was also extended to Belgium and Serbia.

In Brazil, Wilson's intervention was adjudged a complete success. The actual number of delegates proved to be of little significance. Without exception, all the smaller nations found themselves treated with little consideration as the "Big Four" of Great Britain, France, Italy, and the United States dominated the conference proceedings and reserved the important committee appointments for themselves. Far from enjoying a position of influence and being at the cen-ter of events, Brazil had to be content with a place on the commission assigned to draw up the covenant of the new world organization to be known as the League of Nations.

Brazil's international reputation was damaged rather than enhanced by the Versailles Conference as its delegates became visibly preoccupied with what appeared to be a narrow and mercenary assertion of national interests. An unseemly debate arose over the exact amount of financial compensation due on Brazilian assets that had been frozen in German banks during the war. The Brazilian delegation also vigorously contested the proposal that France be allowed to retain the ex-German merchant ships that had been interned in Brazilian ports in 1914 and later chartered to the French government in 1917. After heated discussions the French delegates conceded that the ships were the property of Brazil. Brazilian diplomacy was eventually successful but at the cost of appearing selfish and overly concerned with financial gain.

The diplomatic support of the United States was important to Brazil in its struggle to overcome European objections at Versailles. Domício was espe-cially appreciative of the assistance of Secretary of State Lansing and wrote a gushing note: "your attitude towards us has been most gratifying as one effec-tive manifestation of our old mutual friendship . . . I only wish to thank you for being our friend at the Conference and say this is known here and makes for a stronger inter-American friendship, that is shown in acts."[49]

In the United States, however, politics were dominated by the battle to se-cure the U.S. Senate's ratification of the Treaty of Versailles. Taking his message to the people in a cross-country tour, Wilson suffered a stroke and became an invalid in the White House for the remainder of his presidency. While discus-sions took place with Great Britain and France over the question of the League of Nations, diplomatic relations with minor countries such as Brazil were given little attention. In an attempt to counter criticism of U.S. neglect, the newly appointed secretary of state, Bainbridge Colby, made a goodwill visit to Brazil, Uruguay, and Argentina. Colby arrived in Rio on December 21, 1920, and left four days later. No substantive matters were discussed. In fact, the visit had been arranged rather hurriedly and smacked too much of a contrived public relations exercise. Just like Root in 1906, Colby was greeted with effusive speeches that were full of Pan-American sentiment, but they could not conceal the widely held view that the record of Wilson's policy toward Latin America was uneven and disappointing. As the Wilsonian era drew to a close, diplomatic ties between the United States and Brazil noticeably began to slacken.

4   The Republic under Threat

"Around us there has grown up the absurd legend that we are an ambitious and capricious people who are trying to assume the leadership of the continent," commented a Brazilian newspaper in 1925.[1] During the 1920s, while the Brazilian republic experienced serious political instability, including notably the revolt of the *tenentes* (lieutenants) and the fourteen-thousand-mile march through the interior by the "Prestes Column," the country sought to play an active role in world affairs. However, the attempt to secure a permanent seat on the Council of the League of Nations was rejected by the great European powers and also by the Spanish-American nations who had never accepted the idea that Brazil should have a privileged status. A chastened Brazil left the League in 1926 and returned to its traditional foreign policy in time of need of seeking close relations with the United States. The results were mixed. While U.S. officials appreciated Brazilian diplomatic support at acrimonious sessions of the 1928 Havana Pan-American Conference, they annoyed Brazil by their insensitive handling of the ratification of the Kellogg-Briand Peace Pact.

Relations were improved by President-elect Herbert Hoover's well-received visit to Rio in 1928. U.S. officials, however, showed a characteristic lack of knowledge of Brazilian affairs when they appeared ill-prepared for the 1930 Revolution and were slow to recognize the new regime of Getúlio Dornelles Vargas. The latter retaliated by canceling the contract of the U.S. naval mission that had been in operation since 1922. At first, President Vargas concentrated on consolidating his political authority and showed relatively little interest in foreign affairs. However, he responded favorably to the "Good Neighbor" policy espoused by President Franklin D. Roosevelt, who took office in 1933. The interests of both nations converged in that each desperately wanted to increase trade to help their economies recover from the ravages of the Great Depression. Like the earlier policy of Pan-Americanism, the United States stressed the negotiation of bilateral reciprocal trade agreements involving mutual tariff reductions. Brazil was correctly identified as one of the Latin

American countries most willing to negotiate such an agreement and thereby facilitate the implementation of U.S. policy.

The Naval Mission

During the 1920s the question of naval armaments highlighted the mixture of divergence and convergence that existed in diplomatic relations between Brazil and the United States. Although Americans chose to neglect foreign affairs after the end of World War I, they recognized that their country was now a great power with worldwide political, economic, and strategic interests. This was reflected in President Warren G. Harding's announcement that the United States intended to assist the cause of world peace by actively promoting naval disarmament. A conference to achieve this was held in Washington in November 1921. Invitations were restricted to the great powers and did not include Brazil or any of the other nations of Latin America, even though the Brazilian ambassador to Washington, Augusto Cochrane de Alencar, had made little secret of his government's desire to attend the conference. The State Department informed him that Brazil's participation was ruled out because, if allowed, it would necessitate bringing in similarly sized powers like Belgium and Spain. Furthermore, President Harding was described as "intransigent" in his opposition to any enlargement of the conference.[2]

The Brazilian government was hardly pleased or reassured by the lack of American support for Brazil's diplomatic aspirations and the unflattering reference to the country's lowly international status. Just a year earlier the minister of war, João Pandía Calógeras, had stated: "Nobody respects or seeks the solidarity of the weak."[3] At the Versailles Conference the great powers had sought to enhance their own naval strength at the expense of the smaller nations. It now appeared that the Washington Conference would be used for the same purpose. Moreover, while Brazil might publicly approve the concept of disarmament in principle, it had to consider the current state of its own national security especially in relation to Argentina. This had already resulted in measures to increase the nation's armed strength including the contracting in 1919 of a French mission to train and modernize the army. As the naval conference in Washington drew to a close in early 1922, the Brazilian government raised the idea of appointing a foreign mission to modernize the navy.

The move posed the prospect of a diplomatic battle between Great Britain and the United States. The British appeared as clear favorites to win the contract because the tradition that "Britain rules the waves" exercised a powerful influence among senior Brazilian naval officers. Ambassador Edwin Morgan believed, however, that increased U.S.-Brazilian military cooperation during the world war gave the United States distinct advantages over Britain. In addition, not only was President Epitácio Pessoa a sincere friend of the United States, but he had also confided in Morgan his personal preference for a mission headed by Captain Carl T. Vogelgesang, a much respected U.S. officer who had served as a naval adviser in Brazil at the end of the war. In Morgan's opinion, the appointment of Vogelgesang would clinch the contract for the United States. As usual, however, senior officials in Washington showed little sensitivity to Brazilian opinion. When the Navy Department indicated that Vogelgesang was unavailable for overseas duty, the U.S. naval attaché at Rio gloomily predicted in June 1922: "Unless a miracle happens, the British will get the mission, and the big contract which will later be given."[4]

Contributing to the mood of despondency was awareness of local irritation over reports of American indifference toward the centennial celebration of Brazilian independence scheduled to be held in Rio during September 1922. Evidently the U.S. Congress had objected to the special appropriation of funds requested by the Harding administration to send a U.S. commission to attend the centennial. Just as in previous debates over subsidies for steamship lines, congressmen were generally well disposed toward developing closer links with Brazil, but for political and commercial reasons they queried whether public funds should be used to promote private business interests at overseas expositions. The U.S. chargé d'affaires at Rio, Sheldon Crosby, stated in May 1922 that this news gave the impression of a slight, whether intentional or not, and had created an "unfavorable impression" in Brazil.[5]

In fact, in Washington both Secretary of State Charles Evans Hughes and Secretary of the Navy Edwin Denby were aware of the pending naval contract and wanted to secure it for the United States. A coordinated strategy between the two departments was put into effect. First, the Navy Department announced the release of Vogelgesang for overseas duty. In June the White House disclosed that a commission would be sent to the centennial exposition and subsequently reported that it would be headed by Hughes. "When the exhibition opens," remarked the British ambassador at Rio, John Tilley, "the United States hope to carry everything before them."[6] The positive steps taken by the Harding administration achieved their desired result toward the end of July when the Brazilian government stated officially that the naval contract was awarded to the United States. By the close of 1922 U.S. naval personnel had assembled in Rio to commence their duties.

At the centennial exposition American businessmen displayed the latest technological marvels such as large models of electric light bulbs and stimulated a "radiophone craze" by mounting a broadcasting station on Corcovado. Two U.S. battleships were in attendance in Guanabara Bay, and their crews performed flying displays and a series of drill demonstrations. Although local visitors were duly impressed, the British ambassador reckoned that "the results do not seem to have been commensurate with the efforts made."[7] Partly responsible for this was the fact that Brazilians regarded their centennial as an international occasion and were unable to give any extra attention to their American guests. Consequently, there was no official attempt to create the public relations fanfare associated with Root's visit in 1906. Moreover, in marked contrast to Root, Hughes appeared much more reserved in manner. He stayed "a very short time" and gave "the idea of being conscientiously civil to people whom he despised," reported the British ambassador. Considerably more local interest was attracted by the presence of a commission from revolutionary Mexico and by the visit and eloquent speeches of the president of Portugal.[8]

The whole issue of naval armament was further complicated by the decision of the Pan-American Union in 1922 to revive the Pan-American Conference system. A previous meeting had been scheduled for Santiago de Chile in 1914 but had been cancelled by the outbreak of war in Europe. It would now take place at the Chilean capital in March 1923. The Brazilian government of President Artur da Silva Bernardes publicly welcomed the development as a step toward Pan-American harmony, but it was privately disturbed at the inclusion of the reduction of armaments as one of the most prominent items on the agenda. The new minister for foreign affairs, José Félix Alves Pacheco, feared that the Spanish-American nations intended to thwart Brazil's expressed desire to build up its military forces. Pacheco decided to act preemptively and startled the foreign offices of South America in December 1922 by proposing a preliminary meeting of the ABC countries to discuss specifically the question of disarmament. The proposal, however, received short shrift in both Buenos Aires and Santiago, where it was condemned for being vague and hastily conceived. In effect, Argentina had no desire to be seen as following Pacheco's lead and grasped the opportunity to accuse him of seeking to circumvent the interests of the other Latin American nations in order to pursue Brazil's own selfish militaristic aims.

The Pan-American Conference assembled on schedule in March 1923. Still smarting from the way he believed that Argentina had deliberately chosen to misinterpret his attempt at "open diplomacy," Pacheco feared that the meeting would only cause him further embarrassment.[9] The fact that the Harding administration had taken a negative stance toward the conference was fortuitously helpful to Brazil because it ensured that little substantive progress could be made on the question of limiting armaments. However, as it became evident that the conference had drawn Argentina and Brazil further apart, the State Department showed concern that this would be blamed on the United States. A press communiqué was hastily issued, expressing the hope of the U.S. government that "notwithstanding the inherent difficulties, a satisfactory formula may be found" to resolve the differences between the two countries.[10]

Despite Spanish-American suspicions and any imagined Brazilian pretensions, the naval mission did not mark a special relationship or militaristic conspiracy between Brazil and the United States. Indeed, from the inception of the mission in 1922, U.S. officials consistently downgraded its significance. This attitude appeared to confirm that the primary motivation of the Harding administration had been to prevent the contract falling into the hands of Great Britain. Once this was achieved, the State Department lost interest. Nevertheless, the winning of the contract represented a notable diplomatic success for the United States and served to establish the foundation for the future extension of American influence over the training, operational procedures, and strategy of the Brazilian navy.

External Diplomacy

At the Versailles Conference the Latin American nations approved the establishment of a new world organization known as the League of Nations with its headquarters located in Geneva, Switzerland. In contrast to the United States, they all duly became members of the Assembly of the League. Brazil, as the largest Latin American nation and a co-belligerent in the war, was honored with a temporary seat on the League Council. In addition, the U.S. decision to remain outside the League served to enhance Brazil's sense of its international status and influence. As the only Latin American nation initially represented on the Council, Brazil was able to outshine Argentina and irritated the latter by claiming the leadership of the American continent. "Now, we have become a nation," one diplomat proudly boasted, "that reaches beyond its continent to take part and be heard in the deliberations that concern the world."[11]

But lesser nations such as Brazil enjoyed an equal status in League affairs only in theory and not in practice. This was not particularly upsetting to the Bernardes administration, which considered such matters as European boundary disputes and the fate of German minorities to be peripheral to Brazilian national interests. Nor was there any disposition to exploit the absence of the United States and support Spanish-American proposals to use the League as a forum for the discussion of Latin American issues. From the point of view of President Bernardes and Foreign Minister Pacheco, its principal value lay in Brazil's membership on the League Council. This was a place of signal honor that more than compensated for the country's evident lack of tangible diplomatic influence. Unlike the great European powers, however, Brazil's membership on the Council was nonpermanent and subject to election by the Assembly. According to Edwin Morgan, the securing of permanent status soon became "the principal aspiration" of Itamaraty.[12]

The lukewarm reception given to Brazil's desire for a permanent seat was not entirely due to the insensitivity of the great European powers. In fact, the idea of a special status reserved for Brazil had never been acceptable to the other Latin American governments. During the early 1920s traditional Spanish-American suspicions were heightened by Brazil's evident determination to strengthen and modernize its military forces. As a means of expressing their displeasure, the Spanish-American nations proposed that the two

Council seats reserved for the hemisphere should rotate annually among all the Latin American countries.

The issue came to the forefront of world affairs in 1925 as a result of the Locarno agreement that established postwar boundaries in Europe and paved the way for admitting Germany to the League Council. Brazil was not a party to the agreement made at Locarno and, strictly speaking, was not therefore bound by its provisions. In fact, the Bernardes administration regarded it as a signal opportunity to press once again for Brazil's own permanent seat. At a time, however, when the Brazilian republic suffered from serious domestic political unrest exemplified by the *tenentes* revolt in 1922, a military revolt in the state of São Paulo in 1924, and the existence in the interior of an insurgent army known as the "Prestes Column," the implied claim that Brazil was a member equal to Germany provoked ridicule in Europe. Moreover, a series of clumsy diplomatic maneuvers including the use of the veto to prevent German membership further isolated Brazil and proved counterproductive because they merely revived the widely held impression already gained at the Versailles Conference that Brazilian diplomacy was selfish and unyielding. Not only was a permanent seat on the Council definitely ruled out, but Brazil also faced being defeated in forthcoming elections for the nonpermanent seats. To avoid incurring further diplomatic embarrassment, Brazil announced on June 11, 1926, that it would formally leave the Council and the League.

British officials suspected the involvement of Edwin Morgan, who was known to be a long-time critic of the League. According to the *Diario Oficial*, the ambassador had visited the Catete Palace on June 11 to congratulate Bernardes for deciding to leave the League. "The action of Brazil," a British diplomat claimed, "was largely due to American edging at the psychological moment." The actual role of the United States was hardly so decisive in explaining Brazil's action. The *New York World* reported the suspicion that "it is to Rio's advantage to create an impression among South Americans that the United States approved and applauded the withdrawal." Moreover, the State Department immediately disavowed the report that Morgan had congratulated Bernardes and sought to distance itself from any semblance of complicity in the course of events at Geneva. U.S. reluctance to assist Brazilian pretensions at Geneva did not reflect a Machiavellian strategy to undermine the League. If anything, U.S. diplomats were critical of Brazil's immature international behavior and appeared to wish that Brazil remain a member of the Council. While the argument that the League had become a purely selfish European instrument was not disputed, it was considered that the Bernardes administration had forced the issue to the point where Brazil was compelled to withdraw. The *Philadelphia Public Ledger* bluntly summed up: "It was Brazil that raised the question and Brazil that pushed the answer to its extreme."[13]

The events at Geneva resulted in diplomatic humiliation for Brazil. Ever since the Versailles Conference, Brazil had affected the role of a world power, but the illusion could be sustained no longer. Even though the State Department had been singularly unhelpful over the League issue, Bernardes confided to Morgan in June that Brazil planned "to return to the orbit of her continental relations" and especially to cooperate closely with the United States.[14] The Pan-American Conference to be held in Havana in 1928 provided the opportunity to effect close diplomatic cooperation. The conference coincided with Latin American anger at the Coolidge administration's military intervention in Nicaragua and what was believed to be the exertion of unreasonable U.S. diplomatic pressure on Mexico over disputed oil rights. When the Brazilian delegation assembled in Rio prior to leaving for Cuba, Morgan reported that Foreign Minister Otávio Mangabeira had personally stressed the importance of cooperating fully with the views of the U.S. delegation.

As expected, the Havana Conference provided the arena for the Argentine delegation to launch a vigorous denunciation of U.S. military aggression in Nicaragua. The Brazilian delegates adopted a passive attitude and refused to join the general condemnation of U.S. interventionism. In so doing, they inevitably came to be seen as siding with the United States. After the conference had ended, the Brazilian ambassador to Washington reported the compliment from Secretary of State Frank Kellogg that "Brazil has been a tower of strength to us." The ambassador added jubilantly that "the Government of the United States would never forget the work of the Brazilian delegates" and that the conference had "considerably strengthened the friendship between the two countries."[15]

So long starved of tangible diplomatic successes, Itamaraty could not resist the temptation to boast that a special understanding existed between the two non-Spanish powers. Hopes of a privileged relationship with Washington, however, were rudely shattered by the conclusion of the Kellogg-Briand (Anti-

War) Peace Pact. Ever since the hosting of the Washington naval conference in 1921, Republican administrations had stressed the desirability of preserving world peace. Throughout 1928 Secretary of State Kellogg worked closely with his French counterpart, Aristide Briand, to devise a treaty to outlaw war. Amid a fanfare of international celebration, the Peace Pact was signed at Paris in August 1928 by Kellogg, Briand, and the foreign ministers of the leading European powers. The initial public announcement in June 1928 of the pact's formal conclusion came as a surprise to the governments of Latin America because the State Department had neglected to keep them informed of developments. Morgan reported that Mangabeira was "embarrassed" by the fact that the Brazilian press apparently knew more than Itamaraty. Moreover, the foreign minister was clearly unhappy that Brazil had not been invited to the signing ceremony at Paris, while "minor" nations such as Czechoslovakia and Poland had been included.[16]

Morgan faced a difficult task in soothing bruised Brazilian feelings because the demeaning of Brazil's international status in this instance was attributed directly to action taken by Washington. Only a few days before the holding of the Paris Conference, Morgan recorded the foreign minister's "considerable annoyance" that Brazil was not given "special consideration" in view of the support that the Brazilian delegation had given at the Havana Conference. The anxious tone of the ambassador's dispatch betrayed his concern that officials in Washington had forgotten about the special characteristics of Brazil: "there are always people ready to suggest that the United States is unduly inclined to group Brazil with the South American Powers of Spanish origin and does not differentiate Brazil's peculiar position in view of her racial and linguistic origin and her special economic relations arising from the fact that the United States is the principal consumer of her chief agricultural product."[17]

Since the announcement in August 1927 that he would not be a presidential candidate in 1928, President Calvin Coolidge had presided over a lame-duck administration. The conclusion of the Peace Pact raised morale, and securing its ratification provided a tangible and worthy objective for the administration's last few months in office. By mid-September the process began of asking foreign governments to sign the peace treaty. A State Department memorandum observed that "it is important to play up to the South Americans particularly."

Kellogg informed Morgan that he hoped Brazil would exercise an important influence over its neighbors by being "one of the first formally to adhere to the Treaty."[18]

Now that the State Department had to ask for Brazilian approval, Itamaraty seized the opportunity to show its annoyance over perceived slights. On January 31 Kellogg met with the Brazilian ambassador at the State Department and made a special plea for support, but the Brazilian government remained intransigent. As the Brazilian foreign minister explained, Brazil was a "friend" and not "a servile follower" of the United States.[19] Two years after withdrawing from the League of Nations, Brazil once again adopted a proud and unyielding attitude that appeared to obstruct diplomatic efforts to promote world peace. No longer "a tower of strength," Brazil chose to be uncooperative with the United States. Not only did Brazil pointedly refuse to sign the Kellogg-Briand Peace Pact, but it also resisted being directly associated with U.S. diplomatic efforts to mediate the Chaco territorial dispute between Bolivia and Paraguay.[20] As the election year of 1930 approached, however, foreign affairs were neglected as the Brazilian political world became almost totally absorbed with the question of the selection of the next president of the republic.

Economic Ties

During World War I American business recorded an impressive economic advance in Brazil due largely to the increase in value of American exports. Although the wartime gains were soon challenged by the revival of strong European competition, especially from Great Britain, American exports began to rise again in the second half of the 1920s. This success reflected the emergence of a new pattern of trade in which the United States was the preeminent leader. Whereas Britain's commercial dominance in nineteenth-century Latin America had been largely based on the export of coal and textiles, Brazil and other countries in the region now looked to the United States to supply the new products of the twentieth century such as automobiles, films, radio and telephone communications, petroleum products, and electrical goods. The market for these items grew steadily, restrained only by the financial inability of the local population to buy.

Trade from Brazil to the United States fluctuated during the 1920s. Brazilian exports peaked in 1919 at $233 million and then fell to $96 million in 1921. A slow recovery began until exports were in excess of $200 million by the middle of the decade. However, in marked contrast to the changing pattern of trade in American exports, Brazil had no new lucrative products to sell. Indeed, the long-standing importance attached to exporting coffee increased rather than decreased. In 1925 it was estimated that coffee accounted for 87 percent of Brazil's earnings from all its sales to the United States. Consequently, the latter remained Brazil's single biggest market, with purchases amounting to more than 40 percent of Brazil's total annual exports. The dependent economic relationship with the United States aroused little adverse comment in Brazil. To sell coffee was considered an end in itself and vital for national prosperity. Moreover, the overall balance of trade remained in favor of Brazil. Americans could hardly be criticized not only for being Brazil's best customers but also for purchasing more from Brazil than they sold. "We buy from the people who buy most from us," summed up the *Jornal do commércio;* "these are precisely the great people of the United States who represent the world's greatest consuming market."[21]

The world war also witnessed the decline of the City of London and the rise of Wall Street in New York as the world's leading money market and financial center. U.S. capital investments flooded the world, and substantial sums were directed toward Latin America. Prior to 1914 there had been relatively little American financial involvement in Brazil. While American investment amounted to scarcely $50 million, British loans were valued in excess of $1 billion. But the image of Brazil as a land of unlimited opportunity continued to cast its spell. "No territory in the world," stated the *Wall Street Journal,* "is better worth exploitation than Brazil's."[22] By 1929 American investment in Brazil reached almost $500 million. Although this was only one-third of the corresponding British figure, American investment had grown at a faster rate than that of Britain during the decade and constituted a larger proportion of new capital issues.[23]

In its ever-widening search for markets and raw materials, American business invested directly in Latin America to finance both the acquisition and establishment of local subsidiary companies. Indeed, British and foreign competitors found themselves overwhelmed by the sheer scale of the financial resources available to the giant U.S. corporations, which included Armour, Ford, General Electric, General Motors, International Telephone and Telegraph, Radio Corporation of America, Standard Oil, Swift, United States Steel, and Westinghouse. Corporate investment brought new factories and jobs. It also spread "Americanization" in the form of business skills and cultural values.

The building of "outposts of Yankee enterprise" was visibly symbolized in Brazil by Henry Ford and his Ford Motor Company.[24] At its São Paulo plant in 1919, the company assembled just over 2,000 automobiles in the year. In 1925 production had increased to the same figure per month, with an annual capacity of 45,000. Model Ts, Fordson trucks, and tractors became a regular sight on the roads of Brazil. By 1928 the Ford Motor Company had authorized 700 agencies and more than 2,000 garages all over Brazil to market, distribute, and repair its products. In typical American entrepreneurial fashion, Henry Ford's ambitions were constantly expanding. Acquiring a concession of territory equivalent in size to the state of Connecticut, he ordered work to commence in 1928 on his controversial and ultimately ill-fated scheme to locate a new and prosperous city known as "Fordlândia" in the Amazon jungle.[25]

Like their Spanish-American neighbors, Brazilians were impressed and often overawed by the achievements of American business. They welcomed increased trade with the United States and the inflow of U.S. capital investment that was valued as an important means of promoting their own domestic economic development, but they could also be irritated by the burgeoning symbols of the growing American economic presence, especially in utilities such as telephone and electricity, tramways, and the radio and film industries. Following a pattern already set by the Mexican Revolution, nationalist sentiment was especially alarmed by reports of American capitalists buying up substantial amounts of national territory and seeking to control economic resources. In Brazil, the schemes of the American entrepreneur Percival Farquhar to exploit the vast iron ore deposits located in Minas Gerais raised particular suspicion and prompted the Brazilian Congress in 1926 to pass a constitutional amendment securing the nationalization of all mineral deposits located on federal land.

American economic expansion in Brazil during the 1920s was largely the achievement of private individuals, financial institutions, and industrial corporations. The U.S. government adopted an essentially supportive role. No longer so concerned about foreign competition in international trade, the United States abandoned the pursuit of special tariff concessions and sought equality of commercial treatment. The aim was equal access or the "open door" to the markets of the world. The new commercial strategy was contained in a proviso of the 1922 Tariff Act that ruled that existing tariff preferences should be terminated and replaced by new treaties containing a most-favored-nation clause. However, beyond the bland prediction from Secretary of State Hughes that "in the long run this policy offers larger advantages of amity and trade," there was no tangible reason for Brazil to conclude a new commercial treaty.[26] So long as the large majority of Brazilian products were imported into the United States free of duty, Brazil had nothing to gain from acquiring most-favored-nation status. On the other hand, a treaty containing the most-favored-nation clause would entitle the United States to receive whatever tariff advantages Brazil might grant to other nations. This would apply not only to existing arrangements but any treaty that might be negotiated in the future.

An issue of more immediate concern in U.S.-Brazilian relations was the revival of the controversy over valorization. This occurred after the Brazilian federal government reacted to the dramatic slump in the world coffee price by seeking to regulate supply and thereby maintain, if not raise, prices to higher levels. On this occasion, the term "valorization" was scrupulously avoided in favor of the less pejorative description "the permanent defense of coffee." In a further attempt to escape the difficulties associated with the first valorization scheme, control over stocks was maintained by Brazilians and not assigned to foreign bankers or overseas valorization committees. The policy was highly costly and attracted only reluctant support from the economy-minded Bernardes administration. Growing disenchantment with federal attitudes resulted in the state of São Paulo establishing its own Defense Institute in December 1924. Despite the internal dissensions, the overall strategy was successful in that coffee prices rose in 1924 to a level 50 percent higher than the preceding year.

Officials in Washington were well aware of Brazilian attempts to influence coffee prices. However, it was not considered a matter for either diplomatic protest or discussion at government level. In contrast to the previous valorization controversy, there was little likelihood of legal investigation because there was no discernible evidence of the existence in the United States of a coffee "trust." Indeed, with coffee selling for as little as ten cents per pound in 1922, U.S. officials regarded Brazilian efforts as justified, if not necessary, to alleviate the damaging effects of overproduction. Moreover, the recent experience of implementing wartime emergency measures had altered American attitudes toward the idea of state intervention in the economy.

Just as in the previous "coffee question," the rise in prices after 1922 aroused satisfaction in Brazil but growing displeasure in the United States. One group of American coffee importers represented by the National Coffee Roasters Association was especially critical. Because the matter was not one of diplomatic dispute between governments, the coffee roasters took their case to the Commerce Department. The decision to bypass the State Department also reflected the fact that even since Herbert Hoover had become secretary of commerce in 1921, the Commerce Department had challenged the claim of the State Department to possess the leading role in the promotion of U.S. foreign trade. In December 1924, at the same time that the Defense Institute was being established in São Paulo, the National Coffee Roasters Association met with Hoover to ask for federal government assistance to bring about a reduction in the price of coffee.

Hoover's economic views were well known and guaranteed the roasters a favorable response. The celebrated "rugged individualist" firmly believed in a "free" economy both at home and overseas and was acutely suspicious of attempts by foreign governments to establish monopolies over raw materials. Taking advantage of the retirement of Charles Evans Hughes in January 1925, Hoover seized the initiative. The new secretary of state, Frank Kellogg, found himself relegated to a subordinate role as Hoover launched a public relations campaign against what he described as "the Brazilian coffee cartel." A report prepared by Commerce Department officials estimated that Americans were being overcharged more than $80 million a year for their coffee. By informing and mobilizing the public, Hoover sought to encourage the formation of a countercartel representing American consumers that would employ its own market power to force a reduction in the price of coffee. At the same time he sought to persuade U.S. banks to withhold loans to the Defense Institute.

Hoover had embarked on a battle against the coffee cartel as part of a campaign for free access to the world's raw materials. By the end of 1925 coffee prices had fallen to twenty-two cents per pound. Hoover noted gratifyingly that this difference meant an annual saving to the American consumer of $50 million. While the government of São Paulo wisely avoided entering into a direct confrontation with the most powerful political figure in America, it refused to abandon the policy of defense. In January 1926 it was announced that the Paulistas had successfully raised a loan of five million pounds in London. This represented a considerable boost for the Defense Institute, which was now able to proceed with its plan for substantial coffee purchases. The U.S. commercial attaché at Rio, William Schurz, observed that the loan "has greatly strengthened the British position in São Paulo and has correspondingly reduced our prestige in that field."[27]

Despite his best efforts, Hoover had not been able either to organize an effective boycott of coffee by American consumers or to prevent São Paulo from raising a loan in the international money market. On Capitol Hill there was talk of reprisal against Brazil, but Hoover appeared before a congressional committee to argue that retaliation would only "aggravate" the problem. According to the *New York Times*, the secretary of commerce was acting like "a man trying to put out a fire which he himself had started."[28]

In effect, neither side wished to prolong the controversy. Hoover had somewhat arrogantly believed that the Paulistas must succumb to the combination of financial pressure and the inescapable logic of free-market economics. However, as other U.S. administrations had discovered in past dealings with Brazil, the coffee question was a highly sensitive issue and one in which American demands provoked vigorous Brazilian assertions of independence rather than compliance. Though he might claim credit for bringing down coffee prices to acceptable levels, Hoover's intervention had plainly backfired. He had upset the American banking community and had caused bad feelings in Brazil. By compelling São Paulo to resort to a European loan, he had hindered the strengthening of American economic links with Brazil. Indeed, in this instance the forceful intrusion of the Commerce Department into the making and conduct of U.S. economic foreign policy had proved misguided. The British ambassador at Rio summed up that Hoover "has just been taught a hard lesson."[29]

The 1930 Revolution

It was scarcely surprising that the nomination of Hoover as Republican presidential candidate in June 1928 should arouse some apprehension in Brazil. While the Brazilian press was inclined to be sympathetic toward the Democratic candidate, Al Smith, Hoover was portrayed as "the exponent of dissolving materialism, of mechanical civilization, and of a cold blooded imperialism which characterizes the Yankees."[30] The Brazilian ambassador to Washington, however, reassuringly reported that Hoover's campaign speeches made no mention of foreign monopolies and did not reveal "his ancient hostility to Brazil concerning the coffee question."[31] In fact, now that coffee was no longer a divisive issue between the two countries, Edwin Morgan observed that local attitudes toward Hoover had markedly changed. Any remaining doubts were allayed when Hoover's victory in the presidential election was quickly followed by the announcement that he would make a goodwill tour of Latin America prior to his inauguration.

Rio de Janeiro was the president-elect's final Latin American port of call. When Hoover arrived at Rio, a rapturous welcome awaited him. "Lima, Santiago, Buenos Aires and Montevideo all gave wonderful receptions to Mr. Hoover," reported the correspondent of the *New York Times*, "but in point of numbers, enthusiasm, splendor of decorations and acclaim by the people, none has equaled the great welcome Brazil's metropolis staged today."[32] Brazilians were delighted at the attention paid by the visiting Americans to their country and its capital city. They were flattered to receive a visit from the next president of the United States and were determined to surpass Buenos Aires in their show of hospitality to their distinguished guest. The isolated references in the local press to Hoover as the representative of "a white country" and "the instrument of American imperialism"[33] were ignored as Cariocas warmed to a man who dismissed the bodyguards assigned to his motorcade on the ground that he needed no protection from Brazilians. Hoover was truly moved by his short stay in Brazil, especially by the huge crowds that greeted his arrival and the spectacular display of fireworks that accompanied his departure. Despite the fine speeches and numerous gestures of friendship, little of substance resulted from Hoover's short stay in Rio. Nevertheless, the visit of an American president-elect was an unprecedented event and helped to counter the indifference and misunderstanding that had become a feature of U.S.-Brazilian relations during the 1920s.

Prominent U.S. newspapers now praised Brazil's political and economic achievements. Indeed, Brazil had made considerable economic advances. Under Washington Luís Pereira de Sousa who had held the presidency since 1926, the federal government achieved its first budget surplus since 1908. Symbolic of the country's economic advance was the building of impressive new highways linking Rio with Petrópolis and with São Paulo. The latter city had become such a magnet for business and immigrants that it was known as the "Chicago" of South America. Edwin Morgan was delighted by the visible advance of U.S. economic influence, especially when it was at the expense of British business rivals. Nevertheless, he advised American bankers to exercise caution in making loans. While acknowledging the achievements of the Washington Luís administration, he was concerned that the country's prosperity depended heavily on earning foreign exchange from the export of coffee. Most of all he warned that the availability of foreign capital was tempting the Brazilian federal and state governments "to indulge to an unwarranted extent in what should be considered a luxury and not adopted as an habitual practice."[34]

The Wall Street Crash intervened in October 1929 to render Morgan's strictures unnecessary if not obsolete. During the ensuing months the world plunged into economic depression. No country was left unaffected by the severe contraction of international trade and investment. Indeed, Brazil's export-oriented economy made it more vulnerable than most. In terms of total trade with the United States, Brazilian exports fell by one-third from 1929 to 1930 while purchases from that country declined by almost one-half during the same period. By the middle of 1930 Brazil's foreign debt had climbed to over $1 billion and could only be serviced with great difficulty. As Brazil sank into economic crisis, however, the attention of the Brazilian political elite remained firmly concentrated not upon the state of the economy but upon the 1930 presidential election.

U.S. officials were not perturbed when Washington Luís proposed to flout the political tradition that he, a Paulista, would be succeeded in the presidency by a candidate from the state of Minas Gerais. He favored instead the governor of São Paulo, Júlio Prestes de Albuquerque. As Morgan predicted, the majority of state governors and political bosses duly conformed to the will of Washington Luís so that electoral victory was secured in March 1930 for Prestes over his opponent, the governor of Rio Grande do Sul, Getúlio Vargas. The Brazilian ambassador to Washington was delighted to send Itamaraty a clipping of yet another flattering editorial from the *Washington Post* that likened the Brazilian political system to that of the United States: "The election which has just been held in Brazil offers striking evidence of the success of the representative system of government in Latin America. This great South American republic has demonstrated its ability to maintain a government of the people, by the people and for the people." The editorial dismissed reports of "local disturbances" as "greatly magnified." In fact, the "lively" campaign was viewed as convincing evidence that "Brazil has developed a strong two-party system which has proved effective in expressing the will of the people." In their desire to present Brazil as a mirror image of the United States, the editors overlooked the fact that no more than 5 percent of Brazil's population had actually cast votes in the presidential election.[35]

On September 1, Morgan had a private audience with Washington Luís prior to taking his annual leave of absence in Europe. When the conversation turned to the matter of reports of political unrest, the president assured the ambassador that these were unfounded and that "public order was complete."[36] But the same could not be said for the rest of South America. The Bolivian government had already fallen in March 1930. In September a military coup compelled the resignation of the president in Argentina. Brazil's long-standing immunity from serious revolutionary disorder was suddenly broken on October 3. Insurgent military forces mobilized in the Northeast and the South and demanded the overthrow of Washington Luís and his replacement by Getúlio Vargas. The insurgents quickly secured their military objectives in the Northeast, but it was apparent that the decisive battle would take place in the South when the advancing army of Rio Grande do Sul attempted to enter the state of São Paulo.

In Morgan's absence, the relatively young and inexperienced U.S. chargé at Rio, Walter Washington, was primarily concerned about ensuring the safety of U.S. citizens and their property. He was particularly apprehensive that serious fighting would break out in Pernambuco and suggested that a U.S. naval vessel visit the northeastern coast. "The Department," answered Secretary of State

Henry Stimson, "would be very loath to send any warships to Brazil." In contrast to recent disturbances in Argentina, Bolivia, and Peru, Brazil did not appear to be experiencing widespread public disorder. There was also a concern that the image of the United States in Latin America would be damaged by the sending of gunboats. Nonetheless, Stimson thought it wise to raise the matter at cabinet level on October 10 and to secure agreement to put the cruiser U.S.S. *Pensacola* on standby in Brazilian waters. To Stimson's annoyance, what had been intended as a covert arrangement was made public knowledge next day by the Navy Department. The task of damage limitation was undertaken by Assistant Secretary of State Francis White, who spent the weekend explaining to Brazilian officials that the sending of the U.S.S. *Pensacola* was in no way intended to undermine the authority of the federal government of Brazil. It was described purely as a precautionary measure to assist the evacuation of foreigners should an emergency arise.[37]

While the government of Washington Luís was displeased by the reported dispatch of a U.S. warship to the Northeast, it was delighted to learn of the refusal of the Hoover administration to recognize the belligerent rights claimed by the insurgents. Like Gresham during the Naval Revolt, Stimson argued that "it was the duty as well as the policy of this country to continue its good relations with the existing government."[38] But the decision not to grant belligerent rights to the insurgents implied American sympathy for Washington Luís. This was confirmed in October, when it was announced that the United States was imposing an embargo on the export of weapons to Brazil. Trade under license was not affected, a qualification that permitted continued arms sales to the Brazilian government, while the same privilege was not granted to the insurgents.

"Brazil Coup Stuns Washington Circles," read the headline of the *New York Times* on October 25.[39] Contrary to the expectation, if not the desire of the Hoover administration, the insurgents successfully seized power in Brazil. Stimson was now seen to have backed the wrong side and was facetiously called "Wrong-Horse Harry" by the Washington press corps. The question of the moment, however, was whether the United States would approve the new government. In September the Hoover administration had swiftly established diplomatic relations with the new military governments of Argentina, Bolivia, and Peru. But shell-shocked State Department officials were more circumspect about Brazil. Stimson advised delay, arguing that the unreliable nature of existing information from that country made it difficult to formulate an official response. It was known that a coup had definitely occurred in Rio, but the connection between the military junta and the insurgent forces in the south under Getúlio Vargas was unknown. Moreover, the State Department had made no effort to cultivate relations with the latter and knew very little about his background and personality. Stimson's initial reaction was therefore to proceed cautiously and try to find out what exactly was taking place in Brazil.

Stimson's caution was understandable but was out of step with the pace of events in Brazil itself. The question of recognition became a matter of some urgency as agreement was quickly reached between the military junta and the insurgents. Vargas arrived in Rio on October 31 and three days later announced the formation of a provisional government. The conflict had clearly ended, and it was soon evident that several foreign powers, especially Great Britain, wished to recognize Vargas's government. Edwin Morgan, who had hastily returned to Brazil from his vacation in Europe, also reported that a number of Latin American countries were on the point of establishing diplomatic relations with the new government. On Wednesday, November 5, Stimson sent a telegram asking for his ambassador's opinion on recognition, adding that "we will not be hurried by the British in determining what is the proper action for us to take."[40]

Recognition followed only three days later as Stimson had to confront the reality that the provisional government controlled the country. American behavior in 1930 was evocative of that which followed the fall of the empire. Like Dom Pedro II in 1889, Washington Luís had clearly lost power. In both instances, however, there was a reluctance to admit the overthrow of a friendly ruler, especially when this would entail conferring legitimacy upon a military coup. When recognition was abruptly granted by Stimson in November 1930, the action was not dissimilar to Blaine's impulsiveness in January 1890. Getúlio Vargas was pleased, but he attached no great significance to external diplomatic recognition. The struggle to oust Washington Luís was a purely Brazilian affair and had been conducted without resort to appeals for assistance from any foreign power. Once the revolt was under way the crucial task for the insurgents was to persuade the senior military command in Rio to desert the president. In this the foreign powers had no meaningful role to play.

On the other hand, some resentment did exist toward the Hoover administration on account of the imposition of the arms embargo and its implicit support for Washington Luís. One of the convenient means by which the new government asserted its independence and, at the same time, appeased nationalist supporters was to show its displeasure against the United States by requesting the termination of the naval mission. No objection was raised in Washington. Any attempt to do so would only have provoked retaliation. The State Department was still dismayed by the unexpected turn of political events and desired to be conciliatory. In Rio, Morgan sensed that portentous events were taking place. "The revolution which has occurred in Brazil," he told Stimson, "is fundamental and will affect the future of the country profoundly."[41]

The Vargas Regime

Most U.S. leaders knew little about the political views of the new Brazilian president. He had served as minister of finance in the Washington Luís administration from 1926 to 1927 and was reputed to be competent, honest, and conservative but without a national political base outside Rio Grande do Sul. His enemies looked upon his conciliatory nature as a weakness. In July 1932, the Paulistas directly challenged the authority of the federal government and declared their intention of mobilizing and leading a national movement to overthrow Vargas and restore constitutional government. U.S. officials adopted a policy of watchful waiting. The Hoover administration was unwilling to accord belligerent rights to the insurgents and judged that such action "would be a gratuitous and unfriendly act to the Government of Brazil."[42] On this occasion, the policy was vindicated because the federal army and state militias remained loyal to Vargas. São Paulo was encircled by large land forces and subjected to a blockade by sea and attacks from the air. The insurgents finally surrendered on September 29. Vargas had won a personal victory over his Paulista opponents and the forces of regionalism.

At a time of severe economic depression and political upheaval throughout the world, the foreign policy of the Vargas regime was understandably cautious and reactive. This was especially evident in its attitude to regional affairs. A principal objective was to maintain friendly relations with neighboring countries and most of all with Argentina. Indeed, the dramatic contraction of trade with traditional European markets after 1929 served to enhance Argentina's significance as a trading partner and, in particular, as an important outlet for Brazilian exports. Moreover, diplomatic consultation and cooperation with Argentina was valued as a result of the emergence of serious boundary disputes between Peru and Colombia over Letícia and especially the outbreak of the Chaco War in 1932 between Paraguay and Bolivia. The latter conflict attracted the close attention of Itamaraty and the military because it was feared that the violence might spill over into the adjoining Brazilian territory. Brazilian diplomats cooperated with officials from Argentina, other Latin American countries, and the United States in offering good offices that were eventually instrumental in helping to bring about a peaceful resolution to both border disputes.

The outwardly healthy state of relations between Brazil and Argentina was underscored by the visit of the Argentine president, Augustín Justo, to Rio in October 1933. In turn, Vargas was warmly received in Buenos Aires two years later. The latter occasion was notable in marking the first official visit by a serving Brazilian president to Argentina since Campos Sales in 1900. While both nations desired closer commercial relations, latent national rivalries over the location of territorial boundaries were stimulated by the Chaco War and Brazil's consciousness of Argentina's current military superiority. Brazilian military leaders suspected that Argentina had territorial designs on both Paraguay and Bolivia and was even preparing secret plans for an invasion of southern Brazil. "Our policy has been one of cordial friendship with Argentina and abstention in the Chaco question," Vargas informed the Brazilian ambassador to the United States, Osvaldo de Sousa Aranha, in 1934 and added: "We should maintain it, but we need to take military precautions."[43]

The sense of insecurity and the desire to redress Brazil's perceived military weakness in relation to its neighbor were heightened by the growing conflict in the wider world, especially the Italian invasion of Ethiopia in 1935 and the outbreak of the Spanish Civil War in 1936. These distant wars did not directly threaten Brazilian national security, but they attracted public attention and concern on account of the large number of immigrants from Italy and Spain who were resident in Brazil.

Diplomatic tension with Argentina was particularly visible whenever Brazil considered naval rearmament. In 1936 the Brazilian government expressed a desire to buy six decommissioned cruisers from the U.S. Navy over a period of ten years. "It is rumored with considerable apprehension in Argentine naval circles," telegraphed the U.S. ambassador in Buenos Aires, "that Brazil is to purchase cruisers from the United States Navy."[44] The Brazilian ambassador in Washington privately derided Argentine expressions of concern over Brazil's presumed lofty naval ambitions as "the same as a man armed with a machine gun being afraid of another armed with a simple pocketknife."[45] Accused of aiding a naval arms race, the State Department characteristically took fright and sought to avoid appearing to be choosing sides. It informed the Brazilian government that the order was approved "in principle" but would only be entered into "with the understanding that similar opportunities would be afforded to all of the other American republics should they desire to avail themselves of them."[46]

Reciprocity with the United States

Latin Americans were generally apprehensive over the victory of a "Roosevelt" in the 1932 U.S. presidential election because that surname had become firmly associated with the aggressive policy of the "Big Stick." Unlike his cousin Theodore, however, Franklin D. Roosevelt publicly announced a desire to act sympathetically toward the Latin American nations. As president, he basically continued Herbert Hoover's conciliatory policy toward the region although it now acquired a new name as a result of a section taken from Roosevelt's inaugural address of March 4, 1933, in which he dedicated the United States to the policy of the "good neighbor."

In Brazil, Vargas publicly applauded Roosevelt's inauguration and his proclamation of the "Good Neighbor Policy." In fact, maintaining a close relationship with the United States was an important aspect of Brazilian diplomacy during the 1930s. Despite currently experiencing the depths of economic depression, the United States still remained the most powerful nation in the hemisphere and, as Rio Branco had earlier argued, provided Brazil with its largest market for coffee and a valuable counterweight against any potential hostility from the

Spanish-American nations. The good feelings were reciprocated by President Roosevelt, who appreciated the significance of Brazil's friendship and especially its diplomatic support in helping to promote the Good Neighbor policy throughout the hemisphere. In November 1936 en route to the Pan-American Conference in Buenos Aires, Roosevelt made a point of stopping off at Rio de Janeiro, where he displayed his characteristic personal charm by lavishing praise on Vargas for adopting large-scale social welfare policies. He even lauded the Brazilian president as his coauthor in conceiving the idea of the New Deal.[47]

Especially significant in developing friendly relations between Brazil and the United States was the appointment of Osvaldo Aranha as Brazilian ambassador to Washington in 1934. Like Vargas, Aranha was also from the state of Rio Grande do Sul and was regarded as a protégé and confidant of the president. Aranha had no doubt that Washington was Brazil's most important overseas diplomatic posting, and like Salvador de Mendonça and Joaquim Nabuco, he made a point of cultivating American political society. Most importantly he developed both an excellent working relationship and a personal rapport with Undersecretary of State Sumner Welles. A staunch admirer of the achievements of the North American republic, Aranha was an enthusiast of approximation, which he believed was vital to Brazil for reasons of national security and also for assisting the much needed economic development that would turn Brazil into a modern industrial state. "So far as I can judge," noted the U.S. ambassador to Rio, Hugh Gibson, "he [Aranha] is the initiator of the present definite movement in Brazil to draw away from Europe and throw Brazil's lot in with the United States."[48] Aranha, however, did not envisage a servile relationship because he firmly believed that the United States needed Brazil as a bridge to facilitate the implementation of the Good Neighbor policy throughout the hemisphere. "Without our country," the Brazilian diplomat once remarked, "the United States can do nothing in America."[49]

Behind the uplifting rhetoric of Roosevelt's Good Neighbor policy was also a desire to promote economic integration within the hemisphere that would increase trade and directly help the U.S. economy recover from the Great Depression. This would be achieved by the negotiation of bilateral reciprocal trade agreements involving mutual tariff reductions. As had been the case in the 1890s, the reciprocity policy of the 1930s was very suitable for and mostly aimed at Latin America, where it was known that U.S. exports were losing their share of the market to European competition. The question of reducing tariff barriers and trade restrictions was discussed at the Montevideo Pan-American Conference in December 1933, and a resolution was passed recommending the negotiation of commercial treaties based on reciprocal concessions.

Brazil was a prominent element of this evolving U.S. commercial strategy. Although Brazil was traditionally one of America's largest markets in Latin America, as a consequence of the Depression annual U.S. exports had sharply declined from more than $100 million in 1929 to only around $40 million in 1934. The selection in 1933 of the experienced diplomat Hugh Gibson as the new U.S. ambassador aroused comment in Rio and was regarded by the British Foreign Office as an indication that the Americans "mean to develop their opportunities in Brazil."[50] Indeed, U.S. officials were characteristically confident of securing a favorable commercial treaty with Brazil that would quickly reverse the downward trend in trade. For example, the chief of the division of Latin American affairs, Edwin Wilson, considered that a reduction of Brazil's tariff on American goods was only fair "in view of the fact that Brazilian exports to the United States greatly exceeded Brazilian imports from the United States."[51] It was also believed that tariff reductions could be gained by the judicious application of commercial pressure in the shape of the threat to impose a tax on imports of Brazilian coffee. In the opinion of British officials, Brazil's vulnerability gave it the status of "a conquered country."[52]

In June 1934 the U.S. Congress passed the Reciprocal Trade Agreements Act giving the president authority to implement the reciprocity policy by executive action. Secretary of State Cordell Hull told Gibson of the administration's plan to negotiate a series of trade agreements and its intention "to include Brazil among the first countries with which such agreements are concluded."[53] The progress of discussions in Washington was greatly facilitated by the arrival of Osvaldo Aranha as the new Brazilian ambassador in October 1934. A draft treaty was agreed and signed on February 2, 1935. For American exporters the agreement contained tariff reductions on a variety of goods ranging from capital machinery to flour. In return, around 90 percent of Brazilian exports to the United States, including coffee, would be admitted free of duty. Among the nations of South America, Brazil was the first nation to sign a reciprocity agreement with the United States. Like John W. Foster in 1890, Hull was very pleased at securing a positive response from Brazil. He enthusiastically welcomed the treaty as a step on the road "away from medieval mercantilism" and a representation of the "first break in the logjam of international trade."[54]

Once more, however, ratification of an agreement signed in Washington was subject to delay in Brazil. Although Vargas had secured election as president in 1934, the return to constitutional government stimulated a marked upsurge of political activity that made him reluctant to interfere in the treaty's ratification process that was taking place in the newly formed Congress. The president's passive approach allowed matters to drift. In reality, so long as the vitally important coffee trade was not adversely affected, the fate of the treaty had little significance for Brazil. In June, however, Ambassador Gibson reported that "special interests, principally industrial," were complaining that they had not been consulted over the terms of the arrangement and were vigorously lobbying the Brazilian Congress to reconsider the tariff reductions given to U.S. goods.[55]

Although the treaty was stalled in the Brazilian Congress, the Vargas government recognized that close economic cooperation with the United States was vital in bringing about Brazil's recovery from the economic Depression. Foreign Minister José Carlos de Macedo Soares tactfully informed the U.S. ambassador that President Vargas was "well disposed" to the treaty, but that he was also "apathetic" and "needed to be stirred into action." The foreign minister even promised to speak to the president personally and "impress upon him the necessity for him to take an active part in the drive for ratification." Macedo Soares faithfully kept his word and next day informed Gibson that Vargas had instructed business leaders and members of Congress to cease their "obstructionist tactics" and to proceed to the ratification of the treaty as quickly as possible.[56] To nobody's surprise, the intervention of the president proved decisive in that the treaty passed the Chamber of Deputies by 127 to 51 votes and was ratified by Congress on November 30. The treaty officially came into effect on January 1, 1936, eleven months after it had been first signed with so much fanfare in Washington. The satisfaction of U.S. officials, however, was tempered by awareness that Brazil was also actively looking beyond the United States to Germany as an alternative source of trade and capital investment.

5   The Global Crisis

"Brazil must stand or fall with the United States," President Getúlio Vargas reportedly told his cabinet at a meeting to discuss the global crisis in January 1942.[1] The friendly sentiment was warmly welcomed and reciprocated by leading U.S. officials. For some time they had been disturbed by the fascist sympathies displayed by Vargas ever since the establishment of the Estado Novo in 1937. In fact, Vargas had openly sought to play off Germany against the United States in order to maximize the economic advantages for Brazil. The relationship with the United States, however, was significantly boosted in 1939 by the convergence of national interests arising from the outbreak of war in Europe. The war closed off trade links between Brazil and Germany and greatly enhanced the strategic significance of Brazil's long coastline bordering the Atlantic Ocean. Just as in World War I, Brazil was again highly valued in the United States as a supplier of strategic minerals and raw materials. After the United States entered the war in 1941, the northeastern region of Brazil effectively became a major U.S. military base and staging post for supplying the allied campaign in North Africa and Italy.

Brazil officially declared war on Germany in August 1942. Despite talk of a relationship of equals, Brazil was essentially a satellite of the United States throughout the war. The reward was substantial U.S. financial and material assistance that enabled Brazil to surpass Argentina as the leading military power in South America. In addition, Brazil gained international prestige because it was the only South American country to take on an active combat role in the war. The participation of 25,000 soldiers of the Brazilian Expeditionary Force (FEB), who fought in the Italian campaign under U.S. military command, encouraged Brazil once again to aspire to the status of a world power. The achievement of Brazil's diplomatic ambitions, however, was dependent on the continuation of U.S. diplomatic support, which was effectively ended by President Franklin D. Roosevelt's death in 1945.

The German Challenge

The negotiation of the 1935 reciprocal trade agreement between Brazil and the United States demonstrated the importance that both countries attached to developing trade with each other. But the most notable growth in Brazil's overseas commerce during the 1930s was not with the United States but with Germany. In marked contrast to customary international trading practice and the principle of most-favored-nation treatment, the Nazi government that came to power in Germany in 1933 preferred to conduct foreign trade in what amounted to a barter system in which goods were paid for in a special German currency known as "aski" or compensation marks. These marks were not freely convertible into foreign exchange or gold and could only be used to buy German goods. The arrangement appeared restrictive but was particularly attractive to Brazil and to other Latin American countries not only because it offered a signal opportunity to increase exports at a time of world economic depression, but also because it obviated the need to allocate scarce foreign exchange and gold reserves to finance foreign trade. Moreover, Germany was keen to buy just what Brazil wanted to sell — coffee and agricultural goods — in exchange for manufactured products and capital goods including arms and munitions, which were eagerly desired by the Brazilian military. The barter system was so successful that Brazil doubled its exports to Germany from 1933 to 1938. Germany purchased large quantities of coffee and rubber and also became the biggest single foreign market for Brazilian cotton and cacao. During the same period Germany's share of Brazil's import trade more than doubled from 12 percent to almost 25 percent. In 1938 the value of German exports to Brazil slightly exceeded those of the United States. Only five years earlier Brazil had purchased twice as much from the United States as from Germany.

While Brazil welcomed the opportunity to diversify its foreign exports, the United States was alarmed at the rise of German economic competition and what was considered to be the unfair use of compensation marks. Moreover, Germany's economic drive in Brazil coincided with the start of Cordell Hull's policy of concluding reciprocal trade treaties. Itamaraty was quick to reassure U.S. ambassador Hugh Gibson, who duly reported to Washington that the Germans were not seeking to negotiate a full commercial treaty and that he had been "told definitely that no commitment would be made until Aranha had had an opportunity to conclude his negotiations in the United States."[2]

But in 1934 Germany and Brazil had agreed informally to permit trade in compensation marks, and Hull remained concerned that the growing commerce between the two countries and especially the use of compensation marks undermined his policy of breaking down national barriers to secure preeminence for the United States in hemispheric trade. The Brazilian-German connection had unsettling military implications as well. Prominent military leaders such as Generals Eurico Gaspar Dutra and Pedro Aurélio de Góes Monteiro were avowed admirers of German military achievements and argued that closer contacts and especially trade with Germany should be encouraged. Germany also offered the possibility of providing loans to fund major Brazilian industrial objectives such as the development of a national steel industry based upon the projected steelworks at Volta Redonda in the state of Rio de Janeiro. Indeed, developing closer economic relations with Germany would reduce Brazil's economic dependence on Great Britain and the United States, a point that German politicians and businessmen often stressed.

Playing off the United States against Germany and vice versa was a useful tool for Brazilian diplomacy.[3] The basic reason for the development of closer economic relations with Germany, however, was the economic reality that Germany provided a much needed outlet not only for Brazilian coffee but also for such products as cotton, wool, and tropical fruits, a market that was not readily available in the United States. Furthermore, this trade did not require the expenditure of scarce hard foreign currency, which was a godsend for a country such as Brazil, which was experiencing great difficulty in meeting payments on its overseas debt. Consequently, Brazil had much to gain from the compensation marks system, a fact that was openly acknowledged by U.S. Ambassador Jefferson Caffery in 1938. "From a purely selfish Brazilian point of view," he reckoned that the practice "is highly advantageous" and that the Brazilians "have not the slightest desire to give up this trade unless they are forced to do so." And there was little prospect of that happening. If the United States adopted retaliatory measures, Caffery acknowledged that "Brazil would change her policy overnight [and] would scrap the compensation agreement with Germany," but such measures had never been forthcoming, so "Brazil quite frankly considers all of the many arguments which we have put forth throughout the past several years as 'pure literature.'"[4]

Adopting a broader strategic view, officials in Washington recognized that the application of economic sanctions ran the risk of driving Brazil into closer cooperation, if not even an alliance, with Nazi Germany. The Roosevelt administration, therefore, chose to ignore the fact that Brazil was failing to implement the 1935 reciprocal trade treaty.[5] In effect, the compensation marks arrangement had an inherent defect in that by acquiring too many aski marks, Brazil was compelled to buy more German products so that it began to fear not only the development of an adverse balance of trade but also growing economic dependence on Germany.

Meanwhile, the diplomatic uncertainties arising from growing political tension in Europe after the 1938 Munich Crisis made the Vargas government more guarded in its dealings with Germany and more receptive to the United States. The visit of Foreign Minister Osvaldo Aranha to Washington in February 1939 was arranged to bring about closer economic cooperation. In return for Brazil's resumption of payments on debts held by American bondholders, the United States provided a number of new credits enabling Brazil to finance purchases of American goods. Aranha was disappointed at the actual amount of money that was to be made available, but on his return to Brazil he reassuringly told Caffery that Vargas "had definitely decided on a policy of entire cooperation with the United States."[6]

In fact, the economic agreement reached by Aranha in Washington coincided with the beginning of a rapid collapse of Germany's economic challenge to the United States in the Brazilian market. The outbreak of war in Europe in September 1939 quickly set in motion the establishment of a British naval blockade of the Atlantic, which crippled German trade with Brazil so that during 1940 less than 2 percent of Brazil's foreign trade was conducted with Germany. At the same time, economic cooperation between Brazil and the United States was strengthened by the steady growth of American investment and trade. In 1940 more than 50 percent of Brazil's imports came from the United States, while more than 40 percent of Brazil's exports were destined for the American market.

Estado Novo

The upsurge of German interest in Brazilian affairs was not just limited to commerce. Brazil was one of several Latin American countries that the Nazi government wished to cultivate because its population contained a relatively large number of immigrants of German extraction — estimated at around one million and mostly concentrated in the southern states of Paraná, Santa Catarina, and Rio Grande do Sul. In addition, Germany sought to promote cooperative relations with the Brazilian military by negotiating bilateral arms contracts and establishing personal contact with senior army officers, several of whom were given invitations to attend German army field maneuvers. The Roosevelt administration anxiously observed these developments, which they regarded as a serious challenge not only to their country's political, military, and economic influence in Brazil but also as forming part of a wider threat posed by Germany to the security of all the nations of the Western Hemisphere.

Especially worrying was the visible rise of fascist influence in Brazilian internal political affairs. A right-wing political party had been formed in 1932 that called itself Ação Integralista Brasileira (Brazilian Integralist Action) and proudly imitated the European fascist parties. Dressed in green shirts and jackboots, the "Integralistas" organized massive public rallies and demonstrations. Brazil seemed to have actually become a fascist state on November 10, 1937, when troops surrounded and closed the National Congress. Later that day Vargas made an address over the radio informing the people that he was declaring a state of national emergency in order to save the nation from imminent civil war. More ominously, he canceled the forthcoming presidential election and announced the adoption of a new constitution for what he called the "Estado Novo" (New State).

Vargas, however, was careful not to upset the Roosevelt administration. On the same day as the coup took place, Foreign Minister Macedo Soares visited the U.S. embassy to assure Ambassador Caffery "that the Government intends to continue its present foreign policy, and especially its cordial relation with the United States" and that he hoped "the United States will adopt an attitude of sympathy and understanding toward the present changes."[7] The U.S. press, however, was dismayed by the abrupt cancellation of elections and the imposition of a system of government openly modeled on the ideas and practices of European fascism. A typical reaction was summed up by *Newsweek*, which entitled an article "Getulio Vargas Makes Brazil First Fascist State."[8]

State Department officials were prepared to recognize the establishment of a fascist dictatorship because they regarded a friendly and cooperative Brazil as a vital ally in protecting the hemisphere against the expansion of the Axis powers. However, they did not want the coup to be represented in the international media as a victory for fascism. Consequently, Hull sought to manipulate the U.S. press by quickly arranging a private meeting with journalists at which he emphasized that the recent political changes in Brazil were not inspired by European influences. The coup was presented as entirely the work of Brazilians. As Vargas boasted to Caffery, "it is laughable to think that the Germans, Italians or Japanese had any connection whatever with the recent movement; nor had Integralistas in any way. The new constitution is in no way Integralista or Nazi or Fascist and my Government has absolutely no connection with Rome, Berlin or Tokyo."[9]

Although Vargas assured Washington that Brazil did not endorse Adolf Hitler's growing international ambitions, he continued to maintain friendly relations with Nazi Germany. A particular matter of concern for U.S. officials was Brazil's purchase of German munitions, especially the placing in March 1938 of a $55 million order for nearly nine hundred pieces of artillery from the German armament company Krupp. The order for German weapons reflected the pragmatic approach of Vargas to foreign policy and also the fact that his previous efforts to acquire similar military equipment in the United States had encountered a negative response. At a time of severe economic depression the Roosevelt administration idealistically believed that Latin American governments should cut back on military expenditure and concentrate their scarce financial resources on promoting domestic economic recovery. More realistically, U.S. diplomats were also reluctant to assist the emergence of a powerful Brazilian military that might threaten Argentina and upset the existing balance of power in South America. Attitudes were changed, however, by the sudden outbreak of war in Europe in September 1939.

Outbreak of World War II

When Germany invaded Poland and general war broke out in Europe at the beginning of September 1939, both the governments of the United States and Brazil quickly declared their official neutrality toward the conflict. Vargas followed Roosevelt's diplomatic lead and agreed to send a delegation to attend the Pan-American Conference of foreign ministers subsequently held at Panama City. U.S. officials were delighted when the assembled foreign ministers reaffirmed the policies of neutrality already issued by their governments and subscribed to Roosevelt's fanciful idea of adopting a three-hundred-mile "safety" zone that, it was hoped, would protect and insulate the Americas from the war in Europe.

Although Roosevelt proclaimed neutrality as his government's official policy, he also stated that he did not expect Americans to remain neutral "in thought." Public opinion in the United States was clearly sympathetic to the Allied Powers of Great Britain and France and hostile to Nazi Germany. In Brazil, where the Estado Novo had more associations with fascism than with Western democracy, the attitude was more varied. Although Britain and France continued to attract most public support, admiration mixed with awe was shown at the early military successes of Germany, especially the unexpectedly swift German victory over France in 1940. While he acknowledged that more than at least half of the Brazilian population was indifferent and had no particular opinion on the war, Ambassador Caffery believed that 70 percent of the other half supported the Allied side. The greater support for the Allies, however, had to be qualified by the fact that these elements were "entirely unorganized," while those supporting Germany and Italy were "very well organized."[10]

Just as in the United States, there was initially little public pressure in Brazil to become actively involved in the war on either the Allied or the Axis side. Indeed, the Brazilian government and military leaders were only too well aware that their country was weak and ill-prepared for major military operations whether on land or at sea. Building up and modernizing the armed forces for national defense became a priority but required purchasing armaments from overseas, an option that was severely limited by lack of foreign currency and availability of supplies. "The truth," noted War Minister Eurico Dutra, "is that Brazil is a disarmed State." At times of international conflict, therefore, Brazil's best strategy was to pursue a policy of neutrality while maintaining friendly relations with all the belligerents. As Vargas stated in a speech at Belo Horizonte in May 1940: "Like cautious Ulysses, we should keep our eyes and ears turned away from the enchantments and lure of the sirens which roam our seas, in order that our thoughts may be free to concentrate . . . on Brazilian interests."[11]

On occasion, as in his Navy Day speech of June 11, 1940, delivered on the battleship *Minas Gerais*, Vargas appeared to be admiring the achievements of the Axis nations when he approvingly remarked that "old systems and antiquated formulas" were being swept away and that "a new era" was beginning for the world.[12] The U.S. ambassador explained that Vargas was merely seeking to appease the influential German and Italian elements in the Brazilian population. The president's remarks, however, drew a critical reception in the U.S. press because they came only a day after an important speech made by Roosevelt at the University of Virginia pledging the support of the United States for those nations that opposed fascist aggression. "President Vargas certainly chose a singularly unfortunate moment for his speech," Sumner Welles informed Roosevelt, "but I think you will agree . . . that there is nothing whatever in the speech except one or two ill-chosen phrases which justify the onslaught being made upon President Vargas by the American press today."[13]

Vargas clearly had lots of room to maneuver. U.S. officials chose to ignore the apparently fascist proclivities of his regime because the importance of maintaining friendly and cooperative relations with Brazil had been greatly heightened by the outbreak of war in Europe and the resulting disruption of U.S. trade with Europe. Just as in World War I, Brazil was once again highly appreciated as a vital source and supplier of agricultural products, raw materials, and minerals, especially rubber, iron ore, quartz crystals, and later such items as monazite sands from which uranium and thorium were extracted for the atomic energy project. In 1940, therefore, Vargas found himself in an unusually strong bargaining position and was able to conclude a series of attractive financial arrangements with the United States in which Brazil agreed to guarantee supplies of raw materials and secretly allow American use of Brazilian naval and air bases in return for arms and financial assistance. Included also in the agreement was a substantial loan for the projected government-owned steelworks at Volta Redonda. For some time U.S. corporations such as DuPont and United States Steel had seriously considered becoming actively involved in the steelworks scheme but had eventually withdrawn after concluding that there was likely to be too much political interference from economic nationalists in the Brazilian government and that the financial risks outweighed the possible profits.

The alternative of a direct loan from the U.S. government to finance a wholly foreign-owned economic project operating outside the United States was not only highly unusual but also politically contentious. Writing in August 1940 to Federal Loan Administrator Jesse Jones, Welles stressed that for diplomatic and strategic reasons the State Department regarded the project as "of the utmost importance" and that if U.S. assistance was not offered, Brazil would turn to Germany, which would lead to "Germany's predominance in Brazilian economic and military life . . . for many years." A $20 million credit was duly forthcoming from the Export-Import Bank. The U.S. loan was significant because it gave the go-ahead to the steel mill and essentially brought an end to the long-running diplomatic game in which Brazil had sought to play off the United States against Germany. "I believe unquestionably," Welles informed Aranha, "that this agreement marks the reaffirmation of a policy of close practical and intimate cooperation between our two Governments to our reciprocal advantage and the advantage of the New World."[14] It also definitively marked the ascendancy of the United States over its European rivals in a struggle dating back to the early nineteenth century to be the preeminent foreign influence in the Brazilian economy.

American perception of Brazil's strategic and military significance was also considerably enhanced as a result of the conviction in Washington that Nazi Germany intended to expand the conflict beyond Europe to include Latin America and eventually even the United States. The result was essentially a U.S. commitment to protect the hemisphere. In terms of the security of the Latin American countries, the single most vulnerable and exposed place to Nazi military attack was considered to be northeastern Brazil, especially its easterly extension in the state of Natal. That region, known as "the bulge," was less that 1,500 miles from West Africa — eight hours flying time — and was relatively unprotected because it could not be easily reached by Brazilian troops either by land, sea, or even air. A memorandum prepared in June 1941 summed up the views of U.S. military planners: "With respect to Brazil, the War and Navy Departments have a single objective, the attainment of which at the earliest possible moment is of great concern to this country. That objective is to insure the security of northeastern Brazil against every Axis effort, within Axis capabilities, to obtain a lodgement there."[15] The American people were publicly alerted to the danger by President Roosevelt. "It is time for us to realize," he announced in a radio broadcast, "that the safety of American homes, even in the center of our country, has a definite relationship to the continued safety of homes in Nova Scotia or Trinidad or Brazil."[16]

With Brazil no longer viewed as so remote or peripheral, the defense of Brazil was now deemed vital to U.S. national security. Brazilian military leaders, however, had a very different strategic perspective. For geographical and logistical reasons, they believed that a credible German assault against Brazilian territory was most unlikely to be mounted from West Africa and across the South Atlantic. In fact, the Northeast had not been a scene of major fighting since the expulsion of the Dutch in 1654. Brazilian generals were much more worried about defending the south of the country where they feared that the reported disaffection of local pro-Axis elements might induce major civil unrest or even encourage an opportunistic Argentine invasion. Moreover, the Chaco War between Paraguay and Bolivia had only just ended in 1935 and the possibility of a renewal of military conflict in that region could not be ruled out. Although he acknowledged the need to provide for the defense of the Northeast, the army chief of staff, General Góes Monteiro, advised Vargas that Brazil's "situation in the South American concert of countries required preventively the concentration of its principal Forces in the South Sector of the country."[17]

The first priority according to U.S. military planners was to defend the Northeast, and they argued that the best way to do this was by establishing garrisons of American combat troops. This proposal, however, stimulated a revival of the traditional suspicion and fear of the "American peril" in that the Brazilian government and military believed that American soldiers would be regarded locally as a foreign occupying force and would provide a contentious issue that pro-Nazi groups could use to appeal to nationalist sentiment. Moreover, the U.S. military presence, once established, might prove difficult to remove in the future. Brazilian generals argued instead that Brazil could supply its own forces to protect the region so long as sufficient military assistance in terms of modern weapons, munitions, and equipment, especially tanks and trucks, was forthcoming from the United States. In January 1941 agreement was reached on the Airport Development Program in which American engineering resources would be used to construct a string of airfields from Belém to Salvador. While it was keen on improving communications and transportation infrastructure that had considerable significance in assisting the wider war effort beyond just Brazil, the War Department in Washington appeared unable or unwilling to supply the Brazilian army with the weapons and munitions that it persistently requested. Consequently, an impasse occurred in which U.S. contingency plans to provide garrisons for the defense of the "bulge" were virtually suspended because the Brazilian military withheld their cooperation. Caffery explained that an invitation from the Brazilian government to send U.S. troops to the Northeast would occur only "when the German menace really seems imminent to them," and that "in the meantime they will not do so unless we furnish them with adequate supplies of material for the defense of that region."[18]

There was also the possibility that Germany might be able to exploit any differences that emerged between the two governments. With trade virtually terminated by the British naval blockade, the Germans no longer provided an economic challenge, but their military reputation had soared as a result of their successes in Europe. "Although the great majority of the Brazilian Army is decidedly pro-American," Caffery reported in April 1941, "probable additional victories of the German Army this year will strengthen professional admiration of that military machine, warranting energetic action on our part."[19] In May, during a conversation with the U.S. ambassador, Aranha mentioned that there was a growing belief among Brazilians that Germany would win the war in Europe. He wished to know how the United States would respond to such an eventuality.

But for every expression of doubt about Brazilian intentions, Hull issued reaffirmations of confidence in the Brazilian government and especially in Vargas coupled with pledges that the United States would never permit the domination of the Atlantic and the nations of the Western Hemisphere by any government bent on world domination. Vargas in turn provided his own litany of reassurances with reminders of Brazilian support of U.S. aims at the Panama conference and, later, at a second meeting of hemispheric foreign ministers in Havana in July 1940 after the fall of France. At that meeting, hemispheric governments committed themselves to a continental "no-transfer" principle, prohibiting the cession of any European territory in the Americas to another European power. Vargas instinctively sensed what the U.S. leaders wanted to hear. He told Caffery, "Brazil will honor its obligations contracted at Panama and Habana. In other words you can count on us."[20]

Vargas was also being realistic. Despite Germany's impressive military victories in continental Europe, he recognized that Great Britain still remained undefeated and that the United States was mobilizing its vast resources in preparation for war. Moreover, the boom in trade since 1939 had effectively tied the Brazilian economy tightly to that of the United States. During each year of the war around 50 percent of Brazilian exports were destined for the United States, while American goods took a similar share of the Brazilian import trade. At the same time, Brazilian national security was clearly dependent on receiving U.S. military assistance. A major example of American commitment to defending Brazil was illustrated in the formal extension of Lend-Lease aid of $100 million to Brazil in October 1941.[21]

At War

The United States entered World War II in December 1941 as a result of the Japanese surprise attack on the U.S. Pacific fleet based at Pearl Harbor. In the aftermath of the Japanese assault, a Pan-American Conference of foreign ministers to discuss measures of hemispheric collective defense was quickly scheduled and held at Rio in January 1942. For Cordell Hull, "a life-and-death struggle" was now under way, "the result of which could mean freedom and advancement for Latin America or domination and probably occupation by the Axis."[22] To Washington's delight, Aranha informed Caffery prior to the conference that Brazil would fully support U.S. policy. Sumner Welles, who headed the U.S. delegation at the Rio Conference, duly reported to Hull that Vargas had convened his cabinet, including Generals Dutra and Góes Monteiro, and told them that "Brazil must stand or fall with the United States."[23] In accordance with this instruction and the resolution passed at the Rio Conference,

Brazil severed diplomatic relations with Germany on January 28, 1942. Brazil's action markedly contrasted with its neighbors, Argentina and Chile, who insisted on maintaining normal relations with the Axis powers.

Vargas calculated that his affirmation of solidarity with Washington would be rewarded with a speeding up of the transfer of munitions from the United States. But the U.S. government was currently faced with requests for munitions from all directions, including the urgent mobilization of its own military forces to fight a world war simultaneously on two fronts. "The requirements of our own forces, of the British, and of other Governments actually engaged in resisting aggression," bluntly stated the U.S. Army chief of staff, General George C. Marshall, "take precedence over the needs of Brazil."[24] When expected arms shipments were delayed or did not materialize, Foreign Minister Aranha complained that Brazil was being given the "run around." "Please tell Aranha from me that for once his uncanny intuition has been in error," Welles telegraphed Caffery, and added, "This is no 'run around' and there is not going to be any 'run around.'"[25] Privately, Vargas wrote to the finance minister, Artur de Sousa Costa, then in the United States, that the delivery of war materiel was "very urgent" and would prove "if it is worthwhile or not to be the friend of the United States."[26]

Roosevelt was most concerned that Brazil should not in any way feel slighted. Vargas's cooperation in the war effort was considered vital. To that end, in March 1942 the two governments signed the "Washington Accords," which provided Brazil with a sum of around $200 million in additional Lend-Lease aid for the purchase of military equipment. When news reached Rio of this outcome, Caffery noticed a marked change in the demeanor of Vargas: "From that moment his attitude was definitely changed for the good; he had made his decision; he was on our side."[27]

The desire to conciliate Brazilian feelings coincided with a major effort by the Roosevelt administration to persuade the people of Latin America of the superiority of democracy over fascism. This task was assigned to the Office of Inter-American Affairs that was created in August 1940 and later renamed the Office of Coordinator of Inter-American Affairs (OCIAA). Nelson Rockefeller, who held the office of Coordinator from 1941 to December 1944, saw his primary objective as waging "psychological warfare in the Hemisphere."[28] The emphasis was on extolling the virtues of democracy and the American way of life through radio broadcasting and the distribution of press releases, motion pictures, books, pamphlets, and newspapers. Programs were set up to promote hemispheric unity by sponsoring art exhibitions, concerts, and educational and cultural exchanges. Among notable celebrities to visit Brazil were movie star Douglas Fairbanks Jr. and conductor Arturo Toscanini.

The most famous Brazilian "export" to the United States was popular entertainer Carmen Miranda. The glamorous Miranda in her characteristic "tutti-frutti" hat was much admired and gained the nickname of the "Brazilian Bombshell" in Hollywood.[29] A similar image of Brazil and its people as exotic and lively was exemplified in 1944 by Walt Disney's creation of the comical green parrot "Zé Carioca" to popularize his animated movies *Saludos Amigos* and *The Three Caballeros*. The soundtrack of *Saludos Amigos* also contained "Brazil" ("Aquarela do Brasil"), a Brazilian samba that soon became a popular tune in the United States. In turn, Hollywood movies made Brazilians aware of American popular music, especially jazz and big band dance music.[30]

Walt Disney movies enjoyed popular success in Brazil, as did most OCIAA cultural activities. But some films produced by OCIAA aroused controversy when they touched on the sensitive issue of race relations. *It's All True*, an unfinished documentary largely shot on location in Brazil in 1942 by American actor and director Orson Welles, provoked outrage among the Brazilian elite by depicting Brazil as a mixed-race society and including references to "Indians."[31] Reflecting the views of celebrated social scientist Gilberto Freyre, the Brazilian elite preferred to consider their society as a unique and inclusive "racial democracy" resulting from miscegenation between whites and blacks.[32]

Vargas's decision to draw closer to the United States resulted in German military retaliation. From February 1942 onward, Brazilian merchant ships suffered attacks without warning from German U-boats operating in Atlantic waters. A German submarine offensive specifically directed against Brazilian shipping was launched in July 1942 and resulted in the sinking of several Brazilian ships off the northeastern coast, including six ships within a period of less than a week in mid-August. Four were passenger ships, so the loss of life was heavy. Mass public demonstrations erupted throughout the country demanding retaliation. German- and Italian-owned businesses were attacked. Vargas responded by issuing a declaration of war against Germany and Italy on August 22, 1942. A few days later in an Independence Day speech the president indicated the vital role of public opinion in influencing the decision to go to war: "You asked by every form of expression of the popular will that the Government should declare war on the aggressors, and this was done."[33]

While the actual timing of the decision to join the war reflected the impact of German submarine warfare, Vargas had evidently already decided on a policy of close diplomatic alignment with the United States. Talk of "approximation" was deliberately revived as Brazil once again claimed to be the favorite Latin American ally of the United States. Not only did this enhance Brazil's regional status ahead of that of Argentina, but there were immediate and substantial financial benefits. By breaking off diplomatic relations with the Axis powers, Brazil had been rewarded by the Roosevelt administration with a doubling of the amount of the Lend-Lease aid that had been initially allocated in October 1941.

U.S. assistance increased further after Brazil's formal declaration of war and grew to such an extent that Brazil received more than $350 million or 70 percent of the total amount of Lend-Lease aid given by the United States to the whole of Latin America during World War II. The aid was not only in the form of weapons and munitions. One highly visible element was the arrival in Brazil of substantial numbers of U.S. military and civilian personnel. Many were assigned to the Northeast where they worked to improve and construct local air and sea defenses against possible German attack. The airfields and naval bases of the Northeast soon formed an important staging post for antisubmarine warfare and especially for the preparation and dispatch of U.S. troops, equipment, and supplies in the Allied invasion of North Africa in 1942. Ironically, the relatively "short" distance between northeastern Brazil and West Africa that had once appeared as a strategic liability now became a distinct advantage as Brazil truly became a vital "life-line" for the supply of Allied forces involved in fighting overseas campaigns. "Without the air bases Brazil permitted us to construct on her territory," Hull remarked, "victory either in Europe or in Asia could not have come so soon."[34]

Despite the provision of substantial Lend-Lease aid, there were still persistent Brazilian complaints that the actual amount of assistance was insufficient and too slow in arriving. Caffery warned that "the situation in Brazil" was "delicate if not explosive" because Brazilian leaders believed that the United States was not providing "anything like an equitable quid pro quo" as a return for the "vital military and naval concessions" that had been granted by Brazil. Indeed, Caffery worryingly reported "a general diminution of enthusiasm for the United States," which he attributed to the fact that in a society experiencing low wage levels and rising inflation, "the Brazilian, all the way from Manáos to Santos, has to observe the naturally not (to him) pleasant spectacle of increasing numbers of Americans, both civilians and in the armed forces, receiving 'handsome' wages with which to outbid him and outbuy him in his own land." In the Northeast, in particular, the high price and shortage of food was directly attributed to the presence of well-paid and well-fed American troops.[35]

Another aspect of U.S. wartime policy that caused considerable irritation was interference in Brazilian business affairs. In July 1941 the State Department issued a "Proclaimed List of Certain Blocked Nationals" popularly known as the "Blacklist." The Blacklist contained names of suspected pro-Axis companies and individuals resident in Latin America with whom U.S. companies and citizens were instructed not to do business. More than 250 Brazilian firms were placed on the Blacklist even though Brazilians owned the large majority of them. Itamaraty continually protested to the U.S. embassy and demanded the removal of Brazilian firms from the list. American officials justified the Blacklist as a necessary measure of economic warfare, but Brazilians suspected an ulterior motive to promote the advance of U.S. companies by damaging their competitors. Prior to the meeting of the Rio Conference in January 1942, Foreign Minister Aranha confided in Caffery that the Blacklist had personally caused him "no end of trouble" and was the one single issue that most divided Brazil and the United States.[36]

At the highest diplomatic level, however, relations were very cordial. The secret meeting arranged at Natal in January 1943 between Vargas and Roosevelt, who was returning to Washington from a conference with British prime minister Winston Churchill at Casablanca, was judged to be very successful. Caffery remarked that Vargas appeared "most enthusiastic" about the meeting and reported that Aranha had told him that "he has rarely seen him [Vargas] so pleased with anything." The U.S. ambassador considered that Brazil's status as the leading regional power had been greatly enhanced and, he informed Roosevelt, "at this moment all Latin America (except the Argentine) . . . look to Brazil as the spokesman for and champion of the Americas with and under you."[37]

When news of the Natal meeting became known in Buenos Aires, the Brazilian ambassador reported that local press coverage reflected dismay mixed with a "certain envy."[38] In fact, American friendliness toward Brazil contrasted markedly with the evident difficulties in relations between the United States and Argentina as that country refused to sever diplomatic relations with Germany and Italy. The claim of the Argentine government to be merely seeking to assert national independence, however, was undermined by its outright refusal to restrict the activities of Axis diplomats in Argentina. Cordell Hull believed that Argentina was actually pursuing a pro-Nazi foreign policy and was acting like a "bad neighbor."[39]

When a military coup occurred in Bolivia in December 1943, officials in Washington attributed the development to Argentine instigation and as part of a plan coordinated with German agents to bring about a diversionary Axis counter-offensive in South America. Suddenly, and on this occasion without any prompting from Rio, the United States broke with past attitudes and unilaterally sent military aid to Brazil. Caffery reported that Brazilians were jubilant: "Vargas confidently believes that we will furnish the necessary equipment for his Army, ships for his Navy and planes for his Air Forces to enable him to stand firm in the face of Argentine endeavors to line up the Southern countries against him."[40]

The FEB

Allied and Brazilian military commanders assumed that Brazil had the capability to fulfill limited naval duties but would not be able to commit troops for an effective overseas combat role. In terms of defending its coastline against external attack, Brazil relied upon the U.S. Navy, whose Fourth Fleet was based at Recife. The warships of the Brazilian navy were placed under the operational command of Vice-Admiral Jonas Ingram and joined the U.S. Fourth Fleet in patrolling the South Atlantic. The Brazilian army, like the armies of the other Latin American nations, was expected to concentrate on local defensive and policing roles. Numbering around sixty thousand soldiers, Brazilian forces were mostly stationed in the South to counter potentially pro-Axis activities. "We did not have an organization and a mobilization [plan] to fight overseas," recalled Colonel Humberto de Alencar Castelo Branco, "only for combat in South America and internally."[41]

But Vargas reckoned that a Brazilian expeditionary force in Europe would assure the continuation of a high level of U.S. military aid, boost the nation's hemispheric and international prestige, and thereby enhance its potential for influence in the postwar world. Consequently, and against the advice of some senior generals, he ordered the creation of an expeditionary force known as the Força Expeditionária Brasileira (Brazilian Expeditionary Force or FEB) that would be sent to participate in the fighting in Europe.[42]

U.S. generals considered that the involvement of small foreign armies in combat activities would prove to be more of an operational burden than an asset. They were also concerned that scarce military resources would have to be diverted to train, equip, and transport these forces. Brazil, however, could not easily be ignored because it was the largest country in Latin America, maintained the biggest army, and had proved to be very important in aiding the war effort. Moreover, cooperation in military planning and the deployment of forces was facilitated by the creation in 1942 of a Joint Brazil–United States Defense Commission (JBUSDC) with offices in Washington and Rio. When the idea of a Brazilian expeditionary force was first raised in 1943, State Department official Laurence Duggan informed Caffery that senior U.S. generals such as Dwight Eisenhower, Mark Clark, and George C. Marshall were favorable and that "there therefore exists at this time a good atmosphere in the War Department." Cordell Hull was most enthusiastic a few months later when he noted: "The Department of State, on its part, favors this plan because of important political considerations, such as strengthening of Brazil's present position, and its voice in post-war settlements, equivalent to strengthening our own. Also the plans for active participation in the war by Brazilian troops have given a lift to Brazilian public morale." In addition, a stronger Brazil would act as a counterweight to "bad" Argentina.[43]

With the approval of the Allied supreme commander, General Dwight Eisenhower, it was decided that Brazilian troops would take part in the Allied invasion of Italy. The FEB would serve not as an independent army but would be under U.S. military commanders and dependent upon the U.S. Army for transportation, equipment, and training. Replying directly to reports of a "whispering campaign" among Brazilian officers suggesting that Brazilian troops would not be well treated, Duggan affirmed that they "will be transported abroad in the same sort of troop carriers as American troops and under the same security conditions." He urged Ambassador Caffery to make it known to Brazilian officers that "their troops will be given exactly the same status as our own troops."[44]

In July 1944 the first FEB contingent of just over 5,000 troops left Rio for Italy, where they joined the U.S. Fifth Army commanded by General Mark Clark. "With the presence of these troops we break forth as a great nation among the free powers," proudly declared a Rio newspaper.[45] Around 25,000 Brazilian troops ("Febianos") were eventually sent to Italy and were in active service from September 6, 1944, to May 2, 1945. The Febianos were located in unfamiliar mountainous terrain and exposed to a cold European winter; their exploits, notably their contribution to the hard-fought Allied victory at Monte Castello in March 1945, evoked great pride and patriotic feelings in Brazil and earned them the nickname of "smoking cobras."[46] Vargas's decision to send troops overseas was, therefore, vindicated and brought him considerable political popularity. Although Brazilian troops often found it embarrassing to be so dependent on the U.S. Army for their training, weapons, and even food rations, the FEB was significant in stimulating close professional and personal cooperation between the Brazilian and U.S. militaries and thereby established an enduring relationship that would be a prominent feature of the postwar period. Many Brazilian officers received training in the United States at Fort Leavenworth, Kansas, and acquired considerable respect and admiration for the United States, especially its military and technological skills. "In the War the United States had to give us everything: food, clothes, equipment," summed up one ex-FEB officer, who added, "After the War, we were less afraid of United States imperialism than other officers because we saw the United States really helped us without strings attached."[47]

Participation in World War II enabled Brazil to surpass Argentina and become the leading military power in South America. In addition to the revival of pretensions to regional leadership, there was also the belief that Brazil ought to possess an influential role in the new international organizations that were being formed to shape the postwar world. Indeed, there were high hopes at Itamaraty that much more success would be forthcoming in 1945 than at the end of World War I because Brazil had gained considerable prestige for being the first South American nation to join the war and especially for being the only Latin American country to have actually sent combat troops to fight in Europe.[48]

Brazil's regional and international status had been underscored at the meeting between the two presidents in Natal in January 1943 when Roosevelt had remarked that the United States and Brazil were equal partners in the war and that Vargas would be invited to attend the peace conference of victorious powers that would take place at the end of the war. The U.S. president also mentioned the idea of a new world organization being created. He was delighted to hear from Vargas that Brazil was willing to join the new body. Brazilian diplomats subsequently took an active role in various wartime meetings held in the United States to discuss postwar institutions, including the Conference on Food and Agriculture, the establishment of the United Nations Relief and Rehabilitation Administration, and the Bretton Woods Monetary and Financial Conference.

The structure of what would become the United Nations Organization was discussed at the Dumbarton Oaks Conference in Washington in 1944. From comments made by Cordell Hull, Brazilian diplomats gained the impression that their country might be assigned a permanent seat on the Security Council of the new organization. When the war began in 1939 Brazilian self-esteem was at a low point. However, as the conflict drew to a close in 1945, a confident Brazil was keen to become active in world affairs and demonstrated this by establishing diplomatic relations with the Soviet Union on April 2, 1945, and also by declaring war on Japan on June 5, even though there was no compelling military reason to do so.[49]

In truth, Brazil's pretensions to be a world power were flimsy. Their fulfillment depended upon U.S. support, which proved much more uncertain after Roosevelt's sudden death in April 1945. Welles had resigned his post in 1943, Hull in 1944, and now Roosevelt's death meant that the three Americans who had most valued Brazil's cooperation during the war were no longer in office. At their meeting in Natal Roosevelt had told Vargas that Brazil would be invited to the postwar peace conference. The invitation never materialized. A conference duly took place at Potsdam in July 1945, but it was monopolized by the leaders of the "Big Three" powers of the United States, the Soviet Union, and Great Britain. The "Big Three" were preoccupied with settling the political boundaries of Europe and displayed an attitude of supreme indifference toward Latin America and minor powers such as Brazil. It was a stark indication that few favors would be shown to Brazil in the postwar world. The prospect of financial reparations for wartime losses and the hopes of a permanent seat on the UN Security Council soon evaporated.

Transition to Democracy

During World War II the United States appeared as the international champion of democracy fighting the evil of fascism. This positive image greatly facilitated the aim of the Roosevelt administration to develop unusually close political, economic, military, and cultural relations with Latin America. The region was highly significant for the United States as a source of supply for vital strategic materials and an aid in maintaining military security. In return for their support, the Latin American nations, especially Brazil, received considerable economic aid. They confidently expected that the cooperative wartime relationship and the "Good Neighbor policy" would be carried over into the postwar period. Indeed, the continuation of U.S. financial assistance was considered a crucial element in promoting industrialization and thereby preventing a recurrence of the economically depressed years of the 1930s. The importance of the United States was reinforced by the economic decline of the European great powers, which meant that Europe was temporarily closed as an alternative source of trade and investment.

A very different outcome occurred because the war marked the transformation of the United States from a nation historically on the margin of an international system centered on Europe to the new status of the world's leading superpower. As a result the United States abandoned its traditional policy of avoiding entangling alliances and accepted worldwide commitments to support "democratic" governments notably in Western Europe and the Far East. In the process, the unusual degree of U.S. political and public interest in Latin American affairs that had been shown during the war rapidly diminished. A policy of complacency mixed with indifference was shown toward the region whose diplomatic support was generally taken for granted and not always given very much significance. For Brazil this marked a dramatic change from the special wartime relationship.

As World War II came to an end in 1945, U.S. officials were pleased with what they regarded as a visible trend throughout Latin America to follow the model of the United States and adopt democratic forms of government. This was exemplified in Brazil, where awareness that the nation had joined a war to liberate people in Europe from the tyranny of authoritarian rule stimulated growing public pressure for political reform at home. Gossip focused on Vargas's intentions and whether he would be a candidate in the forthcoming elections for the presidency. As Caffery had predicted before turning over the post of ambassador to Adolf Berle, Vargas felt committed to revitalizing Brazilian democracy.

Berle arrived in Rio in January 1945. The new ambassador was fluent in Spanish, had a good working knowledge of Portuguese, and ensured that he was kept well informed on Brazilian political affairs. He valued Vargas as a friend and a steadfast wartime ally but welcomed the emergence of new political figures competing for the presidency in what would mark a peaceful end of dictatorship in Brazil. Berle elected to facilitate the transition. Believing that a coup was imminent to maintain Vargas in power, Berle decided to make known publicly his government's full support for the holding of elections at their scheduled time in December. On September 29, the ambassador gave a luncheon address in Petrópolis in which he stated that the United States welcomed Brazil's forthcoming transition to democratic government and that "the only way to be a democracy is to practice democracy."[50]

The speech marked a significant change in attitude and convention because U.S. diplomats were usually careful to avoid making public comments on Brazilian political affairs. Although Berle's motive had been to forestall a pro-Vargas coup, his speech with its emphatic support for "democracy" was widely interpreted as indicating the withdrawal of U.S. support for Vargas. Indeed, the Brazilian foreign minister privately described the speech as "deplorable" and considered that such intervention in internal affairs was "without precedent in Brazil's history."[51]

A month later, on October 29, Brazilian generals ended the political uncertainty by staging a coup in which they persuaded Vargas to resign. They were especially fearful of the political power of organized labor, which had played a critical role in Juan Perón's rise to power in Argentina. While the actual extent of Berle's role in encouraging the coup was debatable, the ambassador remained a figure of political controversy in Brazil. When he gave up his post in February 1946, however, the Rio press paid tribute to his personal sympathy for Brazil and his support for political reform.

The presidential and congressional elections that took place in December 1945 were the first national elections to be held in Brazil since 1934. The "official" government candidate for the presidency, General Eurico Dutra, was victorious. Although he had previously served in the cabinet as minister of war, Dutra remained primarily a military figure and was not an experienced politician. His bland personality and reluctance to provide positive leadership were reflected in a conservative approach to foreign affairs that stressed the continuation of close relations with the United States. Brazil was pleased to host the Inter-American Conference at Petrópolis from August 15 to September 2, 1947, and to receive a personal visit from President Harry Truman to close the meeting and also attend the annual celebrations marking Brazil's Independence Day. During the conference Brazilian delegates characteristically worked closely with U.S. officials to secure the smooth negotiation of the Inter-American Treaty of Reciprocal Assistance, a collective security arrangement more popularly known as the "Rio Pact."

Cooperation was also in evidence at the 1948 Bogotá Pan-American Conference where Ambassador João Neves da Fontoura told Secretary of State George Marshall that "the Brazilian Delegation would follow closely the United States Delegation and that every effort would be made to have the points of view of both delegations coincide."[52] At the United Nations in New York, where Osvaldo Aranha was elected president of the General Assembly in 1947, Brazilian delegates provided staunch support for the United States in the emerging Cold War with the Soviet Union. In 1947 the Brazilian government endorsed the U.S. policy of "containing" the threat of International Communism by outlawing the Brazilian Communist Party and severing diplomatic relations with the Soviet Union. In marked contrast to the wartime period, however, Brazil had little to show in terms of economic rewards for its postwar policy of maintaining close diplomatic cooperation with the United States.

6   The Cold War

"I am asking," declared U.S. Congressman William C. Cramer in 1963, "that no further U.S. loans be made to Señor Goulart's government until the Communists are cleaned out of it."[1] Throughout the 1950s Brazilian diplomacy sought U.S. financial assistance to fund large-scale projects for industrial development and economic modernization. When the requested aid did not materialize, Brazil demonstrated its annoyance by its refusal to send a token military expeditionary force to take part in the Korean War. In 1958 President Juscelino Kubitschek proposed "Operation Pan America," a major program of economic development for all the nations of the hemisphere. A negative response, however, was forthcoming from the Eisenhower administration, which interpreted the idea as a calculated ploy to extract American money to finance extravagant expenditures. A separate scheme closely resembling Operation Pan America but devised by the U.S. government later emerged when John F. Kennedy became president in 1961 and was known as the Alliance for Progress.

The U.S. attitude of complacency toward Latin America markedly changed during the 1950s as a result of growing anxiety over the perceived rise in the influence of International Communism in the Western Hemisphere. In Brazil, alarm focused on the danger of Communist infiltration especially in the poverty-stricken northeastern region. There was also concern over the "independent" foreign policy proclaimed by President Jânio Quadros, which stated that Brazil would not automatically take the side of the United States in the Cold War against the Soviet Union. When Quadros resigned in 1961, he was succeeded by the left-wing leader João Goulart. The administrations of John F. Kennedy and Lyndon Johnson distrusted Goulart and suspected that he aimed to establish a personal dictatorship that would be vulnerable to Communist infiltration. U.S. policy showed its displeasure by suspending financial aid to the Brazilian federal government. At the same time, covert assistance was given to Goulart's political opponents, and close relations were cultivated with senior military officers. The personal links were so well known that the coup that overthrew Goulart in 1964 was widely believed to be the work of the U.S. embassy in Brazil. While U.S. officials clearly welcomed and had undoubtedly contributed to the overthrow of Goulart, they denied active involvement in executing the coup.

Brazilian Disillusionment with the United States

The postwar policy of pursuing diplomatic cooperation with the United States resulted in few tangible benefits for Brazil. This was evident in the question of securing preferential support for the modernization and building up of strong Brazilian military forces. The matter was discussed in staff conversations between senior American and Brazilian officers that took place in the spring of 1945. While American military officials appreciated the strategic value of maintaining a close relationship with Brazil in the postwar period, diplomats in the State Department showed less interest. Ambassador Adolf Berle acknowledged that given its territorial size and population, Brazil "is destined to have the major position in the continent," and that, in contrast to Argentina, "Brazil as an essentially pacific country is not likely to abuse her position; whereas certain other South American countries frequently betray a tendency toward expansionism when they are in a position of military supremacy." Nevertheless, he considered that Brazil's ambition to be the leading regional military power was mistaken and ultimately self-defeating because it would be detrimental to the country's long-term economic and social development. "The money which might be used to provide a sixth rate fleet," Berle believed, "will tend to impoverish and weaken the country." True to his New Deal liberalism, he argued that it would be much better spent on mass primary education.[2]

The reluctance of the Truman administration to provide the desired military assistance provoked critical comment from a Brazilian military that nourished the ambition that their country should aim for the status of a world power. In a conversation between the U.S. chargé d'affaires in Rio, Paul Daniels, and Colonel José Bina Machado in December 1945, the Brazilian officer referred to "the recent growth of anti-American sentiment in high Brazilian Army circles" and stated that "the feeling was growing that the us was inclined to treat Brazil as a small brother rather than an important nation pledged to full military cooperation."[3]

Brazilian diplomats concurred with their military colleagues. Most of all, they resented the protracted and difficult negotiations that were required to persuade U.S. officials and bankers to give even relatively small amounts of aid for economic development. This attitude was repeatedly contrasted with the very generous treatment accorded by the United States to the countries of Western Europe in what would be known as the "Marshall Plan." In their meetings with State Department officials, Brazilian diplomats constantly stressed their government's proven friendship and long record of close cooperation and argued that this merited special consideration in the granting of economic assistance. In March 1946 the Eurico Gaspar Dutra administration had optimistically suggested that the United States provide a five-year government-to-government loan of one billion dollars. The State Department replied that it would give "careful and sympathetic study" to the proposal but rendered this virtually redundant by stressing that first of all, Brazil should seek private financing through negotiations with the Export-Import Bank (EXIM) and the International Bank for Reconstruction and Development (IBRD).[4]

Adding to the Brazilian frustration was the fact that the amounts actually discussed were much smaller than the billion dollars mentioned by Dutra. The Truman administration did attempt to help Brazilian economic development through the formation of a Joint Brazilian-American Development Commission known as the Abbink Mission and named after the head of the commission, John Abbink, an American businessman. Abbink, accompanied by around one hundred U.S. financial and technical experts, visited Brazil in 1948. While his final report endorsed the granting of American loans to finance much-needed economic infrastructure and modernization, it also contained a strong emphasis on the universality and importance of American virtues such as individualism and "Self-Help." Crucial significance was therefore given to the role of private Brazilian capital and enterprise. "The United States Delegation considered that one of the principal reasons for its presence in Brazil," bluntly noted the report, "was to make it clear to Brazilian officials with whom it came in contact that Brazil could not expect huge amounts of assistance from the United States, and that the way to get assistance is to do what can be done with the country's own resources."[5]

As part of his sincere effort to improve relations, Truman invited Dutra to the United States in return for his trip to Brazil in 1947. When this was arranged for May 1949, the U.S. ambassador to Rio, Herschel Johnson, pointed out the political significance of the visit when he noted Dutra's need to be seen to be enjoying some success. The ambassador's advice was not heeded. While Truman's meeting with Dutra was cordial and ceremonial, an abrasive discussion took place later between Acting Secretary of State James Webb and Foreign Minister Raúl Fernandes of Brazil. The foreign minister recognized that by helping Brazil, the United States was fearful of stirring up jealousies among other Latin American countries, but he stressed "that in view of the past record Brazil deserved favorable treatment even to the extent of being discriminatory."[6]

A particular concern was the increased cultivation of coffee in Africa. As always, coffee was a most sensitive issue in Brazil. The world price of coffee had remained stable during the 1940s, but its sudden rise in 1949 led to political action in the United States. The matter was investigated by the U.S. Senate Committee on Agriculture and Forestry. In a manner reminiscent of the acrimonious debate over the valorization question some forty years earlier, the committee's chairman, Senator Guy Gillette of Iowa, claimed that the American consumer was being overcharged by $650 million a year. He criticized the Brazilian government and coffee growers for deliberately holding back supplies and for engaging in scaremongering when they stated that future production was decreasing. Brazilian coffee interests were incensed and contended that the price of coffee was being secretly manipulated upward by the actions of American coffee traders and roasters. The Rio newspaper *O Globo* denounced Gillette as "the champion of demagoguery, the chief disseminator of falsehoods, the great promoter and vehicle of injustices that are woven around coffee and the Latin American countries that produce it."[7]

At the same time as they struggled to persuade Washington to understand their need for financial aid, Brazilian officials were stupefied to learn of a reversal of U.S. policy toward Argentina. The U.S. ambassador to Buenos Aires, William Pawley, was well aware of the intense historic rivalry between the two neighbors: "One manifestation of this rivalry," he noted, "is a fear that Argentina may encroach upon the favorable position which Brazil enjoys vis-à-vis the United States and I am sure that Brazilian leaders will be constantly active in efforts to insure that Argentina not obtain any equal footing in this regard."[8] Consequently, the decision of the Truman administration to agree to a transfer of U.S. armaments to Argentina in 1948 provoked considerable dismay. Shortly afterward, the Argentine minister of war, General José Humberto Sosa Molina, visited Washington and returned to Buenos Aires with a pledge of further U.S. assistance. Aware of criticism not only in Brazil but throughout Latin America, Secretary of State George Marshall made things worse by explaining that "a moderate amount of military equipment" had been sold to Argentina and that "this Government is treating Argentina on a no more favorable basis than any other Latin American government."[9]

Return of Vargas to Power

In April 1950 Getúlio Vargas dramatically returned to the center stage of Brazilian politics by announcing that he would be a candidate in the presidential election scheduled for October. The former dictator adopted a "populist" tone in his campaign speeches and lauded the success of the Estado Novo in providing economic benefits and social welfare for the masses. Secretary of State Dean Acheson believed that Vargas was advocating greater state control of the economy, which he described as "a socialistic and definitely nationalistic policy" that ran counter to U.S. aims of promoting a relaxation of barriers to world trade. If Vargas was elected, Acheson reckoned that he would be more difficult to deal with than Dutra because he would make "aggressive and persistent claims upon the United States for financial and other types of assistance in recognition of Brazil's contribution during the recent war." Nevertheless, Acheson regarded Vargas as "an astute, clever and realistic politician" with whom the United States could do business so that relations "would probably not deteriorate."[10]

The campaign for the Brazilian presidency coincided with the outbreak of the Korean War in June 1950. For the Truman administration the invasion of South Korea by North Korea represented the aggressive advance of International Communism. Truman requested an immediate meeting of the Security Council of the United Nations (UN) and secured the adoption of a resolution calling on North Korea to withdraw its forces from South Korea. A second resolution was passed two days later asking members of the UN to provide troops to drive back the invaders. Like other Latin American governments, the Dutra administration initially joined the United States in approving the action of the UN Security Council, but it held back from providing troops on account of the pending presidential election and Dutra's unwillingness to embark on a policy of military participation in an overseas war that his successor might find extremely difficult to reverse.

Vargas won the presidential election in October 1950 and began his official period of office in January 1951. In sharp contrast to Washington, he did not consider the conflict in Korea as a matter of pressing strategic concern for Brazil or the Western Hemisphere. His declared priority was to accelerate Brazil's economic development and modernization, and to achieve this he looked to the United States for capital investment and technical assistance. In a radio broadcast shortly after his election as president, Vargas had unambiguously stated that "whoever wants our collaboration must aid us with our needs."[11] Ambassador Johnson confidently predicted that Vargas would seek a revival of the close wartime relationship.

For the United States, Cold War considerations predominated so that the single overriding objective in its current relations with Brazil was to persuade Vargas to send troops to Korea. A modest contribution was envisaged. In fact, a token expeditionary force of no more than one infantry division was deemed sufficient. At a time when Latin American nations were demurring, it was believed that Brazil's military involvement in the conflict would set a significant example for the others to follow. To secure Brazil's compliance, the State Department began to emphasize the special nature of the relationship with Brazil. A Joint Brazil–United States Economic Development Commission (JBUSEDC) was established to enable U.S. and Brazilian officials to meet and draw up plans for Brazil's future economic development. The new president was also encouraged to outline specific items that he wished to be discussed at a forthcoming Inter-American Conference of Foreign Ministers to be held in Washington. "It is imperative for the future of our relations with Brazil that we give a positive response to the proposals of President Vargas," Assistant Secretary of State Edward Miller informed Acheson.[12]

When Miller subsequently visited Rio in February 1951, he brought a personal letter from Truman stating how much the U.S. president looked forward to maintaining the same close personal relationship that had existed between Vargas and Roosevelt. While acknowledging the importance of close economic cooperation, Truman most of all wanted "collaboration in the military sphere" and in particular the sending of a Brazilian division to Korea, which he said would have "a most important effect and might prove a great influence on the future course of world events."[13] Sensing a window of opportunity, Brazilian officials stressed that they were interested not in letters or words but in substance. They pointed out that their military forces were ill-prepared for mounting an overseas campaign, a condition that could be attributed to American neglect. "If [Washington] had elaborated a recovery plan for Latin America similar to the Marshall Plan for Europe," explained Foreign Minister João Neves da Fontoura, "Brazil's present situation would be different and our cooperation in the present emergency could probably be greater."[14] Confronted with the enormous task of financing the U.S. war effort, Truman had little to offer Brazil. With instructions to discuss the possibility of a loan of no more than $250 million, Miller found that the Brazilian government would not give an undertaking to send troops to Korea.

Vargas temporized further by sending the armed forces chief of staff, General Góes Monteiro, to Washington in July 1951 ostensibly to discuss the formal request made by UN secretary general Trygve Lie asking those UN members like Brazil, who had not so far contributed forces, to send troops. At the State Department, Edward Miller initially dismissed the mission as simply another Brazilian ruse to acquire military equipment. On the other hand, the State Department believed that the possibility of a successful outcome was a prize worth pursuing because a Brazilian decision to join the war would influence other Latin American countries to do the same. Though discussions with Góes lasted for several weeks, they proved inconclusive. Góes complained privately to Osvaldo Aranha that U.S. officials were only interested in talking about Korea. Political and economic issues were avoided, while Latin American affairs were relegated to "a secondary level."[15]

Góes and Miller made some progress on a military accord in which the United States would provide financial assistance toward planning arrangements for hemispheric defense. This was part of a series of bilateral negotiations under the 1951 Mutual Security Act and eventually took the form of a Military Defense Assistance Agreement, which was signed in March 1952. Nevertheless, on the Korean issue Brazilian acquiescence was firmly ruled out because the U.S. government was unwilling to offer Brazil the preferential economic treatment that had been provided during World War II.

Brazil was not alone in feeling aggrieved. With the exception of a small token force from Colombia, all the Latin American nations resisted becoming militarily involved in the conflict in Korea. At issue was a profound difference over the correct strategy to adopt in the Cold War. This tension was evident at the Fourth Inter-American Conference of Foreign Ministers in Washington in March–April 1951. Moreover, in contrast to past Pan-American conferences there was open disagreement between the U.S. and Brazilian delegations, a development that Foreign Minister Neves da Fontoura described as making him "terribly distressed."[16]

The Brazilian delegation contended that the Communist threat in Latin America was primarily an internal issue that could be best countered not by the deployment of military forces for overseas operations, as the United States wanted in Korea, but by countries becoming prosperous and strong through their own programs of national economic development. For Brazil this meant a continued emphasis on industrialization, notably the development of economic infrastructure in transportation and the provision of energy supplies as exemplified in the Five-Year Plan announced in September 1951 by Finance Minister Horácio Lafer. However, the successful implementation of major projects required the inflow of foreign capital mostly in the form of long-term loans from the U.S. government and other U.S. sources such as EXIM and the IBRD.

The issue of foreign investment provoked Brazilian economic nationalism. This was particularly evident in the controversy over the creation of a company to control the exploration and drilling for oil in Brazil. Foreign participation in exploration for oil had been prohibited in 1938 on account of concern over the infringement of national sovereignty. But lack of investment hampered the development of a Brazilian oil industry. A bill was eventually introduced into Congress in December 1951 proposing the creation of a mixed public-private corporation known as Petrobrás (Brazilian Petroleum Corporation). The bill, however, stimulated a fierce debate over the extent of foreign participation to be allowed in the company. Left-wing politicians aided by the Communists condemned any arrangement with the international oil corporations, who were denounced as agents of the capitalist governments of the West. Economic nationalists pointed to the huge financial gains already made by foreign corporations in the international oil business and demanded that strategically important industries such as oil must be nationalized so that control over the company, its reserves, and its earnings would be retained by Brazil.

Contrastingly, Brazilian business interests pointed out the vital importance of providing a welcome for foreign capital and maintaining good relations with overseas trading partners, especially the United States. Leading U.S. corporations such as Ford and General Motors were currently committing huge financial investments to create a massive Brazilian automotive industry located in São Paulo. Moreover, joint ventures in developing oil resources had proved a success in Canada and Venezuela. In addition, elements within the military were also eager not to disturb their close professional links that had been established with the United States. Brazilian public opinion, however, was aroused by the emotive appeal of economic nationalism, which had been summed up in the popular slogan of "o petróleo é nosso" (the oil is ours).

Eventually in October 1953 Congress approved a measure providing for the full nationalization of the oil industry. The outcome was not well received in Washington. Several members of the new Eisenhower administration were former businessmen and strong critics of state intervention in the economy. Acting Secretary of State Walter Bedell Smith described the Petrobrás bill as a "backward step" because it sought to exclude foreign participation. "In Brazil," he noted gloomily, "the outlook is increasingly unfavourable."[17]

The creation of Petrobrás as a state monopoly signified that the Vargas administration was committed to policies of economic nationalism. In fact, a growing feature of the president's public speeches was to blame foreigners for Brazil's difficult economic conditions. Foreign corporations were particularly criticized for the remittance of large profits to their parent firms. In response, Vargas proposed that the annual remittance of profits would be no more than 10 percent. U.S. officials were adamant that such a restrictive action not only penalized American companies in Brazil but was also counterproductive and would arrest economic growth.

End of the Vargas Era

Despite their attachment to free market economic ideas, U.S. diplomats showed some sympathy for Vargas's domestic political difficulties in dealing with the question of foreign investment. Ambassador Johnson listed the political pressures including Communist infiltration and congressional awkwardness that were influencing Vargas to pursue policies of economic nationalism. Johnson was aware of talk in Washington of retaliation, but he considered that a "get-tough attitude" would be a mistake because for political reasons the Brazilian government could not be seen to be giving in to American demands. Such an eventuality, he warned, would simply arouse "a deep and abiding hostility which w[ou]ld play into hands of those elements who for whatever reason desire to diminish Amer[ican] influence and interests here." After a personal meeting with Vargas in May 1952, Johnson reported that the president "has been subjected to considerable anti-Amer[ican] propaganda much of it vicious" and "that it has been so persistent he is beginning to wonder if some of it is not true."[18]

Unfortunately, the understanding approach advocated by the U.S. embassy in Rio was not replicated in Washington. This was exemplified in the question of financial assistance to Brazil that President Dwight Eisenhower encountered in his first weeks in office. A Brazilian request to EXIM for a loan of $300 million had been agreed at the end of the Truman administration. In accordance with its strict free-enterprise principles, fiscal conservatism, and desire to avoid giving commitments to costly foreign aid programs, the new Eisenhower administration decided to reduce the amount to half. Secretary of the Treasury George Humphrey even wanted a reduction of at least two-thirds. At the State Department Deputy Assistant Secretary of State Thomas Mann was more reflective. He considered that Brazil regarded the successful processing of the loan as a test case of the new administration's intentions. Moreover, he pointed out that Brazil was "our traditional and principal ally in the inter-American system," and an effort should be made to "keep them on our side." If such a policy was not pursued, he warned that "Brazil will become more nationalistic and less cooperative in its relations with us." Eisenhower did not see Brazil as a special or deserving case. However, he acknowledged that a binding commitment had been made by his predecessor in the White House and that the loan must be allowed to proceed so as not "to lay the Administration open to possible charges from the Latinos of bad faith."[19]

In his memoirs President Eisenhower remarked that "our sister republics to the south feel that the United States pays too little attention to them and their problems."[20] While Eisenhower began his term of office with talk of reversing his predecessor's neglect of its neighbors, the reality was that his administration valued Latin America for its economic resources and had little interest in political affairs. Moreover, the geopolitics of the Cold War meant that Eisenhower and his formidable secretary of state, John Foster Dulles, were much more concerned, if not preoccupied, with events in Europe, the Middle East, and Asia. By contrast, U.S. leaders were condescending, if not indifferent, to Brazil, and this attitude was damaging to diplomatic relations.[21]

The decision of the Eisenhower administration in March 1953 to terminate JBUSEDC particularly disturbed the Brazilian government. In January 1953, after almost two years of diligent study, the commission had drawn up a plan of long-term economic development costing one billion dollars. The Eisenhower administration took alarm at the size of the sum and the implication that most of it would be funded by the U.S. government. In effect, officials were perturbed that the commission had acquired the characteristics of a self-generating cash machine. "As long as the Joint Commission stays in existence the Brazilians believe they have a chance of squeezing more loans out of the U.S.," summed up State Department official Sterling Cottrell.[22] The decision to terminate the commission, however, was not only unexpected but was also a unilateral act that Brazilians interpreted as definitively removing their preferential status and reneging on what they believed had been an implicit promise made by the U.S. government to fund a major program of national economic development. The resulting annoyance bordering on open hostility was made apparent to the president's brother, Dr. Milton Eisenhower, who visited Rio in July 1953 as the last stop on his goodwill visit of Latin America. "The Brazilians were furious and made no effort to hide their anger," he noted.[23]

The continuation of difficult economic conditions, especially rising inflation, resulted in a growing political crisis for the Vargas administration. In August 1954 the attempted assassination of Carlos Lacerda, a leading critic of the government, was linked with a member of the presidential guard and led to daily public demonstrations outside the presidential palace calling on Vargas to resign. Faced with the imminent prospect of another military coup to remove him from office, Vargas shot himself in the heart on August 24. A political testament was discovered at his bedside, which explained that his decision to commit suicide was caused by "international economic and financial groups."[24] Some public demonstrations took place in which U.S. consulates at Belo Horizonte and Porto Alegre were attacked. The State Department was concerned by rumors that Communists might have been involved in the disturbances but was relieved to discover that that was not the case.

Vargas's death elevated Vice-President João Café Filho to the presidency. Café Filho considered himself a caretaker president and was aware that he lacked a popular mandate to introduce significant political changes. Though he judged the new administration to be "the best group of Brazilian leaders in decades," Sterling Cottrell was not optimistic about the future of Brazil. Quite simply, he believed that the country had "run out of cash and credit" and that "our relations with Brazil will never be on a sound basis until Brazil 'puts its house in order.'" In their typical condescending fashion U.S. officials placed the onus on the Brazilians to act responsibly and show economic good sense and political courage. "As long as they postpone reforms," Cottrell summed up, "they will be broke and crying for help."[25]

The Kubitschek Years

Vargas's prospective successor, Juscelino Kubitschek de Oliveira, initially offered little assurance that he differed from his controversial predecessor. In a decade in which U.S. officials measured the standing of Latin American leaders by their anti-Communist credentials, the former governor of Minas Gerais worried them. His political platform publicly received the endorsement of the Communists. Even more troubling to Washington was Kubitschek's choice of João Belchior Marques "Jango" Goulart of Rio Grande do Sul as a vice-presidential running mate. Goulart's long-standing links with labor unions and his controversial left-wing political views had forced his resignation as minister of labor in 1954. He was also representative of anti-American sentiment that regarded the United States not only as a barrier to economic growth but also as a materialist society that was a threat to Brazilian cultural values.

In victory, Kubitschek proved a confident and energetic candidate who stressed the vital importance of promoting economic growth so that Brazil would be transformed into a modern, industrial nation that would gain international respect and admiration. The showpiece of his administration would be the design and completion of Brasília, a new federal capital in the interior of the country. Brazil, he pledged, would achieve "fifty years' progress in five," and this became the national slogan.

Kubitschek was well aware of the extent of American anxiety over the threat of Communism in Brazil. In his attempt to cultivate close relations with the United States, he recognized the public relations value of appearing as a staunch anti-Communist. After his first meeting with the president-elect, Ambassador James Dunn noted that Kubitschek had expressed regret that some U.S. newspapers were saying that he was linked with the Communists. He told Dunn categorically that he was not a Communist and would not permit the Communists to be active in his government. "I had a very favorable impression of his manner and self-confidence and he struck me as a man even younger than his age (54) vigorous and forthright," reported the ambassador.[26]

Keen to establish a personal rapport with President Eisenhower, Kubitschek visited the United States prior to his inauguration and had lunch with the president at Key West, Florida, on January 5, 1956. The visit was brief because Eisenhower was recovering from an operation. Kubitschek went on to Washington and New York for substantive discussions with administration officials. The themes that he constantly stressed were his resolute opposition to Communism and his desire for the participation of U.S. capital in the development of Brazil. The message was effectively communicated. "One of the reasons for his trip to the United States was to try to inspire confidence in the American business man," approvingly commented a State Department memorandum.[27]

Ambassador Dunn described Kubitschek as "a staunch friend" and was convinced that he sincerely desired close and friendly relations with the United States.[28] This was exemplified when the U.S. government proposed the building of a guided missile–tracking station on the Brazilian island of Fernando de Noronha, which was located around two hundred miles from the northeastern bulge. Kubitschek supported the request and regarded it as an opportunity to gain military assistance from the United States in return. However, he faced criticism from nationalists in Congress that Brazilian sovereignty would be infringed. Opponents also argued that the station would involve Brazil directly in the Cold War and thereby place the country at risk of a nuclear attack from the Soviet Union. Agreement was reached in January 1957 to establish the tracking station, for which Brazil received substantial quantities of military equipment from the United States. To placate nationalist opposition the agreement stipulated that only the Brazilian flag would fly on the island and that the tracking station would be under Brazilian command.

Kubitschek was also supportive of the United States in the Cold War with the Soviet Union. At the UN Brazilian delegates took an active part in endorsing resolutions to promote world disarmament and schemes to aid international economic development. Brazilian troops were assigned to the UN Emergency Forces that carried out peacekeeping duties in the 1956 Suez Crisis and the later Congo Crisis. Though wishing to expand trade with the wider world, including Communist countries in Europe, Kubitschek refrained from establishing full diplomatic relations with the Soviet Union. This was pleasing to Secretary of State John Foster Dulles, who had implied that the consequences of such action would be unpleasant: "To open doors to Soviet agents through a mission in Rio at this time would in our opinion maximise problems Kubitschek will face in difficult months ahead as he tries solve Brazil's basic problems and would make more difficult his constructive cooperation with US this regard."[29]

Operation Pan America

The policy of cooperating closely with the United States was meant to gain financial assistance for Kubitschek's ambitious program of modernizing the Brazilian economy in keeping with his electoral promise of "fifty years' progress in five." In this, like Vargas and Dutra before him, he was sorely disappointed. When Vice-President Richard Nixon visited Brazil for the presidential inauguration in January 1956, Kubitschek took the opportunity to outline his plans for a major economic developmental program, which he estimated would require more than a billion dollars in foreign aid. But respective priorities clearly diverged. While Nixon was only too eager to discuss the need for constant vigilance against the threat of Communism, he was notably noncommittal about an aid program. Eisenhower continued in the same manner when he subsequently wrote Kubitschek, neglecting to discuss the specific issue of governmental loans but reiterating the need to do "everything possible to reassure private initiative as to the great possibilities which exist in Brazil."[30]

The Kubitschek administration found that pursuing a policy of rapid economic growth stimulated both rising inflation and increasing deficits in the balance of payments, which led to a chronic shortage of foreign exchange. U.S. officials regarded the Brazilian government as profligate and the main cause of the country's economic difficulties. Their views were shared by international lending institutions such as the IBRD and the International Money Fund (IMF), which considered that Kubitschek made economic conditions worse by deliberately maintaining an overvalued currency and increasing the money supply to finance anticipated future budgetary deficits. The IBRD was prepared to consider granting loans but only on condition that the government devalue the currency, reduce its expenditures, and implement tight controls over wages and credit. The problem for Kubitschek was that adopting such an austerity policy would inevitably result in a steep rise in the cost of living and create political difficulties extending even to an outbreak of public disorder.

The unsympathetic attitude of U.S. officials motivated both the Vargas and Kubitschek administrations to improve Brazil's political and economic relations with European nations and especially the countries of Spanish-America. At a time of growing frustration over the U.S. economic agenda for Latin America, Kubitschek believed that Brazil should play a leading role in fashioning a Latin American economic union. Such an idea seemed even more appealing and timely following the outburst of anti-American sentiment and violence during Vice-President Nixon's controversial "good will" tour of several Latin American capitals in April and May 1958. To Central Intelligence Agency (CIA) director Allen Dulles, the treatment given to Nixon was a "shock" that "brought South American problems to our attention as nothing else could have done."[31]

Aware of the soul searching taking place in Washington, Kubitschek sensed an opportunity to link the alarm over the expansion of Communism to the broader issue of Latin American economic underdevelopment. He outlined his ideas for hemispheric action in a letter to Eisenhower that was delivered at the White House in person by the Brazilian ambassador. In the aftermath of the Nixon visit, Eisenhower was eager to be seen to be responding positively to Kubitschek's proposal for Pan-American unity and sent Dulles to Rio for personal discussions. In anticipation, Kubitschek made a public announcement of his idea, which he called "Operacão Pan-Americana" (Operation Pan America or OPA) and stated that its aim was to strengthen all the nations of the Western Hemisphere in their fight against the threat of International Communism. Although the approach was multilateral, Kubitschek envisaged the U.S. government acting as the leader of a major economic program to aid all the economies of Latin America and that it would commit billions in aid over a twenty-year period. In a pointed reference to America's recent record of neglect he warned: "The Western cause will unavoidably suffer if in its own hemisphere no help comes. It is difficult to defend the democratic ideal with misery weighing on so many lives."[32]

The Brazilian president stressed that the first step was to obtain hemispheric agreement on the main aspects of a program to address the current economic crisis in Latin America. But Dulles came to Rio clearly unhappy that it was Brazil rather than the United States that was taking the leading role. He stressed that he wanted no precipitate action to be taken. Despite his government's historical propensity to act unilaterally in inter-American affairs, Dulles remarked that, on this occasion, due consideration should be given to the views of the other hemispheric nations. He believed that Brazil and the United States should take things slowly because "it would not be desirable for Brazil and the United States to appear to be getting too far ahead of the other members of the American family." Despite its apparent public support for OPA, U.S. diplomacy was deliberately undermining Kubitschek's initiative. A negative and suspicious attitude prevailed in Washington, where Thomas Mann reckoned that Brazil's real aim, as always, was to commit the United States to underwriting a general program of Latin American economic development. "The United States cannot accept the Brazilian proposals, and the problem is to resolve the issue constructively, with as little discord as possible," he summed up.[33]

In effect, Kubitschek's proposal for a multilateral scheme clashed with and was replaced by Mann's preference for a divide-and-rule approach in which each individual nation would develop its own particular program. The Eisenhower administration eventually agreed to provide general funding in the form of the creation in April 1959 of a new lending institution, the Inter-American Development Bank (IDB). The United States, however, initially contributed only $1 billion to the IDB. This was a much lower figure than the $5 billion originally desired by the Brazilians and essentially ruled out any prospect of aid on the lavish scale of the Marshall Plan. Kubitschek's dismay was increased by the Eisenhower administration's support of the IMF in its reluctance to approve Brazil's request for a loan of $300 million. In June 1959 Kubitschek abruptly broke off negotiations with the IMF and defiantly retorted: "Brazil has come of age. We are no longer poor relatives obliged to stay in the kitchen and forbidden to enter the living room. We ask only collaboration of other nations. By making greater sacrifices we can attain political and principally economic independence without the help of others."[34]

By default, Brazil put more effort into developing trade with the wider world. Notable economic advances were made by West German industrialists, especially in the production of motor vehicles at the Volkswagen factories in São Paulo. Even though full diplomatic relations had not been reestablished with the Soviet Union, an agreement was signed in 1960 to export 1.5 million sacks of coffee in exchange for Soviet oil. Commercial arrangements were also made with Eastern European countries and the People's Republic of China. Meanwhile, Eisenhower sought to counter the impression that the United States was neglecting the region by making a personal visit to several countries, including Brazil, in February–March 1960. Eisenhower visited Brazil from February 23 to 26, 1960, during the time of Carnaval. "The visit of President Eisenhower," reported the U.S. chargé at Rio, Philip Raine, "galvanized the attention of all Brazil for days before and after his presence in the country." The chargé also reported the comments of Brazilians that the visit had revived "the feeling of close kinship with Americans which they had before and during the second world war, but has eroded away in the past 15 years."[35]

In contrast to Hoover's visit in 1928, however, there was disappointment that Eisenhower's entourage contained so many secret service agents that he was effectively removed from personal contact with the people. Moreover, the president's speeches, essentially minilectures preaching the benefits of private enterprise, elicited polite but unenthusiastic applause. Eisenhower's speech to the Brazilian Congress was met with "strong silence."[36] Despite his robust efforts, Kubitschek had clearly failed to establish a personal rapport with the U.S.

president. Nor had he been successful in his strategy of obtaining large-scale preferential aid from the United States.

Independent Foreign Policy

Brazilian prospects for a better relationship with the United States appeared brighter when in the U.S. presidential election of 1960 Senator John F. Kennedy narrowly defeated his Republican opponent, Vice-President Richard Nixon. Kennedy was energetic and forthright. He promised a "New Frontier" for the American people and envisaged an active role for the United States in international affairs. Moreover, Kennedy singled out Latin America as a focal point of the Cold War with the Soviet Union. During the election campaign he had stressed the strategic threat posed by Cuba, where a revolutionary regime had been established in January 1959 under the leadership of the charismatic Fidel Castro. Kennedy was also concerned about Latin America, particularly its economic backwardness and vulnerability to the spread of communism. On one occasion he confided to an aide his anxiety that "the whole place could blow up on us."[37]

In Brazil, Jânio da Silva Quadros was the leading candidate in the 1960 presidential election. A former mayor of the city and governor of the state of São Paulo, Quadros had enjoyed a meteoric political rise during the 1950s capitalizing on the fact that he was a political outsider dedicated to providing honest and efficient government. In the October election Quadros won almost as many popular votes as his two main rivals combined, a result that was regarded not only as a smashing personal triumph but also as a victory for the democratic will of the people and a resounding defeat for the discredited professional politicians. The U.S. ambassador to Brazil, John Moors Cabot, interpreted the result as a significant political watershed bringing an end to thirty years of domination by Vargas and his heirs. Cabot predicted that a "general house cleaning" was expected. Noting that the new Brazilian president would take office and be inaugurated only ten days after Kennedy, Cabot saw this confluence of events as "providing a relatively clean slate on which to record forthcoming phase of us-Brazilian relations."[38]

Officials in the incoming Kennedy administration were imbued with the sense that they were making history. Representing "the best and the brightest" minds of their generation, they were convinced that they possessed the intellectual and technical skills to change the world in the American image. They were therefore keen to take advantage of the opportunity to revamp the relationship with Brazil. Indeed, if the United States was going to be successful in dealing with the problems of the hemisphere, then the support and cooperation of Brazil was regarded as vital. Brazil was not only the largest and most populated Latin American nation, but its image had been greatly enhanced by the architectural achievement of completing the new capital city of Brasília, and major international sporting successes such as Maria Bueno's triumph at the Women's Championship tennis final at Wimbledon in 1960 and Brazil winning the soccer World Cup in 1958. At the same time, the introduction of jet travel was turning Brazil into an accessible tourist destination for Americans, especially the beach at Copacabana in Rio. A fusion of samba and jazz known as "bossa nova" subsequently became very popular in the United States and all over the world. Its success was highlighted by the hit song "The Girl from Ipanema" ("A garota de Ipanema") performed by João Gilberto and Antônio Carlos Jobim.

In place of the reactive attitude of the Eisenhower period, the Kennedy administration adopted a positive approach in which it was decided to show friendship to Brazil and take initiatives to help that country overcome its seemingly endemic financial crisis. As soon as Quadros came into office, Secretary of State Dean Rusk instructed the U.S. embassy in Brazil to "establish effective and productive understanding with Quadros soonest possible" and "to have available constructive suggestions and proposals dealing with economic and financial problems of probable chief immediate concern to Quadros."[39]

While U.S. officials chose to perceive Quadros as similar to Kennedy in that he was also a young charismatic leader representing a generational shift in the political scene, they found it difficult to appraise his character and intentions. They noted with approval his campaign promises to implement administrative efficiency and orthodox fiscal policies that would reverse the financial excesses of his predecessor. However, there was uncertainty over the future direction of Brazilian foreign policy mainly because Quadros did not share Washington's view that Cuba was a serious danger to hemispheric peace and stability. In fact, Quadros had visited the island in April 1960 and let it be known that he was an admirer of the aims of the Cuban Revolution. Moreover, he had constantly stressed during his campaign for the presidency that he would pursue a "política exterior independente" (independent foreign policy).

While Quadros recognized that Brazil was indisputably part of the West, he questioned whether the bipolar division of the world caused by the Cold War was actually relevant to Brazil's national interests, which were essentially the promotion of international trade and world peace. Even though it would produce a divergence with the traditional policy of alignment with the United States, Quadros contended that Brazil should relax its attitude of hostility toward International Communism and fully enter into political and economic agreements with members of the Communist Bloc. In addition, he was particularly keen to cultivate closer commercial and cultural links with the Third World, especially the newly independent African nations. Envisaging his country taking on a leadership role commensurate with its size, population, and natural resources, he also pointed out that Brazil possessed unique historic ties with Africa and that its racially mixed society had much in common with the people of that continent.

The different interpretation of the significance of the Cold War appeared to mark a radical change in diplomatic behavior, but Quadros was not advocating that Brazil break with the West and join the neutralist bloc. In fact, his overall diplomatic aims were hardly new. Successive Brazilian governments since 1945 had recognized that Brazil needed greater access to overseas markets and supplies of foreign capital in order to stimulate industrial development and modernization. If these were not sufficiently forthcoming from the United States and Western Europe, then Brazil must explore alternative sources. Consequently, the Kubitschek administration had attempted to open up new export markets in Latin America and had negotiated trade agreements to sell coffee to the Soviet Union and sugar to the People's Republic of China. There was also an element of political calculation in seeking to placate the nationalists and left-wing political groups who were critical of subordination to the United States. Prior to the presidential inauguration the U.S. chargé, Philip Raine, had predicted that the new president, despite his professions of neutralism, would "avoid an open break with the United States if for no other reason than that he is very aware of the fact that he needs US help." Raine, however, acknowledged that a fundamental change was about to occur and concluded that "there can be little doubt" that "Quadros will change the bases on which relations between the United States and Brazil were traditionally conducted."[40]

To show that he was his own man, and in a deliberate reversal of Kubitschek's behavior in 1955, Quadros ignored an invitation for a preinaugural visit to the United States during which he would have had the opportunity to meet not only President Eisenhower but also President-elect Kennedy. Instead, provocative rumors were allowed to circulate that he might go to Egypt or India for meetings with prominent Third World leaders such as Gamal Nasser and Jawaharal Nehru. The time for a face-to-face conversation came in early March 1961 when the head of Kennedy's Latin American Task Force, Adolf Berle, visited Brazil. At the very start of his meeting with Quadros, Berle made the offer of a U.S. government loan of $100 million. It was soon evident, however, that the offer had strings attached and that Cuba was the topic that the American diplomat most wanted to discuss. Aware that the Central Intelligence Agency (CIA) was currently planning a covert military operation to overthrow Castro, Berle stressed the need for "inter-American action" to combat the Cuban threat. Quadros, however, would not endorse forceful military action and stated that his current priority and preoccupation lay in dealing with Brazil's financial and social problems.[41]

Quadros also turned down the offer of $100 million as too small an amount and countered with the suggestion that if discussions were to take place, they should be pitched at $500 million. If the intention had been to buy Brazilian support for U.S. policy toward Cuba, then this had proved mistaken. In fact, it was counterproductive and prompted Quadros to affirm his country's independence from the United States. Immediately after Berle's visit, the Brazilian president publicly announced the forthcoming state visit of President Tito of Yugoslavia to Brazil and his intention to reestablish full diplomatic relations with Hungary, Romania, and Bulgaria and support the admission of the People's Republic of China to membership in the United Nations.

Not since the Korean War had the United States made a serious effort to secure Brazil's diplomatic cooperation. This was underscored by the sending of a senior cabinet member, Secretary of the Treasury Douglas Dillon, to Brazil in April to discuss economic aid. The figure of $500 million that Quadros had raised at his meeting with Berle was subsequently agreed to in May. State

Department officials were miffed. As Berle noted, "the Brazilian settlement was the most generous in history, but all it got us was rude remarks . . . we can't let them go bankrupt despite their attitude on foreign affairs."[42] Responding to the concern of the U.S. ambassador to Brazil, John Moors Cabot, that the loan would be interpreted as rewarding Quadros despite his neutralist actions, Deputy Assistant Secretary of State Wimberley Coerr explained that "the extent of United States commitment and Brazilian expectations regarding the currently considered financial package is so great that to cancel or delay it at this stage would result in Quadros becoming more rather than less neutralist."[43]

Meanwhile in April 1961, the Kennedy administration had launched its covert military operation to overthrow Castro. The invasion force was defeated at the Bay of Pigs. As news of the operation was broadcast on April 17, anti-American demonstrations occurred in Rio and Recife. Quadros was openly critical of U.S.-sponsored military action to bring down the Castro regime. He stated publicly that Brazil would uphold the principles of self-determination and respect for the sovereignty of nations. A meeting was arranged with the Argentine president, Arturo Frondizi, which affirmed Argentine-Brazilian agreement on the Cuban issue. For Kennedy the Bay of Pigs was a humiliating defeat in the Cold War. By contrast, Castro jubilantly claimed a great victory for the Cuban Revolution over U.S. imperialism.

The Kennedy administration subsequently sought to isolate Cuba and looked for support from the other Latin American governments. Opposing the United States over Cuba was politically advantageous for Quadros because it served to reinforce his claim to be pursuing an "independent" foreign policy and brought him favor with the nationalists and anti-American groups. Moreover, there was no strong political pressure in Brazil calling for punitive action against Cuba. In fact, the tiny island of Cuba was not considered to be a strategic threat either to Brazil or the Western Hemisphere. In addition, there was relatively little commercial contact between Brazil and Cuba. As Kubitschek had indicated during his final year of office, if any Brazilian diplomatic action was required, it should take the form of offering to mediate the differences between the governments of Cuba and the United States. The U.S. chargé in Rio, Niles Bond, concluded: "Any significant future shifts in GOB [Government of Brazil] policy (and same could be said of GOB foreign policy in general) are likely to be determined by President himself on basis of his own assessment [of] his and Brazil's self-interest (which he will define in terms his desire [to] make himself world figure and Brazil [a] major power)."[44]

In conjunction with its policy of seeking to isolate Cuba both politically and economically, the Kennedy administration unveiled policies of substantial financial aid to meet the radical challenge presented by the Cuban Revolution. While Kennedy openly paid tribute to the example set by Kubitschek's Operation Pan America, he stressed that the new program of economic aid called the Alliance for Progress (La Alianza para el Progreso or A Aliança para o Progresso) was his own personal initiative. A conference of hemispheric leaders subsequently met at Punta del Este, Uruguay, in August 1961 to discuss the plan in more detail. Conscious of the danger of becoming entangled in Cold War politics, the Brazilian delegation was under instructions from its government to maintain an independent attitude and avoid taking sides in any controversy that might arise over the Cuban question. In the resulting Charter of Punta del Este, which Brazil signed, the United States agreed to seek to provide the nations of Latin America the substantial sum of $20 billion in government and private aid over a period of ten years. The scheme represented a version of the Marshall Plan that Latin Americans had so long advocated and was similarly politically motivated in seeking to contain the advance of communism in a strategically important region of the world that was visibly suffering from extreme poverty and destitution.

The task of promoting the ambitious aims of the Alliance for Progress were evident in Brazil, where U.S. officials gave particular prominence to the Northeast, a region of long-standing poverty and deprivation made even worse by a catastrophic drought occurring in 1958. The American public had been alerted to the harsh economic conditions and the threat of rampant Communist infiltration by articles written by the journalist Tad Szulc and published in the New York Times in October and November 1960. Fears of a Cuban-style insurgency were stimulated by the activities of a Marxist lawyer, Francisco Julião, who was organizing Peasant Leagues (Ligas Camponesas) to demand land and improved working conditions. Within days of assuming office Secretary of State Dean Rusk noted, "United States Government is vividly aware of distressed region in northeastern Brazil and, subject to GOB [Government of Brazil] desires, suggests the early exploration of joint remedial projects in that area."[45]

Food for Peace program director George McGovern and White House aide Arthur Schlesinger Jr. toured the region in early February 1961 and endorsed a $70 million aid package to purchase supplies of surplus wheat. They also commended the relief work carried out by the Superintendency for the Development of the Northeast (Superintendência do Desenvolvimento do Nordeste or SUDENE), which had been established by the Brazilian Congress in 1959 and was headed by the economist Celso Furtado. "McGovern and I were both appalled by the magnitude of the problem and impressed by the initiatives which Brazil had already taken," summed up Schlesinger.[46]

An Agency for International Development (AID) team led by Ambassador Merwin Bohan visited the Northeast in October 1961 and produced a comprehensive program for economic development in which the U.S. government undertook to give $131 million in aid over two years. But strings were attached. Although the Bohan Report had stressed that SUDENE should be in overall control, the Kennedy administration insisted that AID officials be directly involved in the implementation of the program. In effect, the U.S. government was showing that it had a low opinion of Brazilian abilities and wanted to monitor and evaluate performance. There was also a definite preference for short-term projects, such as constructing houses and classrooms, that would have a quick political impact in promoting a favorable image of the United States while at the same time contradicting Communist propaganda. By contrast, SUDENE thought in terms of a long-term strategy designed to solve the deep-rooted causes of regional economic underdevelopment. Moreover, Celso Furtado disliked American administrative interference and at times proved to be uncooperative. In turn, AID officials complained about Brazilian obstructionism and voiced suspicions that SUDENE was infiltrated by Communists.[47]

From Quadros to Goulart

In the meantime, the political position of President Quadros deteriorated, largely because of his awkward personal style of doing business and his sensitivity to personal criticism, which resulted in increasing difficulties with all the political parties in Congress. Proclaiming the defeat of inflation as the priority of his administration, he introduced austerity measures to cut back federal spending while still seeking to stimulate the economy with the aid of large loans from the IMF and the Alliance for Progress. At the same time, he placed less importance on Brazil's relations with the United States and sought to improve links with Communist countries. Some critics argued that Quadros had swung too far to the left. After the close of the Punta del Este Conference, the revolutionary hero Ché Guevara visited Brazil in August 1961 and received the nation's most distinguished award for foreigners, the Order of the Southern Cross (Cruzeiro do Sul). The award affirmed Brazil's independence in foreign policy but also provoked political opposition. "Quadros is finding it difficult to make progress on Brazil's main problems," noted a U.S. National Intelligence Estimate, which added: "He has already encountered criticism from conservative forces, especially the military, the press, and the Church, primarily on the ground that his foreign policy favors the Bloc."[48]

A week later Quadros suddenly and quite unexpectedly resigned the presidency on August 25, 1961. In accordance with the 1946 Constitution, Vice-President João Goulart would succeed Quadros, but a smooth succession was prevented by the circumstance that Goulart was on a trade mission to a Communist country, the People's Republic of China, at the time of the resignation. Senior military officers led by War Minister Odílio Denys were highly suspicious of Goulart's long-standing left-wing associations and threatened to oppose his succession. The prospect of civil war briefly loomed as the vice-president made his way back to Brazil via stopovers in Paris and New York. A characteristically Brazilian compromise was eventually reached in which the military agreed to Goulart becoming president on condition that his executive powers were considerably restricted. Like Brazilian politicians, U.S. officials were confounded by Quadros's abrupt action but were hopeful that Goulart might well turn out to be easier to deal with than the enigmatic Quadros. A CIA estimate considered that although a Goulart government would continue the "independent" foreign policy, "the need for US financing, as well as domestic political considerations, will probably render it less truculent toward the US than was the Quadros administration."[49]

As the CIA correctly predicted, Goulart's foreign policy was similar to that pursued by Quadros. In his public speeches the new president made critical references to capitalist exploitation of the Third World. He also renewed full diplomatic relations with the Soviet Union in November 1961 and resisted U.S.

diplomatic pressure to isolate Cuba both politically and economically. Brazilian diplomacy continued to stress the importance of nonintervention and self-determination in inter-American relations. In conversation with the new U.S. ambassador, Lincoln Gordon, Goulart remarked that the United States should be patient because the Castro regime would in time "deteriorate under its own weight." In fact, he suggested that "us does itself great disservice by agitating Cuban problem since Latin American masses are instinctive[ly] on side of tiny Cuba whenever it [is] menaced by colossus to [the] North."[50]

In January 1962 at the Conference of Foreign Ministers held at Punta del Este, Secretary of State Rusk denounced Cuba as a satellite of the Soviet Union and sought the mandatory imposition of economic sanctions. The Brazilian delegation led by Foreign Minister Francisco Clementino San Tiago Dantas argued against adopting a confrontational stance and led the "soft six," consisting of Brazil, Argentina, Mexico, Chile, Ecuador, and Bolivia, in abstaining in the votes to impose economic sanctions and to expel Cuba from the Organization of American States (oas). The U.S. ambassador to the oas, Delesseps Morrison, derisively nicknamed the Brazilian foreign minister as "San Tiago de Cuba."[51] In Brazil, however, Dantas earned praise for asserting his country's independence in diplomatic action and resisting what was regarded as crude American pressure.

While Latin American countries generally applauded Castro's defiant stand against the United States, they watched with dismay as the Cuban leader proceeded to align his country with the Communist nations. Cuba became a base for "exporting revolution" in the form of organizing and launching guerrilla operations to overthrow governments on the mainland of Central and South America. The secret attempt of Soviet leader Nikita Khrushchev to construct offensive missile sites on the island of Cuba in 1962 brought the very real prospect of a nuclear war occurring in the hemisphere. In the ensuing "Missile Crisis" of October 1962, Kennedy publicly stated that the whole hemisphere was in danger. But he treated the issue purely as a confrontation between the United States and the Soviet Union and, consequently, preferred to deal directly with Khrushchev.[52] It was only after he had made the decision to place a naval quarantine around Cuba that Kennedy invoked the 1947 Rio Treaty and sought the endorsement of the Organization of American States to approve the use of armed force. An affirmative vote was forthcoming but not unqualified support for Kennedy's technically illegal action. Brazil along with Mexico and Bolivia notably abstained in one of the votes in order to express their misgivings. U.S. officials were irritated at Brazil's reluctance to give its full support. In fact, a majority vote in the OAS for punitive economic sanctions against Cuba was delayed until 1964.

On the other hand, just like his predecessors, Goulart sought to negotiate financial aid from the United States and repeatedly stressed his desire for friendly relations with Kennedy and with Lyndon Johnson, who became president after Kennedy's assassination on November 22, 1963. These efforts ultimately failed because U.S. officials became convinced that Goulart was not to be trusted and was set on establishing a left-wing dictatorship that would pave the way for the Communists to take power in Brazil. This was most visibly exemplified in the controversy over the nationalization of U.S. companies. One of the most contentious issues concerned a subsidiary telephone company of International Telephone and Telegraph (ITT), which had been nationalized by the governor of Rio Grande do Sul, Leonel Brizola, in March 1962. Brizola was Goulart's brother-in-law and a strong nationalist and critic of U.S. imperialism. ITT rejected the amount of $400,000 that was initially offered as compensation by the state government and claimed a much higher figure in excess of $6 million. Although many of his advisers considered that the matter should properly be resolved in the Brazilian courts, Kennedy was convinced that U.S. business interests were being unfairly treated by left-wing political leaders such as Brizola. He determined to raise the issue of compensation directly with Goulart when the Brazilian president visited him in Washington in April.

In that meeting Goulart expressed willingness to settle the compensation claim made by ITT and to include a similar arrangement to nationalize subsidiary telephone companies in Brazil owned by American and Foreign Power (AMFORP). But stiff political opposition meant that little progress was made on this matter after his return to Brazil. Goulart may have believed that nationalization of U.S. companies would please public opinion, but left-wing critics focused on the financial arrangements that were regarded as too generous and an abject surrender to U.S. imperialism. Moreover, conservatives resented interference from the federal government in the right of states to regulate local companies. U.S. officials, however, interpreted the delay as evidence of Goulart's incompetence and untrustworthiness. Concerned over the advance of Communist influence, they decided to become involved in influencing Brazilian political affairs. This mostly took the form of American agencies such as the U.S. Information Service (USIS) and the CIA secretly contributing funds via North American banks to private organizations such as the Instituto Brasileiro de Ação Democrática (Brazilian Institute for Democratic Action or IBAD) and the Instituto de Pesquisas e Estudos Sociais (Institute of Social Research and Study or IPES) to assist the campaigns of anti-Communist candidates in the October 1962 elections. A Brazilian congressional investigation in 1963 uncovered evidence that U.S. agencies had covertly given several million *cruzeiros* for political purposes. IBAD was subsequently declared an illegal organization and dissolved.

As the 1962 elections closed, Kennedy sent General William Draper to Brazil to make a firsthand report on political conditions and assess the effectiveness of U.S. policy. The Draper Commission included representatives from the Defense Department, AID, CIA, and the U.S. Information Agency (USIA). After a study visit lasting just over two weeks and including a meeting with Goulart, the commission pessimistically declared "that Brazil is on the verge of financial collapse." Little confidence was placed in Goulart, who was described as "essentially a clever opportunist, with no strong motivation save his craving for popularity and personal power." The desire for personal popularity was considered highly significant because it meant that the Brazilian president was unwilling to take the hard but necessary economic decisions that were desperately required to save Brazil from imminent bankruptcy. While the commission acknowledged that Goulart hankered after imitating Castro and turning to the Soviet Union for financial support, he was reluctant to take such a step because it would end his hopes of U.S. aid and might also provoke a military coup. The Draper Commission summed up: "As long as Goulart remains in office, the United States should continue its efforts to make him realize the gravity of Brazil's financial and economic situation, and continue to urge the adoption of adequate remedial measures which would justify our large-scale financial help. At the same time we should attempt to influence his political orientation in directions better calculated to serve U.S. interests."[53]

President Kennedy accepted the recommendations made in the report and underscored their significance by assigning the task of influencing Goulart's "political orientation" to his brother, Robert Kennedy. The attorney general duly made a one-day flying visit to Brasília in December 1962 to express the president's growing impatience with Goulart's economic policy and his apparent sympathy with the Communists. After his meeting with Goulart, Kennedy frankly explained the reason for his irritation and its impact on U.S. policy: "When there are people in authority in Brazil who follow the Communist line, it can not be expected that we will work with them effectively."[54]

In March 1963, when the newly appointed finance minister, San Tiago Dantas, came to Washington, he found that his negotiations for a new loan were upstaged by statements from Ambassador Lincoln Gordon in congressional hearings that Communists had infiltrated Brazilian labor unions and even some departments of the federal government. Dantas secured a loan of $398 million, but payments were to be released in stages and only on condition that Brazil met strict fiscal targets that would be monitored by the IMF. When the IMF gave an unsatisfactory progress report in June, the U.S. government essentially suspended financial aid to the federal government but at the same time showed willingness to grant assistance to state governments that were identified as pro-American. This strategy was dubbed by Gordon as the "islands-of-administrative sanity" or "islands of sanity" policy. The new selective policy had little short-term impact because most of the loans were at a preliminary stage, but it served as a clear indication to Brazilians that the United States did not believe that the Goulart administration was capable of overcoming Brazil's financial crisis.

In addition to aiding pro-American, and by definition anti-Goulart, political factions, priority was also given to maintaining the close relationship that had long existed with the Brazilian military. Contacts had been strengthened by the Joint Brazil–United States Military Commission (JBUSMC) in Rio and by the creation in 1949 of the prestigious Escola Superior de Guerra (Higher War College or ESG), which was modeled on the U.S. National War College. The ESG inculcated among elite officers a doctrine of national security that emphasized the danger of International Communism and the importance of close cooperation with the United States in defending the Christian West. Fear of communism had prompted a number of senior military officers to oppose Goulart's succession in 1961. These officers continued to suspect his political motives. "The military," considered a State Department policy paper, "appear to be the only force capable of maintaining and restoring public order — and, if necessary, orderly government — should the political and economic deterioration produced by the policies of the present regime 'get out of hand.'" The policy paper recommended that U.S. policy should seek to "strengthen the basically democratic and pro–United States orientation of the military."[55] An important step in this direction had already been made in October 1962 with the appointment of Colonel Vernon "Dick" Walters as U.S. defense attaché in Rio de Janeiro. Walters had served as a liaison officer and interpreter for the Brazilian Expeditionary Force that had fought in Italy during World War II and personally knew a number of *Febianos* who had since become senior Brazilian military commanders. When he arrived in Rio to assume his duties no less than thirteen Brazilian generals were waiting to greet him at the airport.

The 1964 Coup

In January 1963 a plebiscite restored the executive powers that had been curtailed when Goulart had taken office in 1961. Goulart interpreted the large majority vote in his favor as a personal triumph and proceeded to announce an ambitious and optimistic "Three-Year Plan," prepared by Celso Furtado to combat the economic crisis. In the short term, however, just as the Draper Commission had predicted, economic production lagged and inflation continued its relentless rise. Furthermore, the deficit in the balance of payments widened and the foreign debt increased. The Goulart administration sought to alleviate the financial deficit by raising extra loans from the United States and the IMF but found negotiations severely hampered by its identification with economic nationalism and fiscal irresponsibility.

At the same time, Goulart sought to implement radical social reforms, notably the expropriation of agricultural land for redistribution to landless peasants. This policy reflected a combination of electoral calculation and a response to the increasing violence and disorder that was erupting in the countryside. The Agrarian Reform Bill presented in March 1964, however, provoked a bitter dispute between the president and Congress. Confronted with what amounted to a congressional veto, Goulart chose not to resign like Quadros but to issue a direct appeal to the people, thereby mobilizing "popular forces" to overthrow the reactionary forces blocking reform. In effect, Goulart was continuing the populist policies associated with Getúlio Vargas. But he lacked the political astuteness of his mentor and was also judged by contemporaries as weak and indecisive. Moreover, the attempt to implement radical reforms coincided with a period of increasing economic, social, and political crisis in Brazil. At a conference of U.S. ambassadors in Washington in mid-March 1964 Lincoln Gordon commented that the economic situation in Brazil was "terrible" and that Goulart was "an incompetent, juvenile delinquent" who "seems intent merely on survival." The opposition lacked strong leadership and was content to mark time until the 1965 presidential elections. "Like the Brazilian opposition," summed up one U.S. official, "we hope the ship of state can stay afloat until the elections."[56]

Political events, however, were moving fast in Brazil. Shortly after Gordon returned to Rio on March 22, he reported increased political tension and the important development that Army Chief of Staff General Castelo Branco had agreed to "lead democratic resistance group in military."[57] Earlier on March 20 Castelo Branco had sent a secret letter to senior officers informing them that the nation was in immediate danger of being placed under "the communism of Moscow."[58] As the political crisis escalated, the attitude of the military was clearly crucial. Goulart had pursued a policy of divide and rule in which he had appointed to senior posts men whom he considered loyal, while also cultivating a personal following among noncommissioned officers and enlisted men. Among the senior military, however, confidence in the president was severely shaken in late March when he reacted to a mutiny of sailors in Rio by dismissing the navy minister and granting an amnesty to the mutineers.

Meanwhile, Gordon cabled the State Department on March 27 to inform Rusk that Goulart "is now definitely engaged on campaign to seize dictatorial power, accepting the active collaboration of the Brazilian Communist Party, and of other radical left revolutionaries to this end." If this succeeded, the ambassador felt that "Brazil would come under full Communist control." At the same time, however, organized opposition was emerging under the leadership of Castelo Branco, whom Gordon glowingly described as "a highly competent, discreet, honest, and deeply respected officer who has strong loyalty to legal and constitutional principles." Gordon advised that the United States must support Castelo Branco "to help avert a major disaster here — which might make Brazil the China of the 1960s" and be prepared to provide, if required, weapons and supplies of petroleum. The ambassador issued a stark warning: "that there is a real and present danger to democracy and freedom in Brazil which could carry this enormous nation into the Communist camp. . . . The alternative of risking a Communist Brazil appears unacceptable, implying potentially far great ultimate costs in both money and lives."[59]

The coup began on March 31 when General Carlos Luis Guedes ordered infantry units to march from Minas Gerais and attack Rio. The proclaimed aim was to overthrow the president and restore constitutional government. Support was quickly forthcoming from other senior military commanders and prominent political leaders. On April 1 troops met with minimal resistance as they seized the principal government offices in Rio and Brasília. Meanwhile, Goulart left the capital to fly to Rio Grande do Sul and seek exile in Uruguay.

The relationship between the U.S. embassy and the Brazilian military was known to be so cordial that American complicity was suspected in the military coup. "Our embassy did have far ranging contacts," admitted Gordon, "but we were not participants in the planning of action against Goulart." Indeed, Colonel Walters had informed Gordon on March 30 that the coup was "imminent," but he had been careful not to become directly involved. "Any American attempt to interfere in developments," remarked Walters, "would have been bitterly resented by the Brazilian military, who felt and proved that they were quite competent at handling their own affairs." But the coup organizers could confidently count on the sympathy and support of the United States. This had been made apparent by the visible signs of U.S. disillusionment with Goulart and the adoption of the islands-of-sanity policy. Moreover, in a speech on March 18 the new assistant secretary of state for Latin American affairs, Thomas Mann, had signaled a change in policy — later known as the "Mann Doctrine" — by stating that the Johnson administration would maintain normal diplomatic relations with governments that came to power even if this had been achieved by a military coup. In effect, this reassured military plotters in Brazil that they would not be opposed by the United States. There was also the prospect of valuable logistical aid. In his telegram to Washington of March 27

Gordon had requested that small arms, ammunition, and supplies of petroleum be made available and that a naval task force be sent to Brazilian waters to "demonstrate [American] commitment and some show of force."[60]

While officials in Washington approved the provision of petrol supplies, they were initially dubious about the value of sending a naval squadron that would take up to ten days to reach Brazilian waters. "The punishment doesn't seem to fit the crime," remarked Special Assistant for National Security Affairs McGeorge Bundy.[61] However, on receiving news from Gordon that the coup had begun, a powerful naval task force under the codename "Operation Brother Sam," and consisting of the aircraft carrier U.S.S. *Forrestal*, six support warships, and four oil tankers, was ordered to set sail for the South Atlantic on March 31. The stated aim was "to render assistance at appropriate time to anti-Goulart forces if it is decided this should be done."[62] The prospect of U.S. military personnel becoming involved in serious fighting was therefore a definite contingency. News of the success of the coup meant, however, that the operation was canceled on April 3. A leading Brazilian politician recalled that Gordon expressed himself as "very happy" that U.S. military intervention had not been necessary after all.[63] The Johnson administration was undoubtedly delighted to learn of Goulart's peaceful fall from power. Even though Goulart was still known to be present in Brazil and had not officially resigned, so that the exact constitutional position as to whether he was still head of state was uncertain, Johnson telegraphed his "warmest good wishes" to the new interim Brazilian president, Pascoal Ranieri Mazzilli.[64]

7 The Rise and Fall of Military Government

"Brazil is not a country that is open to external influence with regards to its internal politics," commented Harry Shlaudeman, the U.S. ambassador to Brazil from 1986 to 1989.[1] In the aftermath of the 1964 coup, the United States was unable to moderate the repressive policy of a succession of Brazilian military governments. Moreover, Brazilian diplomacy overtly began to emphasize a "nationalist" approach in what was essentially a return to the idea of the "independent foreign policy." Brazil also looked beyond the United States for alternative export markets and sources of inward capital investment, a strategy that was stimulated by the external "oil shocks" in 1973 and 1979 and the resulting need to earn more foreign exchange from exports to pay for the rising cost of oil imports.

The pursuit of a "nationalist" policy frequently resulted in tension with the United States. The Brazilian government particularly resented criticism that was made public over its record on human rights. Similarly, it insisted on the right to develop atomic energy for peaceful industrial purposes and signed an agreement with a West German consortium for the supply of nuclear reactors. Further examples of Brazil's divergence from the United States were the rejection of President Jimmy Carter's call for a boycott of the 1980 Moscow Olympic Games and unwillingness to endorse the policy of President Ronald Reagan to counter the Communist threat in El Salvador and Nicaragua.

During the 1980s economic factors brought about a return to closer bilateral cooperation because Brazil needed U.S. diplomatic and financial assistance in order to negotiate satisfactory terms for a resolution of the Debt Crisis. The United States, however, diverged from Brazil by forming the North American Free Trade Agreement (NAFTA) with Canada and Mexico in 1992. Brazil opted instead to join with Argentina, Paraguay, and Uruguay in establishing a separate customs union known as Mercosur. By taking the lead to promote

Mercosur, Brazil was implicitly mounting a challenge to U.S. economic leadership of the hemisphere.

The Military in Power

The U.S. government was delighted with the success of the military coup overthrowing João Goulart, an event that Ambassador Lincoln Gordon described "as one of the major turning points in world history in the middle of the twentieth century" and similar in significance "to the Marshall Plan proposal, the Berlin Blockade, the defeat of Communist aggression in Korea, and the resolution of the missile crisis in Cuba."[2] As Gordon's effusive language indicated, instead of being condemned for using violence to overthrow a constitutional government, the Brazilian military was credited with preventing the occurrence of "another Cuba." The perception that they had bravely carried out their patriotic duty in saving their country from an imminent Communist insurrection was relayed in most contemporary newspapers and news magazines in the United States. For example, *U.S. News and World Report* dramatically entitled two articles "Now with Castro Turned Back — A New Start for Brazil" and "How Close the Reds Came to Taking Over Brazil."[3]

U.S. officials envisaged a necessary but temporary period of military rule followed by the resumption of political and legal rights. This was based on a desire to see the installation of democratic government and also their reading of previous Brazilian history, which showed that the military soon gave up political control and returned to barracks. Such an outcome had occurred in 1930 when power had been handed over to civilian politicians, but fear of an imminent countercoup by pro-Goulart forces meant that the same option was ruled out in April 1964. The self-styled "revolutionary high command" representing the junta of senior military commanders likened their situation more to 1889 when the military had considered it incumbent on themselves to hold on to high political office for an indefinite period. Any constitutional barriers to this decision were easily removed. Ten days after the coup, the legal technicalities were dealt with by simply ignoring the 1946 Constitution and unilaterally issuing a series of decrees, beginning with Institutional Act No. 1, which declared the "revolutionary high military command" to be the legitimate government authority. In accordance with the views of military men accustomed to acting within a hierarchical chain of command, the act also substantially increased the executive authority of the office of the president and correspondingly reduced the powers of Congress. Although Congress would continue in session, an indication of its diminished status was reflected in the peremptory instruction to elect an interim president and vice president within the short space of forty-eight hours. General Castelo Branco was duly elected as interim president by a large majority. At the same time, the junta proceeded to implement "Operação Limpeza" (Operation Cleanup) in which a large number of left-wing politicians, organized labor officials, and student leaders were arrested and subjected to summary punishment. The pro-Goulart forces turned out to be demoralized and widely dispersed and proved incapable of organizing effective resistance.

The Castelo Branco administration announced to the people that its aim was to enact a "revolution" in which Brazil would be modernized and reshaped by a policy of ensuring political stability, restoring social order, and promoting economic development with an emphasis on greatly reducing inflation. The new military regime showed, however, that it intended to implement revolutionary change in an authoritarian rather than a democratic manner. This was underscored not only by the adoption of a policy of highly centralized economic control but also by the imposition of severe restrictions on political activities and ruthless repression of civilian opposition. Institutional Act No. 1 notably enabled the government to deprive "political undesirables" such as Goulart and Brizola of their political rights for ten years, a procedure known as *cassação* (cassation). However, the indiscriminate and politically partisan nature of the policy of repression was illustrated by the cassation of ex-President Juscelino Kubitschek. "I am paying for the crime of having fought resolutely for the independence of my country," remarked the ex-president.[4]

Washington was dismayed at the imposition of the institutional act and the ensuing cassation of respected politicians such as Kubitschek. "Brazil may have been thrust into the fire of a right wing police state under the pretext of being saved from Communist infiltration," warned the *New Republic*.[5] An article in the *Washington Post* entitled "Brazil Caught in Grip of Army Dictatorship" estimated that as many as ten thousand arrests had been made in only a few weeks since the coup.[6] Despite the popular conception that the U.S. government possessed considerable influence in Brazil, there was, however, little that it could do to make a material difference in the course of internal political events. In fact, the junta would not be deflected from implementing its authoritarian policies. Interference of any kind, even from the United States, would not be tolerated. Defense Minister Artur da Costa e Silva "gently reminded" Ambassador Gordon and Colonel Vernon Walters that Brazil was a sovereign nation.[7]

Gordon personally wished for the restoration of "constitutional guarantees," but he explained to Washington that the U.S. embassy had only a "limited influence in the circumstances, and I stress that it is limited."[8] Moreover, the Johnson administration undoubtedly wanted the new military government to succeed in its battle to eradicate communism in Brazil. Although he did not personally approve the severity of the coercive measures that had been adopted by the junta, Gordon acknowledged that Goulart had planned a Communist-dominated dictatorship and that "a substantial purge was clearly in order." In the circumstances, the ambassador resolved the dilemma by rationalizing that the best attitude for both himself and his government to adopt was "the closest possible approximation to golden silence."[9] A policy of silence, however, would be publicly interpreted as condoning if not actually supporting the repressive acts of the military government. It also reinforced suspicions that the U.S. government had aided and abetted the military coup.

Conscious that an influential *linha dura* (hard-line) element existed within the military junta, Gordon believed that the "greatest hope for avoidance of undemocratic excesses rests in character and convictions of Castello Branco." Indeed, he gave a very positive appreciation of the personal qualities of the new president after his first official meeting. In comparison to his encounters with Goulart, Gordon found conversing with Castelo Branco was like the difference between "day and night." If Gordon had any misgivings, they were evidently resolved. "I left the interview with the feeling that this was a most auspicious beginning," the ambassador enthusiastically reported. At another meeting some weeks later, Gordon again relayed to Washington a favorable impression of the president's attitude as "one of calm resolve to get on with problems of clean-up, administrative rebuilding, and positive program."[10]

Instead of the anticipated move to democracy, however, the military government consolidated its authority further and decreed a second Institutional Act on October 27, 1965, providing for the dissolution of existing political parties. "It will be obvious to Department," reported Gordon, "that second Institutional Act represents severe setback in our own hopes . . . that Brazil could maintain uninterrupted march on road back to full constitutional normalcy."[11] While Secretary of State Dean Rusk favored a continuation of the attitude of "public silence," he instructed Gordon to make Castelo Branco and other Brazilian leaders "acutely aware [of] our serious concern and deep disappointment." Describing Institutional Act No. 2 as "a backward step," Rusk hoped that the new "arbitrary powers" would be used "with the greatest moderation and restraint."[12] Washington's policy of expressing disapproval in private rather than in public was no doubt pleasing to the Brazilian military. It also indicated that the restoration of democratic government in Brazil was not an absolute priority of the Johnson administration.

Nevertheless, Rusk's concern reflected a widely held belief in Washington that political developments in Brazil had a significance that went beyond just that particular nation. "The emergence of a repressive authoritarian regime," Rusk remarked, "would represent a serious reverse in an otherwise rather encouraging series of developments throughout the hemisphere under the Alliance for Progress." Moreover, pressure for punitive measures was emerging in the U.S. Congress, where Senator Wayne Morse proposed a reduction in U.S. financial aid as a visible protest against the institutional act. Ambassador Gordon recognized that there was a "serious danger of slippage into undisguised military dictatorship," but he cautioned against any thoughts of external interference. In his opinion, Brazil was so big and complex that "we should have no illusions regarding our ability greatly to influence course of political developments" and that attempts to interfere in internal politics could "backfire."[13]

Although the consolidation of military rule in Brazil clearly represented a setback to the advance of constitutional government and would provide instead an influential model of authoritarian political development for neighboring South American nations such as Argentina, Uruguay, and Chile, the Johnson administration raised no objection to the selection of the "hard-line" war minister Costa e Silva to succeed Castelo Branco as president in March 1967. Costa e Silva announced his candidacy in January 1966 and was elected unopposed on October 3. A CIA report on Costa e Silva predicted that under his presidency not only would Brazil become even more authoritarian but that his undisguised nationalist sentiments posed the risk of causing conflict in U.S.-Brazilian relations.[14]

Indeed, the Costa e Silva regime acted in an increasingly arbitrary and ruthless fashion leading to a major political crisis in December 1968 when Congress refused the government's request to lift the parliamentary immunity of a deputy who had made speeches critical of military rule. The attempt by the legislature to assert its constitutional powers against the executive was regarded as an unacceptable act of defiance by Costa e Silva and resulted in his issuing another Institutional Act. The provisions of Institutional Act No. 5 were the most draconian so far. Congress was to be recessed indefinitely, further restrictions were placed on civil rights, and strict censorship was applied to the press, television, and radio. The act demonstrated that Brazil had definitively become a military dictatorship in which the generals ruled not by consent but by force.

Officials in Washington were aghast. "Almost all agree that Costa e Silva and the military overreacted in near cosmic terms to the provocation presented," Rusk informed the U.S. embassy in Rio. Describing the act as a "gross breaching of constitutional restraints and political and civil rights," he believed that it indicated "an almost paranoiac overkill response to provocation presented."[15] Once again, however, the State Department found itself in a state of virtual helplessness. "We must recognize that our influence on internal political events is marginal at best," considered Ambassador John Tuthill.[16] It was felt in Washington, however, that a public sign of displeasure must be made on this occasion. Consequently, even though the Johnson administration was only a few weeks away from leaving office, officials announced the withholding of the release of a $50 million loan installment. Loans to Brazil that were already in the pipeline were suspended and placed under review. The freeze was continued by the Nixon administration until May 1969.

The Economy

The economy was in severe crisis when Castelo Branco became president in April 1964. He turned immediately to civilian "technocrats" and business leaders for advice and quick remedial action. In so doing, he established a collaborative partnership between the military and civilian experts that would be a prominent feature of economic policymaking throughout the period of military government from 1964 to 1985. After the controversial presidencies of Quadros and Goulart, the combination of political stability and the evident commitment of the federal government to the pursuit of orthodox economic policies and financial management successfully restored Brazil's international credit rating. Particularly pleasing to officials in Washington was the appointment of Roberto de Oliveira Campos as planning minister. A former Brazilian ambassador to the United States, Campos was well regarded in U.S. diplomatic and business circles, where he was known as "Bob Fields," a translation of his name into English. After being sworn in as a cabinet minister, he quickly reassured the financial press that "the role of state planning is not to asphyxiate private initiative, but, on the contrary, is to discipline public investments, rationalize government action, and thus construct a framework within which private enterprise should operate."[17] Such views accorded very closely to American financial principles, so that with the backing of Finance Minister Octávio Gouvéia Bulhões, Campos was able to renegotiate improved terms for the servicing of the foreign debt and to secure large loans for economic development from the U.S. government, the IMF, and the World Bank. Whereas the Johnson administration had withheld financial assistance from Goulart, it now gave priority to the promotion of aid and investment in Brazil. During the period from 1964 to 1970 only South Vietnam and India received greater amounts of government loans from the United States. At the same time, the country also became an attractive destination for direct investment from foreign banks and corporations, especially German and Japanese.

The image of Brazil in the United States was further improved by Castelo Branco's successful handling of two issues that had long troubled economic relations between the two countries. He relaxed restrictions on overseas profit remittances by U.S. corporations and secured a vote in Congress to pay the final amount of compensation owing to AMFORP. An American businessman had described the military coup as "the greatest thing that could happen to U.S. interests."[18] The accuracy of this observation was borne out by Secretary of State Rusk's fulsome praise: "Since coming to power in April 1964, the Castello Branco Administration has conducted an admirably tough economic program of stabilization, development and reform . . . We consider that Brazil has made excellent use of the support we have been providing and is today conducting the strongest program of economic self-help in the hemisphere."[19] On the other hand, Brazil was flooded with U.S. advisers and technicians drawn from a multitude of federal agencies such as AID, CIA, and USIS, to supervise the aid programs. In addition, there were hundreds of young American volunteers learning about Brazil by taking part in the Peace Corps program that had begun in 1961. On his arrival in Brazil in June 1966 Ambassador John Tuthill was dismayed to discover that 920 U.S. citizens were on the staff of his embassy and that to Brazilians "the ubiquitous American official" had become "a special irritant." Using what he described as "the shock treatment," Tuthill put in place measures to reduce the staffing levels by up to one-third.[20]

Foreign Policy

Close and friendly relations were evident in diplomatic affairs. In April 1964 the new military government headed by President Castelo Branco immediately announced a reversal of the independent foreign policy pursued by Quadros and Goulart. Instead, the traditional Brazilian policy of seeking a special relationship with the United States was reaffirmed. The move reflected a desire to change the direction of foreign policy away from the left-wing attitude of the previous government. It also expressed the ideology and geopolitical thinking of the ESG in which the military regarded the United States as the leader of the free world in the Cold War currently being fought against International Communism. The influential director of the National Intelligence Service, General Golbery do Couto e Silva, emphasized that Brazil should follow "Washington's wise counsel."[21] In addition, access to U.S. trade and investment and close cooperation on financial matters were considered vital for the successful modernization and development of the Brazilian economy. "What is good for the United States is good for Brazil," later declared the Brazilian ambassador in Washington, Juracy Magalhães.[22]

The change of government in Brazil and its desire to assist the United States in fighting communism in the Western Hemisphere was much appreciated by the State Department. "Brazil is the most important thing outside of Cuba that's happened in the last 20 years in Latin America," Thomas Mann informed President Johnson.[23] Especially pleasing to U.S. officials was Brazil's participation in the policy of isolating Cuba. In contrast to Quadros and Goulart, who had both shown a sympathetic attitude toward Fidel Castro and the Cuban Revolution, Castelo Branco broke off diplomatic relations with Cuba only a few weeks after taking office. "In its international posture the new Brazilian government has now rejoined the free world," summed up a delighted Lincoln Gordon.[24]

In April 1965 political chaos erupted into violence in Santo Domingo, the capital of the Dominican Republic. President Lyndon Johnson suspected that a pro-Castro Communist conspiracy was responsible. More than twenty thousand American troops were dispatched to restore order, the first overt military intervention by the United States in Latin America since Nicaragua in the late 1920s. The unilateral intervention, however, provoked a heated political debate within the United States. Critics in Latin America also pointed out that Johnson had not consulted the Organization of American States (OAS) prior to his decision to send in troops. Johnson belatedly brought the issue to the OAS, and despite considerable misgivings being expressed from some members of the council, he secured agreement for the dispatch of an OAS military presence in the form of token contingents of troops from six Latin American nations, including Brazil, to supervise peace arrangements. In effect, the affirmative vote signified retrospective OAS approval of Johnson's armed intervention.

Brazil played a conspicuously leading role in supporting Johnson's policy. President Castelo Branco, however, informed Colonel Walters that the decision to send Brazilian forces was not motivated simply by a desire to please the United States. Brazil was conscious of a wider purpose to fight International Communism and maintain the security of the Western Hemisphere. "It is because another sister American republic is threatened with losing its freedom as we were threatened with losing ours a short time ago," he explained.[25] From May 1965 to September 1966 around three thousand Brazilian troops served in the Dominican Republic as part of the Inter-American Peace Force. Brazil provided the largest single contingent from Latin America, a fact that was reflected in the placing of a Brazilian officer, General Hugo Panasco Alvim, as commander of the Inter-American Peace Force. This resulted in an awkward personal relationship between Alvim and the commander of the U.S. troops,

General Bruce Palmer, who circumvented the Brazilian's attempts to exercise operational control over U.S. forces. Brazilian troops, however, saw minimal combat and suffered very few casualties so that their deployment overseas provoked little political controversy in Brazil.

The Brazilian government was also publicly sympathetic to the actions taken by the United States to protect South Vietnam from Communist aggression. In August 1964 Foreign Minister Vasci Leitão da Cunha expressed Brazil's solidarity with the United States over the Tonkin Gulf incident. A Brazilian medical team was later dispatched to serve in South Vietnam as a gesture of moral support for the United States. But no Brazilian combat troops were sent. In contrast to the Korean War, there was no UN resolution calling on member states to contribute military forces. Unlike the relatively inexpensive and undemanding intervention in the Dominican Republic, the fighting in Vietnam was steadily escalating in severity and posed the distinct probability of participant nations incurring heavy combat losses. The Johnson administration, however, openly asked for assistance. As a way of putting pressure on Brazil to make a military commitment to the war in Vietnam, Johnson suggested that the request for troops should be directly linked to negotiations over future loans. Gordon argued, however, that any attempt at such linkage would be "disastrous." In his opinion, even a "private hint would arouse resentment from Castello Branco, who although [a] good friend is also [a] very dignified and proud Brazilian."[26]

While Castelo Branco sought close diplomatic cooperation with the United States, the refusal to commit troops to Vietnam demonstrated that Brazil was neither a formal ally nor a satellite state.[27] In fact, the diplomacy of the military government became similar to the independent foreign policies pursued by its civilian predecessors in seeking both to assert and promote the country's sovereignty and national interests. For example, Castelo Branco stressed that Brazil's intervention in the Dominican Republic in 1965 was not at American bidding but was an independent decision and part of a scheme to develop a permanent inter-American "peace force" under the command of the OAS. Similarly, while diplomatic relations were broken off with Cuba, they were maintained with other Communist countries beyond the Western Hemisphere. Indeed, vigorous efforts were made to expand Brazilian trade with the Soviet Union.

Brazil as an Aspiring World Power

U.S. officials found little fault in Castelo Branco. "Cooperation with us on for-eign policy matters could hardly have been closer," remarked Johnson's special assistant on national security affairs, Walt Rostow. In fact, Castelo Branco's pro-American attitude aroused some adverse comment from his military colleagues that he was too subservient to the United States. After he became president in 1967, Costa e Silva chose to emphasize Brazil's autonomy in for-eign policy. He notably resisted U.S. pressure to sign the 1968 Nuclear Non-Proliferation Treaty and to commit Brazilian forces to aid the United States in Vietnam. When the United States declined to provide F-5 jet fighter jets for the Brazilian Air Force, Costa e Silva turned to France for Mirage jets. U.S. officials considered that Costa e Silva was not unfriendly and was being deliberately assertive to suit his own domestic political agenda. In fact, the United States provided a convenient target. Ambassador John Tuthill noted that in both public and private Costa e Silva "made it quite clear that Brazil would find its own way and that it would resist any actions by other governments — which essentially meant the United States — when they infringed upon its rights and authority."[28]

Although the new president was a staunch anti-Communist and made a state visit to the United States early in his presidency, Rostow felt that "there is a puzzling ambivalence in the orientation of the Costa e Silva administration."[29] In effect, Costa e Silva was promoting Brazil's desire to be diplomatically active and thereby implementing what was essentially a return to the "independent" policy of Jânio Quadros and João Goulart. To avoid being associated with the previous left-wing presidents, however, the military preferred the policy to be described in public as "nationalist." But Costa e Silva was similar to Quadros and Goulart in perceiving world affairs as no longer so dominated by the ide-ology and rivalries of the Cold War. In fact, by the beginning of the 1970s the traditional East-West bipolar perspective had become less relevant as the threat of Communist subversion notably receded in Brazil and as the United States withdrew from Vietnam and sought détente with the Soviet Union. Instead, more significance was now attached to the growing divergence between the affluent nations of the North or First World and the less economically devel-oped countries of the South or Third World. Brazil was currently placed in the latter category. Consequently, the priority of Brazilian foreign policy was seen as promoting national economic development so that Brazil could become a member of the First World. "We want," stated Foreign Minister José de Magalhães Pinto, "to put diplomacy at the service of prosperity."[30]

Brazilian self-esteem was boosted by the achievement of internal political stability and the onset of industrial and financial recovery leading to what was hailed as the "economic miracle." From 1967 to 1973 the gross domestic product (GDP) increased by more than 10 percent per year, making Brazil one of the most rapidly growing economies in the world. Simply by projecting the same high annual rate of GDP growth into the future, it was predicted that, by the end of the twentieth century, Brazil would achieve *grandeza* (greatness) and rise to the status of a world power ("O Brasil Grande"), thereby joining the nations of the First World. One diplomat claimed, "we are an emerging power that can no longer be ignored by the kingmakers of the world political scene."[31] The idea of "power" was conceived in terms of economic prosperity and not military strength or territorial conquest. Indeed, the strength of the armed forces was held at a modest level in relation to the country's size and population. More emphasis and expenditure was directed to modernizing and building economic infrastructure in the form of massive domestic projects such as the Itaipú dam and the Transamazon Highway. "We must start up the Amazon clock, which has been losing time for too long," declared President Emilío Garrastazú Médici.[32]

The pursuit of a "nationalist" policy that stressed export-led growth resulted in increasing divergence with the United States. Brazilian exporters complained of protectionist tariff barriers and discriminatory customs duties that seriously affected their sales of such products as instant coffee, shoes, and steel in the U.S. market. Moreover, America's relative decline as the world's leading economic power reduced the value of commercial links. During World War II, the United States had absorbed more than 50 percent of Brazil's total exports. The proportion fell to less than 20 percent during the 1970s. Consequently, Brazil was no longer so economically dependent on the United States and looked farther afield for alternative export markets and sources of capital investment, a drive that was stimulated by the 1973 oil shock and the resulting need to earn more foreign exchange from exports to pay for the greatly increased cost of oil imports. Particular effort was directed by Brazilian diplomats to expanding trade and negotiating loans with the affluent nations of Western Europe. New commercial markets were also developed and cultivated in Africa, the Middle East, and Asia. Trade with the Communist Bloc was markedly increased, especially with the countries of Eastern Europe, where exports rose from $123 million in 1970 to $421 million in 1973. The prospect of trading with the vast Chinese market and gaining access to energy raw materials was presented when full diplomatic relations were established with the People's Republic of China in 1974.

Brazil's remarkable economic progress attracted world attention and some admiration. Impressed by its size, natural resources, and ambition, U.S. national security adviser Henry Kissinger believed that "in 50 years Brazil should have achieved world power status."[33] In a manner reminiscent of Theodore Roosevelt and Elihu Root at the beginning of the twentieth century, President Richard Nixon and Kissinger saw Brazil as America's preferred hemispheric partner in helping to maintain the political stability of South America. Of most importance was Brazil's cooperation in the Cold War. In fact, the success of the military governments in repressing communism was favorably contrasted with events in Chile, where the Marxist Salvador Allende Gossens was elected president in 1970. During the state visit of President Médici to Washington in December 1971, Nixon commented: "We know that as Brazil goes, so will the rest of the Latin American continent."[34]

Nixon's remarks were intended to be flattering, but Brazilians were sensitive to the inference that they were regarded as willing agents in the spreading of American values and business in Latin America. Indeed, the suspicion that U.S. officials and businessmen were seeking to stifle Brazilian commerce and industrial development resulted in calculated efforts to reduce the country's perceived economic dependence on the United States. In what was a veiled but unmistakable reference to the United States, Médici's successor, President Ernesto Geisel, stated in 1974 that there would be "no automatic or aprioristic alignment" with other countries. In its place, Brazil would adopt a multilateral policy based upon "responsible pragmatism."[35] This was exemplified by two presidential visits to Western Europe and the negotiation of large commercial contracts with Great Britain and France.

Conflict over Human Rights

During the 1970s relations were adversely affected by public disquiet in the United States and Western Europe that saw the people of Brazil as suffering under a brutal military regime. Repression had been a feature of the military government since 1964, but the policy of "cleansing" the political opposition did not reach its peak until after the imposition of Institutional Act No. 5 in 1968. During the Médici administration from 1969 to 1974 "search-and arrest" operations conducted by the army and the police became more frequent and were characterized by the systematic use of torture to extract information from those arrested and imprisoned. An influential report published in 1972 by the London-based nongovernmental organization Amnesty International presented documented cases illustrating that torture had become "a routine part of any interrogation" by the army and police in Brazil.[36]

A lively political debate over human rights was already taking place in the United States as a result of concern about the repressive policies of the military government that had seized power in Greece in 1967. In a speech in October 1970 Senator Edward Kennedy linked Brazil with Greece as an example of two countries that received U.S. financial aid while their governments committed violations of human rights. "We stand silent while political prisoners are tortured in Brazil," noted Kennedy, even though "Brazil is ruled by a government that we fully support with money, arms, technical assistance, and the comfort of close diplomatic relations."[37] In May 1971 the chairman of the U.S. Senate Subcommittee on Western Hemisphere Affairs, Frank Church, held secret hearings on "U.S. Policies and Programs in Brazil." While information emerged revealing American participation in the training of some Brazilian police officers who were known to have been implicated in cases of alleged torture, there was a pronounced reluctance to interfere. The current U.S. ambassador to Brazil, William Roundtree, attended the hearings and advised that it was for "the Brazilians themselves to take whatever action is appropriate to end the basis for this criticism."[38] Senator William J. Fulbright concurred and doubted "if [Brazilians] could do any better" than having Médici as their president.[39]

The Brazilian government denied that a policy of systematic torture had ever been adopted. Moreover, it unapologetically justified the need for repressive procedures as a measured and necessary response to the serious threat of revolutionary warfare posed by left-wing urban guerrilla groups such as the ALN (Aliança Libertação Nacional or National Liberation Alliance). In 1969 the ALN switched from its strategy of mainly emphasizing bank robberies to include the kidnapping of foreign diplomats. The most celebrated incident was the kidnapping of U.S. ambassador C. Burke Elbrick in Rio de Janeiro on September 4, 1969. The ambassador was freed after the government agreed to release fifteen political prisoners. The kidnapping of Elbrick and the visible rise of urban terrorism not only in Brazil but also in other cities in South America gave support to those U.S. officials who were prepared to condone the adoption of hard-line methods by the Brazilian government. Nongovernmental organizations such as the North American Congress on Latin America continued to mount a sustained campaign to expose and condemn the use of torture in Brazil, but the passivity shown by the Nixon and Ford administrations meant that the Médici regime could proceed with its policies safe in the knowledge that punitive measures were unlikely to materialize from Washington. In fact, the military rulers were placated by the friendly visit of Secretary of State William Rogers to Brazil in May 1973 and the subsequent sale to the Brazilian Air Force of American F-5 fighter jets that had been previously blocked by the U.S. Congress.

The election to the U.S. presidency in 1976 of a Washington "outsider," James Earl "Jimmy" Carter, however, raised the prospect of a new emphasis in U.S. foreign policy on the obligation of nations to respect human rights. Carter sought to rekindle America's unique historical and self-appointed mission to promote freedom and democracy. While the policy was intended to be worldwide and particularly aimed at the Soviet Union, American officials reckoned that the best chance of initial success lay in Latin America because the United States possessed more influence to effect change there than in other regions of the world.

Carter's stress on respect for human rights found support in the U.S. Congress, which was very keen to participate in the making of a more ethically based foreign policy in the post Vietnam and Watergate era. The passage of the Harkin Amendment to the 1975 Foreign Assistance Act had given Congress authority to limit the U.S. economic assistance given to "any country which engages in a consistent pattern of gross violations of internationally recognised human rights."[40] In compliance with the Harkin Amendment the

State Department published an Annual Report in 1977 on current conditions regarding human rights in countries receiving U.S. economic and military aid. The records of a number of Latin American countries, including Brazil, were singled out for criticism.[41] The U.S. Congress duly reacted by threatening to suspend military assistance unless improvements were made. The impact on Brasília was immediate and sensational. An incensed Geisel administration charged the U.S. government with unacceptable interference in Brazilian domestic affairs and on March 11, 1977, abruptly canceled the military agreement that had been in operation since 1952. The action demonstrated that the termination of military assistance programs would be done by Brazil and not by the United States.[42]

The Brazilian government also pointed out that the United States was unfairly adopting a double standard by not putting the same pressure on Communist countries where human rights were routinely violated. The *New York Times* noted Brazilian criticism that the Carter administration was punishing its long-standing friends but was willing "to cozy up to the Cubans, or the Chinese, or for that matter to any Communist-run countries, which the United States seems no longer to have the stomach to oppose."[43] Brazil subsequently turned to Western Europe and Israel for supplies of weapons and substantially increased investment in its own national arms industry. In so doing Brazil actually became a major exporter of military equipment, especially to the Middle East, and demonstrated that it was not dependent on the United States for armaments.

Conflict over Nuclear Technology

Another cause of diplomatic conflict between the two countries was divergence over nuclear technology. Possessing large reserves of natural resources, Brazil was traditionally suspicious of proposals for international control of strategic materials and declined to support the Baruch Plan in 1946 or to adhere to the 1968 Nuclear Non-Proliferation Treaty. Brazil signed but did not ratify the Tlatelolco Treaty in 1967, which prohibited nuclear weapons in Latin America. In 1970, as part of a long-term program to seek self-sufficiency in energy supplies, Brazil entered into a contract with the American corporation Westinghouse for the construction of a nuclear reactor at Angra dos Reis. Included in the arrangement was the agreement of the U.S. Atomic Energy Commission to provide essential supplies of enriched uranium fuel. However, after India's successful explosion of a nuclear device in July 1974, the United States feared that Latin American nations, especially Brazil and Argentina, would similarly seek to become nuclear powers. Consequently, the U.S. Atomic Energy Commission announced that it would no longer carry out its undertaking to supply enriched uranium fuel for the Brazilian reactor currently under construction by Westinghouse.

Another reason for the halting of exports of enriched uranium was the knowledge that Brazil had sought to break away from its dependence on the United States by entering into secret negotiations with alternative suppliers in West Germany. Much to the disappointment and surprise of the U.S. government and Westinghouse, in June 1975 President Geisel signed a contract with a West German consortium, Kraftwerk Union, for the construction of eight nuclear reactors plus uranium enrichment and reprocessing facilities at a cost of $5 billion. At a time of oil shocks when the country was heavily dependent on expensive oil imports, Brazil claimed that the reactors were intended to generate electric power to meet the growing demands of economic and industrial growth. Mindful of Brazil's constant refusal to join the 1968 Non-Proliferation Treaty, U.S. officials also interpreted the contract as an expression of Brazil's desire to develop its own autonomous nuclear industry and thereby acquire the knowledge and technology to manufacture nuclear weapons. In January 1977 the incoming Carter administration sent Vice President Walter Mondale to Bonn to put private pressure on the West German government to modify the contract so as not to allow Brazil the technology to enrich and reprocess uranium fuel into nuclear weapons–grade plutonium.

Both Brazil and West Germany were determined to proceed with the arrangement that they had already signed. They argued that U.S. criticism reflected irritation at losing a lucrative commercial contract deal rather than issues of technology or security. It was also pointed out that the agreement had been made public and was approved by the European Union. Brazil resented U.S. interference, which was interpreted as a calculated effort to prevent the country's rise to world power status. There was also particular annoyance that Carter had engaged in secret diplomacy with West Germany. To underscore

Brazilian displeasure with the Carter administration, Geisel turned down an invitation to visit Washington and join other hemispheric leaders in celebrating the signing of the Panama Canal Treaties in September 1977. Relations did not improve. In 1978 Geisel visited Great Britain, West Germany, and Japan without including the United States on his itinerary. Later, when Carter visited Brasília, he described Brazil as a "truly great power" but received only "a cool but polite welcoming statement" from President Geisel.[44]

Moreover, Brazil refused to participate in an embargo on exports of grain to the Soviet Union as a protest against the Soviet invasion of Afghanistan in 1979 and to join Carter's call for a boycott of the Moscow Olympic Games. The *New York Times* considered that the Brazilian government took "almost mischievous delight in its refusal to participate in the American action against the Soviet Union."[45] Divergence with the United States was also evident in Brazilian policy toward the Middle East, especially the Arab-Israeli issue. Dependent upon the Middle East for 80 percent of its oil imports, the Brazilian government adopted a pro-Arab attitude. Despite U.S. annoyance, Brazil recognized the Palestine Liberation Organization as the representative of the Palestinians in 1979. A similar diplomatic realism was evident in Brazil's cultivation of friendly diplomatic relations during the mid-1970s with the pro-Marxist governments that won independence from Portugal in Guinea-Bissau, Angola, and Mozambique.

Although Brazilian governments staunchly defended Brazil's sovereignty and secretly sought to develop nuclear weapons, there was no desire to become actively involved in the politics of the Cold War. The primary purpose of Brazilian diplomacy remained the global promotion of the country's commercial relations, a task that became more difficult and demanding as a result of the damaging economic effects of the external oil shocks of 1973 and 1979 and the Debt Crisis of the 1980s. Moreover, domestic factors such as political instability, persistent hyperinflation, and the failure to maintain the high levels of growth of the economic "miracle" created growing strategic and economic insecurity. No longer so optimistic about the inevitability of achieving world power status, successive Brazilian governments were characteristically suspicious of what they regarded as attempts by the great powers to infringe the sovereignty of less powerful nations and to establish international institutions for their own commercial benefit. Brazil was, therefore, extremely distrustful of proposals designed to limit the growth of population, establish international ownership of the seabeds, restrict arms sales, and regulate world trade.

Especially controversial was the issue of the environment and foreign concern over the deforestation of the Amazon region, which argued that Brazilian actions were affecting the rest of the world by destroying many rare plants and animal species. Foreign criticism of deforestation was countered with the argument that "slash and burn" and logging were not only traditional agricultural practices but were also done on a relatively small scale when compared with the massive programs occurring in Central America, West Africa, and Southeast Asia. Furthermore, it was contended that the industrialized nations of the North were actually responsible for much more atmospheric pollution than Brazil. Nevertheless, Brazil did not want to appear too antagonistic or confrontational. Indeed, Brazilian diplomacy during the period of the military governments was inherently conservative and, in matters of dispute, sought to come to an understanding with international political and financial institutions. While Brazil desired friendly relations with the nations of the Third World, it decided not to play a leading role in international meetings and activities of organizations such as the United Nations Commission on Trade and Development (UNCTAD). In fact, Brazil gradually felt that it had less in common with these countries as it became a major exporter of manufactured goods and one of the largest industrial economies in the world.

General João Batista de Oliveira Figueiredo became the last of the military presidents in October 1978. President Figueiredo affirmed his support for the process of allowing broader civilian participation in what was now called the *abertura* (opening) of the political system and its gradual transition to democracy. Institutional Act No. 5 was abolished in 1978 and was followed by the passage of an amnesty act in August 1979 that restored the political rights of nearly all those individuals who had been cassated, imprisoned, or exiled for political reasons. Direct elections were held in November 1982 for Congress, state governors and assemblies, and mayors and municipalities. In 1984 civilian candidates were nominated to run in the 1985 presidential election. Governor Tancredo Neves of Minas Gerais was elected president by an electoral college in January 1985, but his sudden death prevented his formal inauguration and elevated Vice President José Sarney to the presidency in April, so that Sarney became the first civilian president to hold office since 1964. A new constitution was approved in 1988. The transition from military authoritarianism to civilian democracy was symbolically made complete in 1989 by the holding of direct popular elections for the presidency for the first time since 1960 and resulting in the election of Fernando Collor (de Melo).

Diplomatic Divergence during the 1980s

After twenty-one years of authoritarian rule, U.S. diplomats welcomed the return to constitutional government in Brazil and saw the "Nova República" (New Republic) as an encouraging example of democratic political achievement for the whole hemisphere. But U.S. diplomats in Brazil lacked the self-confidence and brashness shown by Berle in 1945 and took care not to be seen as interfering in the slow and sometimes tortuous course of domestic political events. Mindful of local sensitivities and the lingering resentment over suspected U.S. involvement in the staging of the 1964 coup, U.S. officials praised the process of *abertura* while recognizing that "abertura will be defined for Brazilians by Brazilians."[46]

Relations between Brazil and the United States noticeably improved after Ronald Reagan's victory over Jimmy Carter in the 1980 presidential election. A leading influence on Reagan's foreign policy was Jeane Kirkpatrick, who believed that authoritarian governments in Latin America were worthy of support because they were friendly to the United States and were anti-Communist. During his 1980 electoral campaign Reagan accordingly criticized Carter's policy of stressing the importance of human rights as divisive and particularly mistaken in its application to Latin America. On taking office in 1981, the new Reagan administration pleased the Brazilian government when it acknowledged that Brazil was markedly different from Argentina and Chile in that cases involving the violation of human rights had clearly diminished as a result of the implementation of *abertura*. On the contentious issue of the transfer of nuclear energy, Vice President George H. W. Bush visited Brazil in October 1981 and stated that a special exemption would be given by the U.S. government to enable Brazil to buy enriched uranium fuel from a consortium of European companies.[47] "Mainly, we were trying to re-establish a relationship with the Brazilian government which had reached a nadir in the Carter days," recalled U.S. ambassador Langhorne Motley.[48]

In December 1982 President Reagan traveled to South America and included a stop in Brasília. Despite committing the gaffe of thanking "the people of Bolivia" in a farewell toast to his hosts, Reagan believed that he had generated personal goodwill. U.S. officials considered the presidential visit important because they wanted Brazil's assistance in the reinvigoration of the Cold War against the Soviet Union. Reagan was deeply distrustful of communism and was determined to implement a robust foreign policy that would confront and defeat what he described as the "evil empire" of the Soviet Union. The Central American and Caribbean region, which State Department officials referred to as America's "backyard," was a cause of particular alarm because the local revolutionary movements were regarded as instruments of Soviet expansionism. It was hoped that Brazil would endorse U.S. policy to defeat the Communists in El Salvador and Nicaragua. Now serving as a roving ambassador, General Vernon Walters was sent on a mission to Brasília to use his personal influence to seek Brazilian support. The Reagan administration also wanted Brazil to help in providing stability in the South Atlantic at a time when the Soviet Union and Cuba were pursuing interventionist policies in Africa. Officials in Washington developed the idea of forming a South Atlantic Treaty Organization that would include Brazil, Argentina, and South Africa.

Brazilian governments, both military and civilian, were traditionally reluctant to assume the active military role desired by Washington in the Cold War. For Brazil the threat of communism was regarded as arising from internal rather than external factors. While prepared to endorse UN resolutions criticizing the Soviet invasion of Afghanistan as an act of aggression, Brazil was not violently anti-Soviet in principle. This was demonstrated by the refusal to join in Carter's ban on grain exports to the Soviet Union and to boycott the Moscow Olympics. Moreover, much to Washington's irritation, Brazil maintained friendly diplomatic relations with the left-wing Sandinista government in Nicaragua and did not regard the Sandinistas as posing a serious military danger to hemispheric security. On the other hand, American arrogance was openly criticized. "The idea of being a backyard, or a vacant lot, is naturally upsetting," remarked President José Sarney.[49]

When Sandinista leader Daniel Ortega visited Brazil in March 1985 to attend the presidential inauguration of Tancredo Neves, his speech to the Brazilian Congress was greeted with a standing ovation. Although preferring to assume a minor supportive role, Brazil assisted the Contadora Group of Latin American governments in working independently for a peaceful diplomatic resolution of the Central American crisis. "In relation to Central America, Brazilian policy for the past five years was marked by the central aim of finding a negotiated solution for regional problems," explained Foreign Minister Ramiro Saraiva Guerreiro in 1984.[50]

Brazil was disturbed by Reagan's aggressive interference in Central American affairs and was critical of his decision to send U.S. military forces to intervene in Grenada in 1983. "When Washington's concern is security; its solution, [is] military," considered President Sarney.[51] By contrast, the main objective of Sarney's foreign policy was to promote national economic growth and prosperity rather than automatically take the side of the United States in the Cold War. The Reagan administration, therefore, was infuriated to learn of Brazil's decision to sell tanks and missiles to Libya, a country that the United States accused of aiding international terrorism and on which an arms embargo had been placed. In Washington, the State Department formally conveyed its displeasure to the Brazilian ambassador. Brazil firmly maintained, however, that it regarded arms as a legitimate item of international trade and that producing advanced weapons systems was necessary to develop a self-sufficient Brazilian armaments industry. "This 'Have guns, will travel' attitude has made Brazil the largest third world arms seller," noted the *New York Times*.[52]

Debt Crisis

A similar divergence was evident over respective attitudes toward the international Debt Crisis. During the 1970s Brazil vigorously pursued a strategy of "debt-led growth," which involved contracting large overseas loans that were readily made available from foreign private banks rather than governments or international lending institutions as had been the case in previous decades. The theory was that borrowing would stimulate economic development and that the resulting growth would be sufficient to service and ultimately pay off the foreign debt. As Finance Minister Antônio Delfim Neto explained in 1982: "Brazil did not take dollars to throw them away. The country went into debt to grow."[53]

While annual economic growth of up to 10 percent was recorded for the period from 1965 to 1979, the figure dropped sharply to little more than 2 percent during the ensuing "lost decade" of the 1980s as the greatly increased cost of imported oil exerted a negative effect. At the same time, rising international interest rates pushed the servicing of the foreign debt to a crippling level because the loans had been originally contracted at floating rather than fixed rates of interest. By the end of 1982 Brazil had the dubious distinction of possessing the largest foreign debt in the world, estimated at $87 billion. Foreign exchange reserves became so depleted that in 1983 Brazil followed Mexico in declaring a suspension of payments to foreign creditors.

The response of the Brazilian government to what was initially termed the "Latin American Debt Crisis" was to turn to the IMF for funding to meet short-term financial obligations. The action was taken reluctantly because it implied that Brazil was acting as a supplicant and was not able to manage its own economic affairs. In 1959 Kubitschek had broken off negotiations. The economic position was so desperate in 1983, however, that the Figueiredo administration felt compelled to agree to the austerity measures demanded by the IMF. There was, however, little sympathy for Brazil in the United States, where traditional liberal economic views prevailed. Just as in the Kubitschek years, U.S. officials considered that recent Brazilian governments had been irresponsible if not profligate in embarking on vast developmental projects, most of which involved creating state-owned enterprises that were inefficiently managed and excessively funded. Instead of Brazil resorting to the palliative of borrowing, the Reagan administration wanted the nation to implement free market economic reforms such as lifting trade restrictions and deregulating the banking industry and financial markets. "Brazil, like its neighbors, still leans too heavily on big government to solve economic problems," remarked a prominent U.S. business magazine, which characteristically added: "Until the country sheds that attitude, placing more faith in the dynamism of its society and entrepreneurial sector, the capital Brazil needs to solidify its hopeful democracy will remain in short supply."[54]

Brazil countered with the argument that the domestic economic policies of the Reagan administration had directly resulted in high international interest rates and an overvalued U.S. dollar that greatly increased existing budgetary deficits all over the world. Despite its predominant role in international financial institutions, the U.S. government was unwilling to accept responsibility or take the leading role in developing a coherent strategy to resolve the crisis. It was only after the Latin American debtor nations threatened collective action in 1985 that the Reagan administration made available substantial funds through the World Bank in the form of the Baker Plan, named after Secretary of the Treasury James A. Baker. The Debt Crisis came to the forefront of international attention once again in 1987 when Brazil unilaterally declared another moratorium on its repayments. Emergency financial measures were implemented on this occasion. As former secretary of state William Rogers conceded, the U.S. government was able "to stave off disaster," but "there was no evidence that Washington was preparing anything more systematic for the longer term."[55]

Commercial relations between Brazil and the United States were further upset by persistent friction over commercial issues. Both nations continued to accuse the other of being overly protectionist. Brazilian businessmen cited the discriminatory tariff duties and surcharges that had long affected their exports of shoes and steel but were now imposed on new high-value products such as orange juice and aircraft. Likewise, U.S. pharmaceutical companies complained that Brazilians pursued unfair trade practices in ignoring their international patent rights. A new grievance was the restriction on imports of American computers and software products and the prohibition of their manufacture by U.S.-owned subsidiary companies based in Brazil. The U.S. Congress retaliated by placing Brazil on a blacklist of countries carrying out unfair trade practices and thereby eligible for economic sanctions. In November 1987 the Reagan administration imposed punitive tariffs covering more than $100 million worth of imports from Brazil. Brazilians argued that such measures were counterproductive and only contributed to the worsening of the Debt Crisis. "The irrationality of protectionist mechanisms becomes even more evident at a time in which countries like Brazil have to honor heavy financial commitments," remarked Brazilian foreign minister Saraivo Guerreiro.[56]

Mercosur and NAFTA

As part of the strategy of expanding overseas trade and acquiring greater economic independence, Brazilian diplomacy sought to cultivate closer political and commercial relations with neighboring countries. In 1979 President Figueiredo declared that Latin America would be a priority in Brazil's diplomacy. A similar statement had been made by President Geisel, but Figueiredo differed from his predecessor in putting policy into action and making a state visit to Buenos Aires in May 1980. The occasion attracted considerable publicity because it marked the first visit of a Brazilian president to Argentina since Getúlio Vargas in 1935. Figueiredo followed up his initiative with further presidential visits to Venezuela, Paraguay, and Chile in what was described in the U.S. press as Brazil's attempt "to woo its neighbors."[57]

Conscious of traditional Spanish-American suspicion of Brazilian ulterior motives, Figueiredo was keen to reassure his hosts that Brazil had no expansionist aims. The president sought to project an image of his country as a peaceful and trustworthy partner. In this he was helped by the poor state of current relations between his government and the Carter administration, which meant that Brazil did not appear on this occasion as a U.S. agent or surrogate. The diplomatic initiative was also aided by the fact that it took place when regional rivalries were muted by an awareness of the value of working together to promote shared mutual interests at a time of internal political and economic weakness.[58]

Ironically, the process of improving diplomatic relations with Argentina was assisted by the end of Figueiredo's term of office in 1985 and the return of civilian government in Brazil, two years after the election in Argentina of a civilian president, Raúl Alfonsín. In 1985 both governments agreed to the Iguaçu Declaration, which created a commission to study the feasibility of economic integration of the two countries. An understanding was signed in the following year that envisaged the creation of a customs union and later a common market within the next ten years. In 1988 the governments of Brazil and Argentina signed the Treaty of Integration, Cooperation and Development. A subregional customs union came into being in 1991 and was known as the Common Market of the Southern Cone (Mercado Commún del Sur or Mercosur or Mercosul). The founding members were Brazil, Argentina, Paraguay, and Uruguay.

The negotiations for Mercosur coincided with the presidential election in the United States of George H. W. Bush in 1988 and the ending of the Cold War symbolized by the dramatic dismantling of the Berlin Wall in November 1989. In accordance with the liberal economic ideas that would become known as the "Washington Consensus," the new Bush administration sought to develop more integrated economic relations with all the countries of the Western Hemisphere. The "Enterprise for the Americas Initiative" was launched in June 1990 in which Bush unveiled the idea of a free trade area covering all of the Americas and extending from Alaska to Tierra del Fuego. The timing of the initiative was propitious for Brazil in that it came shortly after the inauguration of a new Brazilian president, Fernando Collor de Melo, who took office in March 1990. In contrast to his predecessor, Collor made the improvement of commercial relations with the United States a priority of his administration. The U.S. press acclaimed the new president as a man of energy who held "a vision of Brazil Novo — New Brazil," which included significant economic reforms and encouragement for foreign investment.[59]

The friction over trade relations was noticeably lessened as Brazil reduced a number of tariffs and agreed to open its computer industry to foreign investment and direct competition from imports. In return, the United States removed Brazil from the blacklist. In September 1990 Collor visited the United States. But no special commercial agreements were forthcoming. Two months later when Bush visited Brazil in December 1990, the *New York Times* reported that the president's reception in Brasília was "oddly subdued" and that "no crowds lined the streets." "The modernistic chamber of the Brazilian Senate was only partly filled and many seats on the main floor and in the balcony were empty," noted the American newspaper.[60]

In effect, while Bush talked of a hemispheric-wide free trade area, he was clearly much more interested in pursuing the separate negotiations that had already informally started with his immediate neighbors, Canada and Mexico. This resulted in a separate regional arrangement known as the North American Free Trade Agreement (NAFTA), which was signed in October 1992. Latin American governments initially regarded NAFTA as the first step toward what would become a hemispheric free trade area to be known as the Free Trade Area of the Americas (FTAA) or Associação de Livre Comércio das Américas (ALCA). At the Summit of the Americas meeting in Miami in December 1994 the goal was proclaimed of achieving FTAA by 2005. But progress was slow in expanding membership because neither President Bush nor his successor, Bill Clinton, would provide positive leadership. The apparent inertia was attributed to the unexpected strength of domestic political opposition and controversy generated in the U.S. Congress over the ratification of NAFTA.

In common with several other Latin American countries, Brazil had growing reservations over NAFTA. There was disquiet that a special preferential economic status had been given to Mexico, and that Chile had been singled out as the next prospective member. Ever sensitive, Brazil complained about having been assigned an inferior standing. Moreover, the concept of a free trade area based on and revolving around NAFTA implied economic subordination to the United States and was not therefore attractive to Brazilian nationalists. Furthermore, the stated U.S. preference for admitting future members one by one posed the likelihood of the negotiation of separate bilateral agreements that would lead to the withering away of subregional organizations such as Mercosur. In fact, Brazil's export trade, especially in manufactured goods, was expanding faster with its Mercosur partners rather than with NAFTA. "Mercosur is not a stage toward a Free Trade Area of the Americas," stated the Brazilian diplomat Luiz Felipe Lampreia in 1997, adding, "It is an end in itself."[61]

Consequently, Brazilian diplomacy sought to promote the development of Mercosur for its economic benefits and, in addition, to provide a stronger bargaining position in future trade negotiations with the new economic "megablocs" of the world such as NAFTA and the European Union.[62] In the process, Brazil became the senior partner in Mercosur and took the lead in suggesting a separate South American Free Trade Area (SAFTA) or Área de Livre Comércio da América do Sul (ALCSA) as a logical next step in regional economic integration. Conscious of its growing strength and status, Brazil was implicitly mounting a challenge to U.S. economic leadership of the hemisphere. The divergence was evident to Secretary of State Madeleine Albright when she privately described Mercosur as "harmful" to the interests of the United States.[63]

Epilogue

In October 1994 U.S. officials welcomed the victory in the presidential election of Fernando Henrique Cardoso over Luis Inácio "Lula" da Silva, the organized labor leader and candidate of the left-wing Partido dos Trabalhadores (Workers' Party). A former college professor and finance minister, Cardoso was well regarded in the United States for implementing the financial measure known as the "Real Plan" that had achieved considerable success in reducing inflation and stabilizing government finances. With his election to the presidency, Brazil's economic prospects began to look very attractive to U.S. diplomats and businesspeople. "You can't put a limit on the possibilities," remarked U.S. ambassador Melvyn Levitsky. "Suddenly, it is all coming together in Brazil," enthused the *New York Times*; it added that after only a few months in office Cardoso's liberal reforms had produced "a high-demand, low-inflation economy that is sucking in imports by the billions of dollars and encouraging an invasion of foreign investment."[1]

The American public, however, showed that it still possessed little interest in Brazilian affairs. Even though the 1994 Brazilian presidential election was a keenly fought political contest that took place in "the hemisphere's second largest democracy," the *New York Times* tellingly noted that the event failed to draw any live television coverage in the United States. "Without a military coup to grab headlines or a nuclear bomb to inspire fear, Brazil is huge in just about everything but the amount of outside interest it generates," concluded the U.S. newspaper.[2] President Bill Clinton demonstrated that a similar attitude of benign neglect prevailed at the highest level of U.S. policymaking. While making regular trips to Europe and the Middle East, Clinton did not visit South America during his first term of office. He belatedly sought to remedy this deficiency by a short visit to South America, including Brazil, in October 1997. "This is the first visit of his Presidency to Brazil, and Mr. Clinton appeared anxious to play catch-up," remarked the *New York Times*.[3] Despite causing consternation among Brazilian diplomats when he delivered a speech that singled out Argentina for particular praise and described that country as an "extra-NATO ally,"[4] Clinton used his charm to establish a friendly relationship with Fernando Henrique Cardoso. The Brazilian president acknowledged that there were definite disagreements between the two countries, especially the "particularly contentious issue" of trade. "Unlike in the past, however, these differences were handled with a tremendous amount of respect," he noted graciously.[5] In turn, Clinton took a liking to Cardoso and described him as "a modern, effective leader."[6]

The congenial meeting with the U.S. president and its attendant publicity served Cardoso's purpose of enhancing both his own and Brazil's international prestige. Under his leadership Brazil resolved to play a more significant role in the activities of the United Nations and revived its long-standing aim of securing a permanent seat on the Security Council.[7] During the 1970s some members of the military government had fondly predicted that Brazil would be a world power by the end of the twentieth century. In 2000 Brazil had not quite achieved the status of a world power, but the hosting of the first-ever meeting of South American presidents at Brasília in August demonstrated that the country had successfully risen to a leading position in the region. "Brazil has earned respect for its international positions, its international goals," declared Foreign Minister Luiz Felipe Lampreia, and he proudly added: "We have to be taken seriously."[8]

Brazil, however, was not "taken seriously" in Washington and still remained peripheral to U.S. national interests. Moreover, the replacement of Clinton by George W. Bush as U.S. president in 2001 was regarded with mixed feelings among Brazilian political leaders. Some concern was expressed over Bush's evident lack of experience in conducting foreign affairs, and there was apprehension that his background as governor of Texas would lead him to favor Mexico at Brazil's expense. President Cardoso met Bush in Washington in March 2001 but was not able to develop the personal rapport that he had established with Clinton. "I have had much less contact with George W. Bush," stated Cardoso.[9]

Having served two terms of office (Cardoso was reelected president in 1998), he could not be a presidential candidate in 2002. Nevertheless, his conduct of diplomatic relations between Brazil and the United States became a key issue in the election campaign when the Workers' Party leader, Lula da Silva, castigated the Cardoso administration for being too friendly and "submissive" to

Washington. Lula was also highly critical of the U.S. proposal for FTAA, arguing that completion of the scheme would result in the "annexation" of Latin America by the United States.[10] According to Lula, the proposed free trade area was nothing "but a policy of annexation," and he forthrightly declared that "our country will not be annexed."[11] Some politicians in the U.S. Congress were alarmed by the strident language and condemned Lula as a danger not just to economic stability but to hemispheric security as well. Showing no concern for Brazilian sensitivity, Congressman Henry J. Hyde of Illinois sent an open letter to President Bush warning of "a real prospect that Castro, Chavez, and Lula da Silva could constitute an axis of evil in the Americas."[12]

When Lula won the presidential election, U.S. officials pondered the likely negative diplomatic consequences. Lula had sharply spelled out his differences with the United States, but once elected he was characteristically Brazilian in preferring discussion to confrontation. In fact, Lula was willing to visit the United States prior to his inauguration as president and talk face-to-face with leading U.S. officials. When Lula came to Washington in December 2002, the first impressions that he gave were most reassuring. He was described as bringing a "conciliatory message to the White House." Quoting the president-elect's own public comments that he had "an excellent impression" of Mr. Bush and that "I will go back to Brazil knowing that I can count on President Bush as an ally," the New York Times facetiously remarked, "Such assurances might come as a minor shock to people in Brazil."[13]

Despite initial U.S. apprehension, the Lula administration did not destabilize government finances or implement radical measures such as defaulting on Brazil's foreign debt. It chose instead to pursue economic and foreign policies that basically reflected a continuation from the Cardoso regime. Nevertheless, Lula was determined that Brazil did not appear as "submissive" to any of the great powers and especially to the United States. In fact, he was severely critical of the U.S.-led war in Iraq, which was seen as unilateral, aggressive, and showing a lack of proper concern for the role of international institutions such as the UN. "The whole Iraq situation has brought back memories of the big stick—American power as used in Nicaragua or Chile during the cold war," remarked former foreign minister Luiz Felipe Lampreia.[14] Moreover, Brazil would not be bullied or treated as an inferior. When U.S. immigration officials instituted the fingerprinting and photographing of Latin Americans entering the United States at international airports, Brazilian immigration officials were instructed to retaliate by subjecting American visitors to the same treatment. In contrast to the U.S. public, Brazilians did not regard the War on Terror as equivalent to the Cold War against International Communism. Violence did concern Brazilians in their daily lives, but the threat came not from al-Quaeda but from local drug barons and their armed militias operating in the *favelas* of Rio de Janeiro and São Paulo. "After September 11, 2001, Bush seemed to care very little about Brazil," considered Fernando Henrique Cardoso.[15]

Bush's attitude of indifference was misleading. Indeed, the United States could not ignore Brazil for very long because the country was simply too economically important. Trade had formed the bedrock of the U.S.-Brazilian relationship ever since the early nineteenth century. During the 1990s annual trade between the two countries doubled to $26 billion, while total U.S. investment in Brazil tripled to around $38 billion. Not only was the United States the biggest investor in Brazil, but from the mid-1990s onward it reversed its previously asymmetrical trading relationship by achieving an annual trade surplus with that country.

U.S. officials also appreciated the significance of Brazil's diplomatic support in launching initiatives to promote hemispheric trade. This had been previously demonstrated in the policy of commercial reciprocity in the 1890s and the 1930s. At the beginning of the twenty-first century, Brazilian participation was once again regarded as vital for the successful completion of an integrated free trade area covering the whole hemisphere. "Without cooperation from Brazil, it is doubtful that the Bush administration could achieve its goal of extending NAFTA to the entire hemisphere, especially with the growing protests against the agreement in the United States," commented the *New York Times*.[16] Moreover, Brazil's economic significance and influence were likely to increase rather than diminish on account of the discovery of major petroleum deposits in the South Atlantic. As a member of the "BRICS," Brazil was linked with Russia, India, and China as one of the fastest-growing economies in the world.

During the first decade of the twentieth century a "new" Brazil had arisen with a revitalized foreign service and a robust approach to foreign affairs masterminded by Rio Branco. A century later, a similar combination of political stability and economic growth revived Brazilian diplomatic ambitions to be both a regional and world power. "Brazil fancies itself, not Venezuela, as South America's natural leader," remarked the *New York Times*.[17] Echoing the sentiments expressed by Elihu Root at the 1906 Rio Pan-American Conference, Secretary of State Condoleeza Rice acknowledged Brazil as "the regional leader and our global partner."[18] Much to Brazilian delight, the comment suggested a special relationship based on U.S. recognition that Brazil not only was the biggest country in South America but also deserved to be treated as an equal. In fact, a convergence of shared interests between Brazil and the United States was evident when President Bush visited Brazil in March 2007 for discussions with Lula about cooperation in energy production and proposals to stimulate hemispheric economic growth. Brazilians were pleased at what they regarded as the respect shown them by the United States, with Lula going so far as to describe the newly established "strategic alliance" between Brazil and the United States as a "historical moment."[19] It was a bold statement to make, and time will be the test of its veracity, but it was one that was in keeping with the changes taking place in the world economic order. It was also consonant with the past efforts of distinguished Brazilian diplomats such as José Silvestre Rebelo, Salvador de Mendonça, Rio Branco, Joaquim Nabuco, and Osvaldo Aranha. Their pursuit of a special relationship with the United States had been based on admiration for the achievements of the northern colossus and the belief that it was the hemispheric power that could do most to assist Brazil's economic advancement and national security.

Washington's response, however, has been varied. The relationship was at its most cordial during World War II when Brazil's cooperative attitude was rewarded with substantial U.S. economic aid and diplomatic support. More often, Brazilian aspirations and requests for aid encountered a combination of U.S. indifference and self-serving calculation. It seemed that Brazil only acquired significance when the United States was at war or was launching a major policy initiative involving all the nations of the hemisphere.

In the nineteenth century, Brazil gradually but successfully broke away from its political and economic dependence on Great Britain. In the twentieth century, Brazil sought to avoid a similar subordination to the United States. When the U.S. government was unwilling to grant economic assistance during the 1950s and 1960s, Brazil turned to Western Europe and Japan as alternative sources of trade and investment. During the Cold War Brazilian governments pursued "independent" and "nationalist" foreign policies even though they clashed with U.S. objectives and marked a reversal of the strategy of approximation. In recent international negotiations over reforms to world trade, Brazil has been prominent in condemning the high tariff policies of the United States.[20] The approach has gained respect. "As the largest democracy in South America, Brazil is a leader, and today, Brazil is exercising its leadership across the globe," said President George W. Bush on his visit to Brasília in 2005.[21] The president's words showed that Americans were finally taking note of the impressive political and economic progress made by their giant neighbor and the important and independent role that it was playing in both hemispheric and world affairs.

Notes

1. The South American Empire

1. James Watson Webb to William Henry Seward, January 24, 1867, Department of State, *Foreign Relations of the United States (FRUS), 1868* (Washington, D.C., 1862), 2:251.

2. José Correa da Serra to John Quincy Adams, December 18, 1818, quoted in Phil Brian Johnson and Robert Kim Stevens, "Impossible Job, Impossible Man! Thomas Sumter, Jr., and Diplomatic Relations between the United States and the Portuguese Court in Brazil, 1809–1821," in *United States–Latin American Relations, 1800–1850: The Formative Generations,* ed. T. Ray Shurbutt (Tuscaloosa, Ala., 1991), p. 94.

3. The establishment of republics in the United States and France had influenced the 1789 outbreak of a republican movement in Minas Gerais known as the Inconfidência Mineira. Brazilian travelers in Europe sought support from Jefferson, then serving as U.S. minister to France. Jefferson limited his response to passing on the information to U.S. Secretary for Foreign Affairs John Jay.

4. *Boston Patriot,* May 3, 1817, quoted in Stanley E. Hilton, "The United States and Brazilian Independence," in *From Colony to Nation: Essays on the Independence of Brazil,* ed. A. J. R. Russell-Wood (Baltimore, 1975), p. 115.

5. Joseph Ray to John Quincy Adams, February 18, 1818, quoted in Gerald Horne, *The Deepest South: The United States, Brazil, and the African Slave Trade* (New York, 2007), p. 21. See Moniz Bandeira, *Presença dos Estados Unidos no Brasil (Dois Séculos de História)* (Rio, 1978), pp. 36–37.

6. John Quincy Adams, *Memoirs of John Quincy Adams* (Philadelphia, 1874–77), 4:339. In public correspondence, Adams defended his minister's actions and showed little inclination to be conciliatory toward Brazil. In private, however, Adams acknowledged that the U.S. government was not blameless when he admitted that Sumter had not been "a fortunate choice" as minister because he "has been repeatedly involved in quarrels of personal punctilio, even with members of the royal family." Ibid., 4:340.

7. P. Sartoris to John Quincy Adams, March 4, 1822, quoted in William R.

Manning, *Diplomatic Correspondence of the United States Concerning the Independence of the Latin-American Nations*, 3 vols. (New York, 1925), 2:732; Condy Raguet to John Quincy Adams, October 1, 1822, February 1, 1824, quoted in ibid., 2:749, 775.

8. *Memoirs of John Quincy Adams*, 6:319. On Rebelo see Arthur P. Whitaker, "José Silvestre Rebello: The First Diplomatic Representative of Brazil in the United States," *Hispanic American Historical Review* 20 (1940): 380–401.

9. Raguet to John Quincy Adams, October 5, 1824, quoted in Manning, *Diplomatic Correspondence*, 2:807. See also José Silvestre Rebelo to Adams, January 28, 1825, cited in ibid., 2:808–10; Henry Clay to Rebelo, April 13, 1825 2:233–34; Rebelo to Clay, April 16, 1825, ibid., 2:814–15.

10. Letter dated July 1823 from Felisberto Caldeira Brant Pontes (later Marquis of Barbacena) to José Bonifácio, quoted in Alan K. Manchester, *British Pre-eminence in Brazil: Its Rise and Decline* (Chapel Hill, N.C., 1933), p. 193, n. 25. "Brazil in imitation of Portugal," lamented Raguet, "has completely thrown herself into the arms of England and, to a certain extent, has transferred her colonial allegiance from one country to another." Raguet to Clay, November 23, 1825, quoted in Horne, *Deepest South*, p. 28.

11. George Proffitt to Secretary of State, February 27, 1844, quoted in Lawrence F. Hill, *Diplomatic Relations between the United States and Brazil* (Durham, N.C., 1932), p. 121.

12. José Bonifácio, quoted in Ron Seckinger, *The Brazilian Monarchy and the South American Republics, 1822–1831* (Baton Rouge, La., 1984), pp. 27–28.

13. Rebelo to Clay, November 14, 1827, quoted in Manning, *Diplomatic Correspondence*, 2:862–63.

14. John Quincy Adams, quoted in Lawrence F. Hill, *Diplomatic Relations*, p. 55.

15. For British influence see Richard Graham, *Britain and the Onset of Modernization in Brazil, 1850–1914* (Cambridge, England, 1968). The cultural impact of France is examined in Jeffrey D. Needell, *A Tropical Belle Epoque: Elite Culture and Society in Turn-of-the-Century Rio de Janeiro* (Cambridge, England, 1997). There is no reference to any Brazilian accounts in Jack Ray Thomas, "Latin American Views of United States Politics in the Nineteenth Century," *Journal of the Early Republic* 12 (1992): 357–80.

16. Henry M. Brackenridge, *Voyage to South America*, quoted in Hilton, "U.S. and Brazilian Independence," p. 119; John C. Calhoun to Henry Wise, May 25, 1844, quoted in Horne, *Deepest South*, p. 55; Daniel P. Kidder and James C.

Fletcher, *Brazil and Brazilians Portrayed in Historical and Descriptive Sketches* (Philadelphia, 1857), p. 21.

17. Professor and Mrs. Louis Agassiz, *A Journey in Brazil* (Boston, 1868), p. 496.

18. Thomas Ewbank, *Life in Brazil* (New York, 1856), p. 436; Ewbank, quoted in Horne, *Deepest South*, p. 25; Henry Hill to Adams, May 1821, quoted in John J. Johnson, *A Hemisphere Apart: The Foundations of United States Policy toward Latin America* (Baltimore, 1990), p. 72; Ewbank, *Life in Brazil*, p. 430.

19. John Codman, quoted in Manoel Cardozo, "Slavery in Brazil as Described by Americans, 1822–1888," *Americas* 17 (1961): 254. Codman's comment reflected views held by whites in the southern United States who saw Brazil as a natural ally in their defense of slavery.

20. Brackenridge, quoted in ibid., p. 270.

21. Ewbank, *Life in Brazil*, p. 135.

22. Kidder and Fletcher, quoted in Cardozo, "Slavery in Brazil," p. 256. Ewbank, as well as Kidder and Fletcher, however, did not distinguish between the mulatto and the rest of the black population. See Carl N. Degler, *Neither Black nor White: Slavery and Race Relations in Brazil and the United States* (New York, 1971), p. 219.

23. Frederick Douglass, speech dated January 14, 1865, quoted in Horne, *Deepest South*, p. 13.

24. William E. Curtis, *The Capitals of Spanish America* (1888; reprint, New York, 1969), p. 661.

25. Letter from Henry Shipley Stevens, December 17, 1865, quoted in Horne, *Deepest South*, p. 200. Just as the existence of slavery in the United States prior to the American Civil War gave support to slave owners in Brazil, the ending of slavery in the United States aided the Brazilian abolitionist movement. See Robert Conrad, *The Destruction of Brazilian Slavery, 1850–1888* (Berkeley, Calif., 1972), pp. 141–42. Emperor Pedro II believed that slavery placed Brazil in a moral dilemma and that the country would suffer further international opprobrium and isolation so long as it retained the institution of slavery. See Roderick J. Barman, *Citizen Emperor: Pedro II and the Making of Brazil, 1825–91* (Stanford, Calif., 1999), p. 195.

26. George Barnsley, letter dated August 20, 1871, quoted in William Clark Griggs, *The Elusive Eden: Frank McMullan's Confederate Colony in Brazil* (Austin, Tex., 1987), pp. 122–23.

27. The exception was the illegal transatlantic slave trade in which ships, espe-

cially fast schooners, constructed and registered in the United States played a prominent role especially during the 1840s.

28. Letter by Sérgio Teixeira de Macedo, May 16, 1854, quoted in Graham, *Britain and the Onset of Modernization*, p. 73.

29. Kidder and Fletcher, *Brazil*, p. 195.

30. Ibid., pp. 611–12; Matthew Fontaine Maury, *The Amazon and the Atlantic Slopes of South America* (Washington D.C., 1853), p. 5.

31. John Codman, *Ten Months in Brazil* (Boston, 1867), pp. 41, 51.

32. Maury, *Amazon*, p. 45.

33. James Partridge to Hamilton Fish, no. 102, March 24, 1873, *FRUS* (1873), p. 96.

34. Maury, *Amazon*, p. 62. Maury also had ambitious plans for the relocation of slaves from the American South to the Amazon region.

35. Kidder and Fletcher, *Brazil*, p. 579.

36. Seward to Webb, no. 210, June 17, 1867, *FRUS* (1867), 2:255.

2. From Empire to Republic

1. H. Clay Armstrong to Thomas Bayard, November 28, 1888, RG59, Brazil, Dispatches, 48.

2. Professor and Mrs. Louis Agassiz, *A Journey in Brazil* (Boston, 1868), p. 496. American visitors at the Philadelphia exposition were also impressed by the Brazilian pavilion, which displayed a wide variety of goods including precious gems, stuffed parrots, and a Brazilian-made rifle. "Brazil was everywhere at the Centennial Exhibition, presenting a higher profile even than most European nations." See John H. Williams, "Brazil's Most Curious Monarch," *Americas* 36 (1984): 26.

3. *Congressional Record*, 45th Cong., 3rd sess., p. 2131.

4. Christopher C. Andrews, *Brazil: Its Condition and Prospects* (New York, 1891), p. 103. In an 1885 survey, the U.S. Latin American Trade Commission paid scant attention to Brazil, which prompted the American chargé d'affaires at Rio, Charles Trail, to conclude that "one is led to infer that Brazil is the least important of all the countries in this Hemisphere south of the Equator." Trail to Bayard, no. 72, January 21, 1886, National Archives, State Department, Record Group (RG)59, Dispatches, Brazil, 18.

5. Carlos Süssekind de Mendonça, *Salvador de Mendonça: Democrata do Império e da República* (Rio de Janeiro, 1960), pp. 126–27.

6. James G. Blaine to Thomas A. Osborn, no. 9, December 1, 1881, RG59, Brazil, Instructions, 17.

7. Robert Adams to Blaine, no. 20, November 19, 1889, RG59, Brazil, Dispatches, 48.

8. For the debate of December 20, 1889, see *Congressional Record*, 51st Cong., 1st sess., pp. 313–24.

9. The foreign minister supported the idea of a political alliance between the two countries, but just as in 1825 the U.S. government gave Brazil no encouragement to enter into substantive discussions. See Quintino Bocaiúva to Salvador de Mendonça, no. 11, September 2, 1890, Arquivo Histório do Itamaraty, Missões Diplomáticas Brasileiras, Ofícios (AHI) 273/3/5.

10. *New York Daily Tribune*, June 25, 1890; *New York Times*, June 24, 1890.

11. John W. Foster, *Diplomatic Memoirs* (2 vols., Boston, 1909), 2:7.

12. Edwin Conger to Blaine, no. 27, February 26; no. 30, March 6; and no. 40, April 2, 1891, RG59, Brazil, Dispatches, 50.

13. Alvey A. Adee to Conger, May 23, 1891, RG59, Brazil, Instructions, 17; Foster to Salvador de Mendonça, June 16, 1891, enclosed in Salvador to Justo Chermont, no. 8, June 19, 1891, AHI 233/4/10.

14. Conger to Blaine, no. 159, November 13, 1891, RG59, Brazil, Dispatches, 52 and 53.

15. Hugh Wyndham to Lord Salisbury, no. 88, May 6, 1892, FO 13/695.

16. Julian Pauncefote to Salisbury, no. 154, July 10, 1891, FO 5/2120.

17. On Salvador de Mendonça's activities to buy warships in the United States leading to the creation of "Flint's Fleet," see Steven C. Topik, *Trade and Gunboats: The United States and Brazil in the Age of Empire* (Stanford, Calif., 1996), pp. 155–77.

18. Thomas L. Thompson to Walter Q. Gresham, October 22 and 24, 1893, RG59, Brazil, Dispatches, 55; Gresham to Thompson, October 25, 1893, ibid., Instructions, 18.

19. Gresham to Thomas L. Thompson, January 9 and 30, 1894, RG59, Brazil, Instructions, 18.

20. Gresham to Thomas L. Thompson, January 30, 1894, ibid.

21. Gresham to Bayard, January 21, 1894, Library of Congress, Walter Q. Gresham Papers.

22. *New York Times*, January 21, 1890; Picking to Herbert, October 14, 1893, Records of the Department of the Navy, National Archives, RG 45.

23. Report of the Secretary of the Navy, November 17, 1894, 53rd Cong., 3rd sess., House Document part 1, p. 23.

24. Wyndham to Lord Rosebery, no. 37, February 2, and no. 48, February 5, 1894, FO 13/724.

25. Thompson's dispatch of October 12, 1895, cited in 54th Cong., 1st sess., House Document no. 377, part 1, p. 92.

26. Gresham to Salvador, August 29, 1894, enclosed in Salvador to Carlos de Carvalho, no. 1, February 7, 1895, AHI 233/4/11.

27. *South American Journal* (London), September 29, 1894.

28. Salvador to Richard Olney, December 20, 1895, *FRUS* (1895), 1: 76. Later, in their boundary dispute with France over the Guyana region of Amapá, Brazilian diplomats believed that the example of Cleveland's resolute action against Great Britain was helpful in persuading the French government to accept arbitration. The award was made by the president of Switzerland in 1900 and represented a triumph for Brazil and Rio Branco. See E. Bradford Burns, *The Unwritten Alliance: Rio-Branco and Brazilian American Relations* (New York, 1966), p. 33.

29. Charles Page Bryan to John Sherman, no. 20, May 5, 1898, RG59, Brazil, Dispatches, 62. A Brazilian editorial summed up that Spain recognized that it had been a mistake to fight "an enemy incomparably superior in resources." See *Journal do commércio* (Rio), July 25, 1898.

30. John Hay to Bryan, no. 115, March 4, 1899, RG59, Brazil, Instructions, 18.

31. Salvador to Dionísio Cerqueira, no. 5, April 3, and to William E. Curtis, April 6, 1897, AHI 234/4/12.

32. Constantine Phipps to Salisbury, no. 40, August 13, 1899, FO 13/786.

33. Hay to Bryan, no. 213, October 2, 1900, RG59, Brazil, Instructions, 18.

34. Bryan to Olinto de Maghalães, September 21, 1900, AHI 280/2/6.

35. Memorandum by Chapman Coleman to Elihu Root, January 3, 1906, RG59, Brazil, Dispatches, 72.

36. Hay to Joaquim Francisco de Assis Brasil, May 29, 1899; Assis Brasil to Hay, June 10, 1899, *FRUS* (1899), p. 119.

37. Memorandum by Bryan, July 19, 1902, AHI 280/2/6.

38. Eugene Seeger to Hay, January 20, 1903, RG59, Brazil, Dispatches, 68.

39. Thomas L. Thompson to Hay, no. 147, May 12, 1904, and no. 252, January 15, 1905, RG59, Brazil, Dispatches 70 and 71.

40. Hay to Thomas L. Thompson, June 13, 1904, RG59, Brazil, Instructions, 18.

3. The New Era

1. *O Paiz* (Rio), January 26, 1905.

2. Theodore Roosevelt, *Through the Brazilian Wilderness* (New York, 1914), p. 217. Roosevelt attributed the economic achievements that he observed to the activities and work not of native Brazilians but of the "large European, chiefly south European immigration." While acknowledging the "mixed blood" of many of the inhabitants of the Amazon region, he contended that "the dominant blood . . . that is steadily increasing its dominance is the olive-white." Ibid., p. 345.

3. As a crude average about 250 Americans migrated annually to Brazil in the two decades before World War I. For statistics see T. Lynn Smith, *Brazil: People and Institutions* (Baton Rouge, La., 1963), p. 137.

4. Roosevelt, *Brazilian Wilderness*, p. 348.

5. Marie R. Wright, *The New Brazil* (Philadelphia, 1907), p. 102.

6. Gilberto Freyre, *Order and Progress: Brazil from Monarchy to Republic*, trans. Rod W. Horton (New York, 1970), pp. 202–3.

7. Rio Branco, December 11, 1905, quoted in E. Bradford Burns, *The Unwritten Alliance: Rio Branco and Brazilian-American Relations* (New York, 1966), p. 148.

8. For contemporary Brazilian concern over the advance of American economic imperialism see Eduardo Prado, *A ilusão americana* (Paris, 1896).

9. Rio Branco to Gomes Ferreira, no. 1, January 31, 1905, AHI 235/2/6.

10. *Jornal do commércio* (Rio), March 16, 1905. Nabuco was typical of most members of the Brazilian elite who visited the United States and came away with admiration for the energy and drive of American society especially in its industrial achievements. On the other hand, they still regarded Europe as culturally superior. See Joaquim Nabuco, *Minha formação* (São Paulo, 1934), pp. 146–57.

11. Elihu Root to Ben Tillman, December 13, 1905, quoted in Philip C. Jessup, *Elihu Root* (2 vols., New York, 1938), 1:469.

12. Charles Richardson to Root, no. 113, December 1, 1905, RG 59, Brazil, Dispatches, 71; Joaquim Nabuco to Rio Branco, January 3, 1906, AHI 234/1/4.

13. Nabuco, quoted in Burns, *Unwritten Alliance*, p. 110.

14. *Times* (London), August 9, 1906.

15. Jessup, *Elihu Root*, 1:483; William Haggard to Lord Grey, no. 23, April 7, 1907, FO 371/200.

16. While Rui regarded himself as quintessentially an English liberal, he was a keen student and admirer of the political and legal history of the United States. See Homero Pires, *Anglo-American Political Influences on Rui Barbosa: A Spiritual Child of the Anglo-Saxon* (Rio, 1949).

17. Haggard to Grey, no. 83, October 21, 1907, FO 371/201.

18. David Thompson to John Hay, no. 252, January 15, 1905, RG 59, Brazil, Dispatches, 71.

19. A. M. Beaupré to Root, no. 592, August 19, 1907, RG 59, NF 6047/2.

20. Beaupré to Root, no. 592, August 19, 1907, RG 59, NF 6047/2; Nabuco to Rio Branco, no. 1, January 3, 1907, AHI 234/1/6.

21. See minutes dated October 22, 1908, on Spencer Eddy to Root, no. 18, September 16, 1908, RG 59, NF 15865/1; Alvey A. Adee to Eddy, tel., December 19, 1908, ibid., NF 1070/25.

22. Irving Dudley to Philander Knox, no. 582, August 27, 1910, RG 59, DF 1910–29, 732.35/20.

23. Dudley to Rio Branco, December 31, 1909, AHI 280/2/9.

24. Francis Huntington-Wilson to Domício da Gama, January 20, 1912, RG 59, DF 1910–29, 832.3421/26A.

25. Rio Branco to George L. Rives, no. 8, December 28, 1911, enclosed in Rives to Knox, no. 788, January 7, 1912, 832.34/73; Rio Branco to Domício, December 31, 1911, quoted in José Honório Rodrigues, *Interêsse nacional e política externa* (Rio, 1966), p. 31.

26. Haggard to Grey, no. 14, February 14, 1912, FO 371/1302.

27. Dudley to Knox, no. 626, December 16, 1910, and no. 694, April 11, 1911, 832.00 and 832.34/52.

28. *New York Herald*, May 28, 1912.

29. Huntington-Wilson to Henry Janes, September 24, 1912, RG 59, DF 1910–29, 832.6133/103.

30. A Harvard graduate in history, Morgan represented the new breed of U.S. career diplomats. After a period as U.S. minister in Korea he was assigned to a succession of Latin capitals beginning with Havana, followed by Montevideo, Lisbon, and finally Rio in May 1912. While Morgan regarded Brazil as just another step up the ladder to a choice European posting, he also made it evident both to his staff and foreign diplomatic colleagues that he intended to earn his promotion. "He is very active and takes his work extremely seriously, and is determined to make a success of mission here,"

noted the British minister. See Haggard to Grey, no. 6, January 13, 1913, FO 371/1580.

31. Francisco de Paula Rodrigues Alves to Lauro Müller, December 17, 1912, quoted in Afonso Arinos de Melo Franco, *Rodrigues Alves* (São Paulo, 1973), p. 675.

32. Müller to Domício, March 6, and Domício to Müller, April 3, 1913, AHI 234/2/1.

33. *New York Times*, March 12, 1913.

34. Domício to Müller, tel., no. 74, November 5, 1912, AHI 234/1/13; Domício to William Jennings Bryan, March 31, 1913, RG 59, DF 1910–29. 832.6133/153.

35. Domício to Müller, tel., no. 16, September 29, 1915, AHI 234/2/4.

36. William G. McAdoo, *Crowded Years* (Boston, 1931), p. 351.

37. Edwin Morgan to Bryan, tel., August 3, 1914, RG 59, DF 1910–29, 832.51/71; Malcolm Robertson to Grey, no. 19, April 21, 1915, FO 371/2294.

38. Colloquy, August 30, 1916, quoted in Arthur S. Link, ed., *The Papers of Woodrow Wilson* (Princeton, N.J., 1966–) 38:116.

39. Domício to Müller, no. 6, February 24, 1917, AHI 234/2/7.

40. *New York Evening Post*, April 11, 1917; October 25, 1917, quoted in Frederick C. Luebke, *Germans in Brazil: A Comparative History of Cultural Conflict during World War I* (Baton Rouge, La., 1987), p. 159.

41. Arthur Peel to Arthur Balfour, no. 23, March 25, 1918, FO 371/3167.

42. Brazil's actual combat contribution to the Allied war effort was slight and was limited mainly to the dispatch of a small naval squadron that arrived too late in Europe to experience active wartime service.

43. Josephus Daniels to Robert Lansing, November 16, 1917, RG 59, DF 1910–29, 732.35/29.

44. Henry L. Stimson, *My United States* (New York, 1931), p. 294.

45. Morgan to Lansing, no. 1473, March 20, 1919, RG 59, DF 1910–29, 763.72119/4509.

46. Rui, quoted in Peel to Balfour, no. 134, December 14, 1918, FO 371/3653.

47. Department of State, Papers Relating to the Foreign Relations of the United States: The Paris Peace Conference, 1919 (13 vols., Washington D.C., 1942–47), 1: 386.

48. Domício to Ipanema Moreira, no. 5, January 9, and no. 11, January 18, 1919, AHI 234/2/11; Frank Polk to Lansing, tel., January 10, 1919, RG 59, DF 1910–29, 763.72119/3325.

49. Domício to Lansing, April 18, 1919, RG 59, DF 1910–29, 711.32/23.

4. The Republic under Threat

1. *O Jornal* (Rio), September 25, 1925.

2. Azevedo Marques to Augusto Cochrane de Alencar, tel., no. 62, October 10, 1921, AHI 235/4/5; Cochrane de Alencar to Azevedo Marques, tels., no. 64, September 26 and no. 80, December 30, 1921, AHI 235/3/8b.

3. Quoted in Stanley E. Hilton, "Brazil and the Post-Versailles World: Elite Images and Foreign Policy Strategy, 1919–1929," *Journal of Latin American Studies* 12 (1980):343.

4. Captain Sparrow to Luke McNamee, June 8, 1922, RG 59, DF 1910–29, 832.30/69.

5. Sheldon Crosby to Charles Evans Hughes, tel., no. 49, May 19, 1922, RG 59, DF 1910–29, 832.415/23.

6. John Tilley to Lord Curzon, no. 162, June 6, 1922, FO 371/7184.

7. Tilley to Curzon, no. 62, February 22, 1923, FO 371/8431.

8. Tilley to Curzon, no. 257, September 21, 1922, FO 371/7184, and no. 261, September 24, 1922, FO 371/7193.

9. See Afonso Arinos de Melo Franco, *Um estadista da República: Afrânio de Meo Franco e seu tempo* (Rio, 1955), 1113–48.

10. Memorandum by J. Butler Wright, April 28, 1923, and "Department of State Press Release," June 4, 1923, RG 59, Santiago Conference, Entry 126, Box 358.

11. Hélio Lobo to MRE (Ministério das Relações Exteriores), April 8, 1923, quoted in Hilton, "Brazil and Post Versailles World," p. 352.

12. Edwin Morgan to Frank Kellogg, no. 2398G, July 12, 1925, RG 59, DF 1910–29, 832.00/522.

13. See minutes on Beilby Alston to William Tyrell, tel., no. 42, September 15, 1927, FO 371/11965; *New York World*, June 18, 1926; *Philadelphia Public Ledger*, June 15, 1926.

14. Morgan to Kellogg, no. 2594, June 23, 1926, RG 59, DF 1910–29, 832.00/583.

15. Silvino Gurgel do Amaral to MRE, no. 51, February 20, and no. 70, February 23, 1928, AHI 234/4/12.

16. Morgan to Kellogg, no. 3028, July 6, 1928, RG 59, DF 1910–29, 711.3212/AntiWar/5.

17. Morgan to Kellogg, no 3049, August 22, 1928, 711.3212/AntiWar/11.

18. William R. Castle to Wallace McClure, September 14, 1928, 711.3212/AntiWar/no document file number; Kellogg to Morgan, tel., September 14, 1928, AntiWar/13.

19. MRE to Silvino Gurgel do Amaral, tel., no. 36, February 15, 1929, AHI 235/3/12.

20. Brazil eventually gave its adherence to the pact in December 1933.

21. *Jornal do commércio* (Rio), February 17, 1928.

22. *Wall Street Journal*, September 10, 1924.

23. The economic prospects of Argentina continued to be more alluring so that out of total American investment in the region, the proportion held by Brazil actually fell from 29 to 20 percent during the decade.

24. *Saturday Evening Post* (New York), October 24, 1925. General Motors was also successful in selling automobiles to Brazil beginning with the production of the Chevrolet in 1925.

25. In 1945 Ford sold Fordlândia at an estimated loss of $20 million. In 1967 the American shipping millionaire Daniel Ludwig started a similarly vast agricultural project at Jarí in the Amazon region. The scheme also collapsed with large financial losses in 1981.

26. Hughes to Morgan, tel., January 6, 1923, *FRUS* (1923), p. 454.

27. William Schurz to Julius Klein, January 13, 1926, Hoover Papers, Commerce, Box 231.

28. *New York Times*, January 8, 1926.

29. Patrick Ramsey to Austen Chamberlain, no. 7, January 8, 1926, FO 371/1115.

30. *O Paiz* (Rio), December 21, 1928.

31. Silvino to MRE, no. 287, August 18, 1928, AHI 235/1/2.

32. *New York Times*, December 23, 1928.

33. *A Crítica* (Rio), December 21, 1928.

34. Morgan to Kellogg, no. 2884, October 12, 1927, RG 59, DF 1910–29, 832.52/505.

35. *Washington Post*, March 7, 1930.

36. Morgan to Henry Stimson, tel. no. 53, September 2, 1930, RG 59, DF 1930–39, 832.00/66.

37. Walter Washington to Stimson, tel., no. 78, October 9; Stimson to Washington, tel., no. 57, October 8, and tel., no. 60, October 11, RG 59, DF 1930–39, 832.00/Revolutions/29, 37 and 44. The *Pensacola* did not actually reach Bahia until October 25, by which time the civil war was over.

38. Memorandum of Press Conference, October 24, 1930, RG 59, DF 1930–39, 832.00/Revolutions/169.

39. *New York Times*, October 25, 1930.

40. Stimson to Morgan, tel., no. 78, November 5, 1930, RG 59, DF 1930–39, 832.00/Revolutions/199.

41. Morgan to Stimson, November 12, 1930, RG 59, DF 1930–39, 832.00/ Revolutions/227.

42. William R. Castle to Charles Cameron, tel., August 2, 1932, *FRUS* (1932), 5:408.

43. Getúlio Vargas to Osvaldo de Sousa Aranha, December 24, 1934, quoted in Stanley E. Hilton, *Brazil and the Great Powers, 1930–1939: The Politics of Trade Rivalry* (Austin, Tex., 1975), p. 120.

44. Alexander W. Weddell to Cordell Hull, tel., March 18, 1936, *FRUS* (1936), 5: 299.

45. Osvaldo Aranha quoted in Hilton, *Brazil and the Great Powers*, p. 182.

46. William Phillips to Weddell, tel., March 19, 1936, *FRUS* (1936), 5: 299–300. Brazil turned to Britain and placed an order for destroyers to be supplied by British company Armstrong Vickers.

47. Roosevelt is reported as having said that Vargas was "one of the two people who invented the New Deal." See Robert M. Levine, *Father of the Poor? Vargas and His Era* (Cambridge, England, 1998), p. 13. Postmaster General James Farley recalled a conversation with Roosevelt in 1941 in which the president said, "Vargas was not the least like other South American leaders, being more progressive in his views and a more capable administrator." Quoted in Stanley E. Hilton, "The Overthrow of Getúlio Vargas; Diplomatic Intervention, Defense of Democracy, or Political Retribution?" *Hispanic American Historical Review* 67 (1987):10.

48. Hugh Gibson to Franklin D. Roosevelt, September 4, 1934, quoted in Hilton, *Brazil and the Great Powers*, p. 51. Gibson had replaced Edwin Morgan as U.S. ambassador in May 1933 and served in Brazil until December 1936.

49. Aranha to Vargas, November 24, 1939, quoted in Frank D. McCann, "Brazil, the United States, and World War II: A Commentary," *Diplomatic History* 3 (1979):62.

50. Foreign Office minutes, February 21, 1934, quoted in Hilton, *Brazil and the Great Powers*, p. 132. Gibson's previous post was U.S. ambassador to Belgium. He soon became unhappy at what he considered were primitive living conditions in Rio and described the American embassy as "about the poorest dump I've ever seen." Gibson to Arthur B. Lane, February 1, 1934, quoted in Irwin F. Gellman, *Good Neighbor Diplomacy: United States Policies in Latin America, 1933–1945* (Baltimore, 1979), p. 16.

51. Memorandum by Edwin Wilson, August 11, 1933, *FRUS* (1933), 5:16.

52. See Hilton, *Brazil and the Great Powers*, p. 50.

53. Hull to Gibson, June 20, 1934, *FRUS* (1934), 4:544.

54. *New York Times*, February 3, 1935, quoted in Allen F. Repko, "The Failure of Reciprocal Trade: United States–Germany Commercial Rivalry in Brazil, 1934–1940," *Mid-America* 60 (1978), p.9. The treaty with Brazil was predated by a special commercial arrangement that had been signed between the United States and Cuba in August 1934.

55. Gibson to Hull, tel., June 29, 1935, *FRUS* (1935), 4:304–5.

56. Gibson to Hull, tels., August 27 and 29, 1935, *FRUS* (1935), 4:313, 315–16.

5. The Global Crisis

1. Getúlio Vargas, quoted in Sumner Welles to Cordell Hull, tel., January 18, 1942, *FRUS* (1942), 6:633.

2. Hugh Gibson to Hull, tel., October 10, 1934, *FRUS* (1934), 4: 595–96.

3. The policy has been described as "pragmatic equilibrium." See Gerson Moura, *Autonomia na dependência: A política externa brasileira de 1935 a 1942* (Rio, 1980).

4. Jefferson Caffery to Hull, no. 567, May 6, 1938, *FRUS* (1938), 5:346. Caffery was appointed ambassador to Brazil in July 1937 and served at this post until September 1944.

5. In addition to the compensation marks system, there were many other practices such as exchange control, currency depreciation, withholding of debt service obligations, and import and export controls that restricted U.S. trade with Brazil.

6. Caffery to Hull, tel., July 5, 1939, *FRUS* (1939), 5:365. Aranha ended his term as Brazilian ambassador to Washington in 1937 and was appointed minister of foreign affairs in March 1938.

7. Caffery to Hull, tel., November 10, 1937, *FRUS* (1937), 5: 313–14.

8. *Newsweek*, November 22, 1937, quoted in Stanley E. Hilton, *Brazil and the Great Powers, 1930–1939: The Politics of Trade Rivalry* (Austin, Tex., 1975), p. 172.

9. Caffery to Hull, tel., November 13, 1937, *FRUS* (1937), 5: 315. On relations between Vargas and the Integralistas see Ricardo Antônio Silva Seitenfus, *O Brasil de Getúlio Vargas e a formaçao dos blocos, 1930–1942: O processo do envolvimento brasileiro na II Guerra Mundial* (São Paulo, 1985).

10. Caffery to Hull, tel., June 17, 1940, *FRUS* (1940), 5: 623.

11. Dutra's remarks are quoted in Frank D. McCann, *Soldiers of the Pátria: A History of the Brazilian Army, 1889–1937* (Stanford, Calif., 2004), p. 423; those of Vargas, in Frank D. McCann, *The Brazilian-American Alliance, 1937–1945* (Princeton, N.J., 1973), pp. 181–82.

12. McCann, *The Brazilian-American Alliance*, p. 185.

13. Welles to Franklin D. Roosevelt, June 12, 1940, *FRUS* (1940), 5:620.

14. Welles to Jesse Jones, August 7, 1940, *FRUS* (1940), 5:609–10; Welles to Aranha, tel., October 1, 1940, ibid., 5:614.

15. Memorandum by Marshall and Welles, June 17, 1941, *FRUS* (1941), 6:498–99. The need to address the vulnerability of northeastern Brazil had been recognized the previous year in late May 1940 when France was being overrun by German forces and the Roosevelt administration had hastily devised the "Pot of Gold" contingency plan to dispatch 100,000 U.S. troops to defend Brazil against a Nazi attack.

16. Radio Broadcast, May 31, 1941, cited in ibid., p. 499.

17. Pedro Aurélio de Góes Monteiro to Vargas, July 10, 1939, quoted in McCann, *Brazilian-American Alliance*, p. 140.

18. Caffery to Hull, tel., August 21, 1941, *FRUS* (1941), 6:511.

19. Caffery to Hull, tel., April 29, 1941, *FRUS* (1941), 6:532.

20. Caffery to Hull, tel., May 28, 1941, *FRUS* (1941), 6:496.

21. Of the total amount of $100 million, only $16 million was allocated to immediate purchases so that by the time of the attack on Pearl Harbor Brazil had received only a few searchlights and a token shipment of tanks and trucks. See Stetson Conn and Byron Fairchild, *The Framework of Hemisphere Defense: U.S. Army in World War II* (Washington D.C., 1960), p. 293. The terms were generous, but countries receiving Lend-Lease aid also made a financial contribution. In the agreement signed on March 3, 1942, Brazil undertook to pay 35 percent of the cost of material provided. See Dean Acheson to Harry S. Truman, May 14, 1946, *FRUS* (1946), 11:444–45.

22. Cordell Hull, *The Memoirs of Cordell Hull* (2 vols., New York, 1948), 2:1145.

23. Welles to Hull, tel., January 18, 1942, *FRUS* (1942), 6:633.

24. George C. Marshall to Welles, October 24, 1941, quoted in Conn and Fairchild, *Framework of Hemisphere Defense*, p. 296.

25. Welles to Caffery, tel., February 9, 1942, *FRUS* (1942), 5:642.

26. Vargas to Artur de Souza Costa, February 14, 1942, quoted in McCann, *Brazilian-American Alliance*, p. 262.

27. Caffery, February 6, 1943, quoted in McCann, *Brazilian-American Alliance*,

p. 269. Following the signing of the Washington Accords, American officials sought to aid the war effort by devising ways of promoting Brazil's long-term economic growth. A U.S. Technical Mission, headed by Morris L. Cooke, visited Brazil in 1942.

28. Nelson Rockefeller to Marshall, August 28, 1942, quoted in Elizabeth A. Cobbs, *The Rich Neighbor Policy: Rockefeller and Kaiser in Brazil* (New Haven, Conn., 1992), p. 40. On the activities of OCIAA see Gerald K. Haines, "Under the Eagle's Wing: The Franklin Roosevelt Administration Forges an American Hemisphere," *Diplomatic History* 1 (1977):379–88, and Antonio Pedro Tota, *O imperialismo sedutor: A americanização do Brasil na época do segunda guerra* (São Paulo, 2000).

29. After her first successes in Hollywood movies Miranda returned to Rio in 1940 and upset the audience at her homecoming show by greeting them in English and then singing the rumba "South American Way" from the movie of the same name, which was set not in Brazil but in Argentina. Miranda's evident "Americanization" elicited a hostile response. See Antonio Pedro Tota, "Seductive Imperialism: The Americanization of Brazil during World War II" in *Brazilian Perspective on the United States: Advancing U.S. Studies in Brazil,* ed. Paulo Sotero and Daniel Budny (Washington, D.C., 2007), pp.39–40.

30. See Bryan McCann, *Hello, Hello Brazil: Popular Music in the Making of Modern Brazil* (Durham, N.C., 2004), p. 138.

31. See Robert Stam, *Tropical Multiculturalism: A Comparative History of Race in Brazilian Cinema and Culture* (Durham, N.C., 1997), pp. 107–32.

32. Freyre's *Casa Grande e Senzala* was first published in 1933. An English translation, *The Masters and the Slaves*, appeared in 1946 and received much acclaim in the United States. Freyre's ideas were influenced by his travels in the United States and especially his study of the history of slavery and race relations in the states of the Deep South.

33. Vargas, speech dated September 7, 1942, quoted in R. A. Humphreys, *Latin America and the Second World War, 1942–1945* (London, 1982), p. 67.

34. Hull, *Memoirs,* 2:1423.

35. Caffery to Hull, no. 10509, March 22, 1943, *FRUS* (1943), 5: 623–24. Friction between Brazilian civilians and U.S. military personnel continued in the immediate postwar period. See Sonny B. Davis, *A Brotherhood of Arms: Brazil–United States Military Relations, 1945–1977* (Niwot, Colo., 1996), pp.80–81.

36. See R. A. Humphreys, *Latin America and the Second World War, 1939–1942* (London, 1981), p. 167.

37. Caffery to Hull, tel., January 30, 1943, *FRUS* (1943), 5: 656. Caffery to Roosevelt, February 9, 1943, quoted in McCann, *Brazilian-American Alliance*, pp. 309–10.

38. Rodrigues Alves, quoted in Gary Frank, *Struggle for Hegemony in South America: Argentina, Brazil and the United States during the Second World War* (Coral Gables, Fla., 1979), p. 41.

39. The title of a chapter in Hull, *Memoirs*, 2:1377–89.

40. Caffery to Hull, tel., July 13, 1944, *FRUS* (1944) 7: 585.

41. Humberto de Alencar Castello Branco, quoted in Frank D. McCann, "The Brazilian Army and the Problem of Mission, 1939–1964," *Journal of Latin American Studies* 12 (1980):118.

42. A Brazilian air squadron also served in the Italian campaign.

43. Laurence Duggan to Caffery, October 8, 1943, *FRUS* (1943), 5:643; Hull to Leahy, April 15, 1944, *FRUS* (1944), 7:566.

44. Duggan to Caffery, December 15, 1943, *FRUS* (1943), 5: 651.

45. *Diário da Noite* (Rio), July 19, 1944, quoted in McCann, *Brazilian-American Alliance*, p. 404.

46. Shortly after Brazil declared war on Germany, Adolf Hitler is alleged to have remarked that snakes would smoke cigars before Brazilians fought in Europe. The Febianos adopted the regimental insignia depicting "smoking cobras" as a mark of their pride and defiance.

47. General Edson de Figueiredo, quoted in Alfred Stepan, *The Military in Politics: Changing Patterns in Brazil* (Princeton, N.J., 1971), p. 242.

48. Brazil was not the first Latin American country to join the war. Mexico did this on May 22, 1942.

49. By officially remaining at war, Brazil could have continued use of Lend-Lease equipment. See Joseph Grew to Paul C. Daniels, tel., June 6, 1945, *FRUS* (1945), 9:627.

50. Adolf Berle Diary, September 29, October 1, 1945, quoted in Jordan A. Schwarz, *Liberal: Adolph A. Berle and the Vision of an American Era* (New York, 1986), p. 269. See also Stanley E. Hilton, "The Overthrow of Getúlio Vargas; Diplomatic Intervention, Defense of Democracy, or Political Retribution?" *Hispanic American Historical Review* 67 (1987): 23. A more celebrated example of American diplomatic intervention took place in Argentina when Spruille Braden attempted to influence Argentine voters not to elect Juan Perón in the 1946 presidential election.

51. Velloso to Washington, October 1, 1945, quoted in Hilton, "Overthrow of

Vargas," p, 27. Berle had actually met with Vargas the previous day and had shown the president a copy of his speech.

52. Memorandum by Pawley, April 2, 1948, *FRUS* (1948), 9:27–28.

6. The Cold War

1. William C. Cramer, March 18, 1963, quoted in Ruth Leacock, *Requiem for Revolution: The United States and Brazil, 1961–1969* (Kent, Ohio, 1990), p. 140.

2. Adolf Berle to Secretary of State, no. 2196, July 27, 1945, and no. 2186, July 26, 1945, *FRUS* (1945), 9:615,605.

3. Paul Daniels to Secretary of State, tel., December 28, 1945, *FRUS* (1945), 9: 621.

4. Memorandum by Department of State to the Brazilian Embassy, March 27, 1946, *FRUS* (1946), 11:487.

5. John Abbink to Secretary of State, March 17, 1949, FRUS (1949), 2:555. Abbink reported, "Expectations of a 'Marshall Plan' are no longer entertained in Brazil." Ibid., 2:560.

6. Memorandum by Harold Midkiff, May 26, 1949, *FRUS* (1949), 2:576.

7. Quoted in Robert H. Bates, *Open-Economy Politics: The Political Economy of the World Coffee Trade* (Princeton, N.J., 1997), p. 101. Controversy with the United States over the international price of coffee continued beyond 1949, but Brazil's pre-eminent ability to manipulate the market was undermined by increased competition in coffee production from Colombia, Central America, and Africa.

8. William Pawley to Daniel Braddock, December 16, 1946, *FRUS* (1946), 11:461.

9. George Marshall to U.S. Diplomatic Representatives, airgram, August 10, 1948, *FRUS* (1948): 9:327.

10. Memorandum by Dean Acheson, May 1, 1950, *FRUS* (1950), 2:760. Acheson visited Brazil for a week in July 1952 and described the country as "undisciplined, as full of energy as a colt, rich, vulgar, cultivated, poor, technically competent, naïve, administratively hopeless . . . I am in love with it." Quoted in Robert L. Beisner, *Dean Acheson: A Life in the Cold War* (New York, 2006), p. 574.

11. Getúlio Vargas, November 1950, quoted in Sonny B. Davis, *A Brotherhood of Arms: Brazil–United States Military Relations, 1945–1977* (Niwot, Colo., 1996), p. 122.

12. Edward Miller to Acheson, January 25, 1951, *FRUS* (1951), 2:1190.

13. Memorandum by Ivan White, February 6, 1951, FRUS (1951), 2:1191–92.

14. João Neves da Fontoura to Vargas, February 1951, quoted in Stanley E. Hilton, "The United States, Brazil, and the Cold War, 1945–1960: End of the Special Relationship," *Journal of American History* 68 (1981): 609.

15. Goés Monteiro to Osvaldo Aranha, July 30 and August 3, 1951, quoted in Moniz Bandeira, *Presença dos Estados Unidos no Brasil (dois séculos de história)* (Rio, 1978), p. 332.

16. Neves da Fontonia, quoted in ibid., p. 610, n. 41.

17. Memorandum by Walter Bedell Smith to NSC, November 20, 1953, *FRUS* (1953–54), 4:32.

18. Herschel Johnson to State Department, tel., March 11 and May 9, 1952, *FRUS* (1952–54), 4:573, 576.

19. Memorandum by Thomas Mann for Secretary of State, February 20, 1953, *FRUS* (1952–54), 4:607–8; Minutes of the Secretary's Staff Meeting, February 24, 1953, ibid., 4:609.

20. Dwight D. Eisenhower, *The White House Years*, vol. 1: *Mandate for Change, 1953–1956* (Garden City, N.Y., 1963), p. 420.

21. The Eisenhower administration did attempt to promote a positive image of the United States in the Brazilian media. The United States Information Agency was particularly concerned to counter the view that racial prejudice and crime were widespread features of American society. See Gerald K. Haines, *The Americanization of Brazil: A Study of U.S. Cold War Diplomacy in the Third World, 1945–1954* (Wilmington, Del., 1989), pp. 170–73.

22. Sterling Cottrell, March 9, 1953, quoted in Haines, *Americanization of Brazil*, p. 120.

23. Milton Eisenhower, *The Wine Is Bitter: The United States and Latin America* (Garden City, N.Y., 1963), p. 152.

24. Letter by Vargas, quoted in E. Bradford Burns, ed., *A Documentary History of Brazil* (New York, 1966), pp. 370–71.

25. Memorandum from Cottrell to Roland Atwood, January 28, 1955, *FRUS* (1955–57), 7:639.

26. James Dunn to State Department, tel., October 19, 1955, *FRUS* (1955–57), 7:678.

27. Memorandum, January 6, 1956, *FRUS* (1955–57), 7:686–87. After his visit to the United States Kubitschek traveled to Western Europe.

28. Dunn to State Department, tel., July 3, 1956, *FRUS* (1955–57), 7:711.

29. John Foster Dulles to American Embassy in Brazil, tel. March 3, 1958, *FRUS* (1958–60), 5:663.

30. Dwight Eisenhower to Juscelino Kubitschek de Oliveira, May 8, 1956, quoted in Hilton, "The United States, Brazil and the Cold War," p. 618.

31. Memorandum by Allen Dulles to John Foster Dulles, May 27, 1958, *FRUS* (1958–60), 5:253.

32. *Time*, "Operation Pan American," June 30, 1958.

33. State Department memorandum, August 5, 1958, *FRUS* (1958–60), 5:699; Memorandum from Mann to Douglas Dillon, January 26, 1959, ibid., 5:708–9.

34. Kubitschek, speech dated June 27, 1959, quoted in Thomas E. Skidmore, *Politics in Brazil, 1930–1964: An Experiment in Democracy* (New York, 1967) p. 181. Brazil still remained a member of the IMF. The transaction of substantive diplomatic business between Washington and Rio was "paralyzed" for some weeks in 1959 as the Eisenhower administration sought to accommodate Clare Boothe Luce's wish to become the new U.S. ambassador to Brazil. Her nomination was vigorously opposed by Senator Wayne Morse, and the resulting clash became a public spectacle. Luce was the wife of Henry Luce, the owner of *Time/Life*. See Ellis O. Briggs, *Proud Servant: The Memoirs of a Career Ambassador* (Kent, Ohio, 1998), p. 364, and "The Compromised Mission," *Time*, May 11, 1959.

35. Philip Raine to State Department, April 20, 1960, *FRUS* (1958–60), 5:771–2.

36. John Moors Cabot, quoted in Stephen M. Streeter, "Campaigning against Latin American Nationalism: U.S. Ambassador John Moors Cabot in Brazil, 1959–1961," *Americas* 51 (1994): 208, n. 64.

37. John F. Kennedy, quoted in Stephen G. Rabe, *The Most Dangerous Area in the World: John F. Kennedy Confronts Communist Revolution in Latin America* (Chapel Hill, N.C., 1999), p. 19. The sense of urgency was reflected during the transition period before Kennedy officially became president when he set up a Latin American Task Force headed by the former ambassador to Brazil, Adolf Berle, to make a study of current conditions in Latin America and formulate policy recommendations. The task force included Lincoln Gordon, a professor of economics at Harvard University, who later served as U.S. ambassador to Brazil from 1961 to 1966.

38. Cabot to State Department, tel., October 7, 1960, *FRUS* (1958–60), 5:790.

39. Dean Rusk to American Embassy in Brazil, tel. February 3, 1961, *FRUS* (1961–63), 12:424.

40. Raine to State Department, December 13, 1960, *FRUS* (1958–60), 5:794–96.

41. Cabot to State Department, tel., March 3, 1961, *FRUS* (1961–63), 12:426–67.

42. Berle, quoted in W. Michael Weis, *Cold Warriors and Coups D'État: Brazilian-American Relations, 1945–1964* (Albuquerque, N.M., 1993), p. 146.

43. Memorandum from Wimberley Coerr to Chester Bowles, May 14, 1961, *FRUS* (1961–63): 12:434.

44. Niles Bond to State Department, tel., May 31, 1961, *FRUS* (1961–63), 12:437–38.

45. Rusk to American Embassy in Brazil, tel., February 3, 1961, *FRUS* (1961–63), 12:426.

46. Arthur M. Schlesinger Jr., *A Thousand Days: John F. Kennedy in the White House* (London, 1965), p. 163.

47. Riordan Roett, *The Politics of Foreign Aid in the Brazilian Northeast* (Nashville, Tenn., 1972), pp.82–86. The agreement that followed from the Bohan Report was signed by Kennedy and Goulart in April 1962.

48. National Intelligence Estimate, August 8, 1961, *FRUS* (1961–63), 12:442.

49. Special National Intelligence Estimate, December 7, 1961, *FRUS* (1961–63), 12:453–54.

50. Lincoln Gordon to State Department, tel., October 21, 1961, *FRUS* (1961–63), 12:449.

51. DeLesseps S. Morrison, *Latin American Mission: An Adventure in Hemisphere Diplomacy* (New York, 1965), p. 169.

52. On the use of Brazil as an intermediary between Kennedy and Castro see James G. Hershberg, "The United States, Brazil, and the Cuban Missile Crisis, 1962 (Parts 1 and 2)," *Journal of Cold War Studies* 6, no. 2 (2004):3–20, 6, no. 3 (2004): 5–67.

53. Report from the Inter-Departmental Survey Team on Brazil to Kennedy, November 3, 1962, FRUS (1961–63), 12:472–75.

54. Robert F. Kennedy, quoted in Leacock, *Requiem for Revolution*, p. 137. See also *Time*, "A Kennedy Comes Calling," December 28, 1962. In a reference to the notorious American organized labor leader, Robert Kennedy famously said that he took a dislike to Goulart because he looked "like a Brazilian Jimmy Hoffa." See Arthur M. Schlesinger Jr., *Robert Kennedy and His Times* (London, 1978), p. 628.

55. State Department Policy Paper, September 30, 1963, *FRUS* (1961–63), 12:509, 512.

56. Memorandum from Gordon Chase to McGeorge Bundy, March 19, 1964, *FRUS* (1964–68), 31:408–9.
57. Gordon to State Department, tel., March 26, 1964, *FRUS* (1964–68), 31:411.
58. Castelo Branco, 20 March 1963, quoted in Luiz Alberto Moniz Bandeira, *O governo João Goulart: As lutas sociais no Brasil, 1961–1964* (Rio, 2001), p. 167.
59. Gordon to State Department, tel., March 28, 1964, *FRUS* (1964–68), 31:412–18.
60. *Washington Post*, March 8, 1977; Vernon A. Walters, *Silent Missions* (Garden City, N.Y., 1978), pp. 386–87; Gordon to State Department, tel., March 28, 1964, *FRUS* (1964–68), 31:416.
61. Bundy, Memorandum, March 28, 1964, *FRUS* (1964–68), 31:419.
62. Rusk to American Embassy in Rio, tel., March 31, 1964, *FRUS* (1964–68), 31:434.
63. Carlos Lacerda, quoted in Moniz Bandeira, *O governo João Goulart*, p. 173.
64. Acting Secretary of State George Ball later explained that he had sent the telegram at 3 a.m. without Johnson's knowledge. When he later heard about the telegram, Johnson was furious with Ball for not informing him. See "Editorial Note," *FRUS* (1964–68), 31:448.

7. The Rise and Fall of Military Government

1. The Foreign Affairs Oral History Collection of the Association for Diplomatic Studies and Training, Interview with Harry W. Shlaudeman, May 24, 1993, p. 21.
2. Lincoln Gordon, quoted in Thomas E. Skidmore, *The Politics of Military Rule in Brazil, 1964–85* (New York, 1988), p. 28.
3. *U.S. News and World Report*, April 21 and May 27, 1964, quoted in W. Michael Weis, "Government News Management, Bias and Distortion in American Press Coverage of the Brazilian Coup of 1964," *Social Science Journal* 34 (1997):44.
4. *O Estado de São Paulo*, June 9, 1964, quoted in John W. F. Dulles, *President Castello Branco: Brazilian Reformer* (College Station, Tex., 1980), p. 39. "The Kubitschek thing is bad," remarked Assistant Secretary of State Thomas Mann, adding, "we are urging them [Brazilian Government] to set up an appeals procedure for Kubitschek and all of the others, so they'll have a chance to be, for their day in court, to be heard." Telephone Conversation between Johnson and Mann, June 11, 1964, *FRUS* (1963–68), 31:45.

5. *New Republic*, May 2, 1964, quoted in Weis, "Government News Management," p. 47.

6. *Washington Post*, May 3, 1964.

7. Vernon A. Walters, *Silent Missions* (Garden City, N.Y., 1978) p. 390.

8. Gordon to State Department, tel., April 7, 1964, *FRUS* (1963–68), 31:460.

9. Gordon to State Department, tel., April 10, 1964, *FRUS* (1963–68), 31:462. At one point Gordon was so depressed that he considered resigning his ambassadorial post.

10. Gordon to State Department, tel., April 10, 1964, *FRUS* (1963–68), 31:463; April 20, 1964, 31:450; June 10, 1964, 31:470.

11. Gordon to State Department, tel., October 27, 1965, *FRUS* (1964–68), 31:486.

12. Dean Rusk to U.S. Embassy in Brazil, November 7, 1965, *FRUS* (1964–68), 31:494.

13. Rusk to U.S. Embassy in Brazil, November 7, 1965, *FRUS* (1964–68), 31:494 and November 14, 1965, 31:495.

14. National Intelligence Estimate, "The Outlook for Brazil," August 18, 1966, *FRUS* (1964–68), 31:505.

15. Rusk to U.S. Embassy in Brazil, December 19, 1968, *FRUS* (1964–68), 31:530, and December 25, 1968, 31:535.

16. John Tuthill to State Department, tel., December 28, 1968, *FRUS* (1964–68), 31:538.

17. *O Estado do São Paulo*, April 21, 1964, quoted in Dulles, *Castello Branco*, p. 22.

18. *Wall Street Journal*, April 9, 1964, quoted in Weis, "Government News Management," p. 49.

19. Memorandum by Rusk to Lyndon B. Johnson, December 3, 1965, *FRUS* (1964–68), 31:499.

20. John W. Tuthill, "Operation Topsy," *Foreign Policy* 8 (1972): 62, 67.

21. Golbery do Couto e Silva, quoted in Carlos Estevam Martins, "Brazil and the United States from the 1960s to the 1970s," in *Latin America and the United States: The Changing Political Realities*, ed. Julio Cotler and Richard R. Fagen (Stanford, Calif., 1974), p. 280. For the geopolitical idea that Brazil should cooperate with the United States by acting as the "aircraft carrier of the Northeast," see General Golbery do Couto e Silva, *Geopolítica do Brasil* (Rio, 1967), pp. 137–38.

22. Juracy Magalhães, quoted in Robert Wesson, *The United States and Brazil: Limits of Influence* (New York, 1981), p. 51. The statement caused embarrass-

ment and controversy. See Juracy Magalhães, *Minha experiência diplomática* (Rio, 1971), p. 275.

23. Telephone Conversation between Lyndon B. Johnson and Thomas Mann, June 11, 1964, *FRUS* (1963–68), 31:45.

24. Gordon to Mann, August 10, 1964, *FRUS*, 1964–68, 31:478.

25. Walters, *Silent Missions*, p. 401.

26. Gordon to State Department, tel., December 12, 1965, *FRUS* (1964–68), 31:503, n. 2.

27. The escalation of the war in Vietnam by the United States stimulated the growth of anti-Americanism in Brazil, especially among left-wing university students. The image of the United States as a model democracy was also damaged by the widely held perception that U.S. officials approved and supported the continuation of military government in Brazil.

28. Memorandum from Walt Rostow to Lyndon B. Johnson, June 14, 1967, *FRUS* (1964–68), 31:509; Tuthill, "Operation Topsy," 67.

29. Memorandum from Rostow to Johnson, June 14, 1967, *FRUS* (1964–68), 31:510.

30. José de Magalhâes Pinto, quoted in J. Jon Rosenbaum, "Brazil's Foreign Policy: Developmentalism and Beyond," *Orbis* 16 (1972):63.

31. Novais de Oliveira, quoted in Ronald M. Schneider, *Brazil: Foreign Policy of a Future World Power* (Boulder, Colo., 1976), p. 32. In a country whose society is fanatical about soccer (*futebol*), Brazilian national pride was greatly boosted by the success of the national team in winning the World Cup in Mexico City in 1970. This was particularly pleasing because Brazil was the first country to win the cup on three separate occasions. Brazilians were also delighted by the international fame acquired by the outstanding black soccer player Edson Arantes do Nascimento, better known as "Pelé."

32. Emilío Garrastazú Médici, quoted in Skidmore, *Politics of Military Rule*, p. 146.

33. Henry Kissinger, quoted in Hal Brands, "Third World Politics in an Age of Global Turmoil: The Latin American Challenge to U.S. and Western Hegemony, 1965–1975," *Diplomatic History* 32 (2008): 130.

34. Richard M. Nixon, quoted in Jan Knippers Black, *United States Penetration of Brazil* (Philadelphia, Pa., 1977), p. 55. Nixon and Médici discussed the overthrow of Allende during their private meeting at the White House. A secret back channel was also set up to maintain communications between both presidents. See White House memorandum, December 9, 1971, National Security

Archive Electronic Briefing Book no. 282 at http://www.gwu.edu/~nsarchiv/ NSAEBB/. In February 1976 Secretary of State Henry Kissinger and Foreign Minister Antônio Azeredo da Silveira of Brazil signed a memorandum of understanding to include semi-annual meetings of foreign ministers — only Saudi Arabia had such an arrangement with the United States. For the view that the concept proved to be "a flawed device from the start," see Albert Fishlow, "Flying Down to Rio: Perspectives on U.S.-Brazil Relations," *Foreign Affairs* 57 (1978–79):399.

35. Ernesto Geisel, quoted in Moniz Bandeira, *Relações Brasil-EUA no contexto globalização, II, Rivalidade Emergente* (São Paulo, 1977), p. 126.

36. *Guardian* (London), September 6, 1972.

37. Edward Kennedy, quoted in Kathryn Sikkink, *Mixed Signals: U.S. Human Rights Policy and Latin America* (Ithaca, N.Y., 2004), p. 58.

38. William Roundtree, quoted in James N. Green, "Clerics, Exiles, and Academics: Opposition to the Brazilian Military Dictatorship in the United States," *Latin American Politics and Society* 45 (2003): 103.

39. William J. Fulbright, quoted in Martha K. Huggins, *Political Policing: The United States and Latin America* (Durham, N.C., 1998), p. 161.

40. Quoted in Green, "Clerics, Exiles, and Academics," p. 89.

41. The State Department did not mention the secret activities of "Operation Condor," which involved cooperation between the military intelligence services of Brazil, Argentina, Chile, Uruguay, Paraguay, and Bolivia in assassinating several thousand alleged left-wing political dissidents.

42. Another indication of the extent of the annoyance of the Geisel administration was its decision to bring an end to the activities of the Peace Corps in Brazil. Several hundred Peace Corps volunteers had been assigned to Brazil from 1961 onward, but the number had been greatly reduced during the 1970s.

43. *New York Times*, April 26, 1977.

44. *Guardian* (London), February 3, 1977; "Whirling through the Third World," *Time*, April 10, 1978.

45. *New York Times*, January 17, 1980.

46. The Foreign Affairs Oral History Collection of the Association for Diplomatic Studies and Training, Interview with Langhorne A. Motley, March 7, 1991, p. 19. Motley was U.S. ambassador from 1981 to 1983.

47. U.S. anxieties over the nuclear deal with Germany had been relieved by the fact that implementation of the program proved difficult for technical reasons

and a shortage of funds caused by the Debt Crisis. No new reactors were actually completed in Brazil until 1995.

48. Foreign Affairs Oral History Collection, Interview with Langhorne Motley, p. 7. Ironically, it could be argued that Carter's championing of human rights had actually given encouragement to the opponents of the military government and thereby contributed to the success of *abertura* in Brazil.

49. José Sarney, "Brazil: A President's Story," *Foreign Affairs* 65 (1986): 115.

50. Ramiro Saraiva Guerreiro, August 31, 1984, quoted in Carlos Federico Domínguez Avila, "O Brasil Frente ao Conflito Regional na America Central: Oposição ao Intervencionismo e Apoio à Solução Negociada, Justa, Equilibrada e Duradoura (1979–1996)," *Revista Brasileira de Política Internacional* 46, no. 1 (2003): 77.

51. Sarney, "Brazil: A President's Story," p. 115.

52. *New York Times*, September 8, 1990. Brazil also sold weapons to Iraq and had sent a technical mission to modernize that country's air-to-air missile defenses. In marked contrast to Argentina, Brazil declined to cooperate militarily with the United States in the 1991 Persian Gulf War.

53. Antônio Delfim Neto, quoted in Eul-Soo Pang, "Brazil and the United States," in John D. Martz, ed., *United States Policy in Latin America: A Decade of Crisis and Challenge4*(Lincoln, Neb., 1995), p. 144.

54. "Brazil's Tomorrow Is Finally in Sight," *Fortune*, September 1986.

55. William D. Rogers, "The United States and Latin America," *Foreign Affairs* 63 (1984): 578. When President George H. W. Bush visited Brazil in December 1990, he disappointed Brazilian officials by implying that the renegotiation of the country's foreign debt was "a private affair between Brazil and the banks." *New York Times*, December 5, 1990.

56. Saraivo Guerreiro, October 1, 1984, quoted in Riordan Roett, "Brazil and the United States: Beyond the Debt Crisis," *Journal of Inter-American Studies* 27 (1985): 9.

57. *Washington Post*, July 16, 1981.

58. In the South Atlantic War between Great Britain and Argentina in 1982, Brazil remained officially neutral but secretly favored Argentina. Brazil recognized Argentina's claim for sovereignty over the islands.

59. *New York Times*, March 15, 1990.

60. *New York Times*, December 4, 1990.

61. Luiz Felipe Lampreia, quoted in *New York Times*, September 18, 1997.

62. Brazil has also been an active participant in the global trade negotiations organized under the auspices of the World Trade Organization.
63. See Luiz Alberto Moniz Bandeira, *Conflito e Intergração na América do Sul: Brasil, Argentina e Estados Unidos: Da Tríplice Aliança ao Mercosul, 1870–2003* (Rio, 2003), p. 507.

Epilogue

1. Melvyn Levitsky, quoted in the *New York Times*, October 10, 1994; *New York Times*, April 17, 1995.
2. Ibid., October 9, 1994.
3. Ibid., October 15, 1997.
4. Bill Clinton, quoted in David Scott Palmer, *U.S. Relations with Latin America during the Clinton Years* (Gainesville, Fla., 2006), p. 42.
5. Fernando Henrique Cardoso, *The Accidental President of Brazil: A Memoir* (New York, 2006), p. 258.
6. Bill Clinton, *My Life* (New York, 2004), p. 766.
7. In July 1998 Brazil signed the 1968 Nuclear Non-Proliferation Treaty and joined with Argentina in advocating a ban on the development of nuclear weapons in South America.
8. *Washington Post*, August 6, 2000.
9. Cardoso, *Accidental President*, p. 260. Bush evidently knew very little about Brazil. At the meeting Cardoso remarked that Brazil possessed one of the largest populations of black people in the world, which drew the question from Bush: "Do you have blacks in Brazil?" Ibid.
10. *New York Times*, December 3, 2002.
11. *Folha de São Paulo*, September 24, 2002, quoted in Moniz Bandeira, *As Relações Perigosas: Brasil-Estados Unidos (De Collor à Lula, 1990–2004)* (Rio, 2004), p. 284.
12. Henry J. Hyde, October 24, 2002, quoted in ibid., p. 285.
13. *New York Times*, December 11, 2002.
14. Luiz Felipe Lampreia, quoted in *New York Times*, December 5, 2004. President Lula argued that military forces should be employed as a means of securing peace not fomenting war. This was demonstrated in 2004 by his sending a contingent of 1,200 Brazilian troops to take on the leading role in UN peacekeeping activities in Haiti.

15. Cardoso, *Accidental President*, p. 260. Brazilians were annoyed that the Bush administration took more than a year to appoint a new U.S. ambassador to Brazil after the departure of Anthony Harrington in February 2001.

16. *New York Times*, November 10, 2003.

17. Ibid., March 6, 2007.

18. See remarks of Eliot E. Engel, "U.S.-Brazil Relations," Hearing before the Subcommittee on the Western Hemisphere, Committee on Foreign Affairs, House of Representatives, September 19, 2007, p. 1.

19. *Guardian* (London), March 10, 2007. Another development of historic significance is the influx of Brazilians into the United States. From the 1980s onward increasing numbers of Brazilians have been drawn to the United States either as affluent tourists, especially for shopping sprees in New York or the attractions of Disney World in Florida, or as immigrants seeking employment and advancement. U.S. Census reports revealed that less than 100,000 Brazilians were resident in 1990 and estimated that this figure had risen to 350,000 by 2006. The number did not take into account those Brazilians who were living in the United States illegally. See *New York Times*, September 1, 2008.

20. In 2009 President Lula cast his net of criticism more widely when he famously blamed the current world economic crisis on financial mistakes made by "white people with blue eyes." See *New York Times*, April 3, 2009.

21. November 6, 2005, quoted in Russell C. Crandall, *The United States and Latin America after the Cold War* (New York, 2008), p. 160.

Bibliographical Essay

There are many works on the history of U.S. relations with Latin America, but relatively few specifically deal with bilateral relations between the United States and Brazil. For a long time the only single-volume study was Lawrence F. Hill, *Diplomatic Relations between the United States and Brazil* (Durham, N.C., 1932), a fine example of traditional diplomatic history that concentrated on relations during the nineteenth century and ended at the beginning of the twentieth century. The more recent studies by Roger W. Fontaine, *Brazil and the United States* (Washington D.C., 1974), Robert G. Wesson, *The United States and Brazil: Limits of Influence* (New York, 1981), and Mônica Hirst, *The United States and Brazil: A Long Road of Unmet Expectations* (New York, 2005), briefly mention the historical background and then focus their attention on analyzing events dating from the 1960s. The subtitles of the last two works convey their major themes of a relationship characterized on both sides by constraints and disappointment. Lincoln Gordon, *Brazil's Second Chance: En Route toward the First World* (Washington D.C., 2001) is mainly concerned with Brazil's future development as a world power but mentions U.S.-Brazilian relations in the chapter "Brazil and the World," pp. 194–220. An important resource that provides a selection of historical documents in digital form is *The United States and Brazil: Expanding Frontiers, Comparing Cultures*, a collaborative project between the U.S. Library of Congress and the Biblioteca Nacional that can be accessed at http://international.loc.gov/intldl/brhtml/brhome.html.

A reliable work on the history of Brazilian foreign policy is Amado Luiz Cervo and Clodoaldo Bueno, *História da política exterior do Brasil* (Brasília, 2002). The foremost historical study of U.S.-Brazilian relations by a Brazilian scholar is Luiz Alberto Moniz Bandeira, *Presença dos Estados Unidos no Brasil* (Rio, 2007, first published in 1978), which provides considerable factual detail on diplomatic exchanges and stresses the importance of economic factors in promoting a conflicting relationship between the two countries. See also the same author's *Conflito e integração na América do Sul: Brasil, Argentina e Estados Unidos (da tríplice aliança ao Mercosul)* (Rio, 2003), and "Brazil as a Regional Power and Its Relations with the United States," *Latin American Perspectives* 33 (2007): 12–27. A brief and perceptive historical overview of Brazilian attitudes toward the United States is Thomas

E. Skidmore, "Brazil's American Illusion: From Dom Pedro to the Coup of 1964," *Luso-Brazilian Review* 23 (1986): 71–84.

Basic factual information on diplomatic relations during the period of the empire is presented very clearly in Hill, *Diplomatic Relations*. A short study of the first U.S. minister to serve in Rio is Phil Brian Johnson and Robert Kim Stevens, "Impossible Job, Impossible Man! Thomas Sumter, Jr., and Diplomatic Relations between the United States and the Portuguese Court in Brazil, 1809–1821," in *United States–Latin American Relations, 1800–1850: The Formative Generations*, ed. T. Ray Shurbutt (Tuscaloosa, Ala., 1991), pp. 86–101. Caitlin A. Fitz, "'A Stalwart Motor of Revolutions': An American Merchant in Pernambuco, 1817–1825," *Americas* 65 (2008): 35–62, is a detailed case study. The diplomacy leading up to U.S. recognition of the empire in 1824 is expertly analyzed in Stanley E. Hilton, "The United States and Brazilian Independence," in *From Colony to Nation: Essays on the Independence of Brazil*, ed. A. J. R. Russell-Wood (Baltimore, 1975), 109–29. On the diplomatic mission of the first Brazilian minister to the United States see Arthur P. Whitaker, "José Silvestre Rebello: The First Diplomatic Representative of Brazil in the United States," *Hispanic American Historical Review* 20 (1940): 380–401. Ron Seckinger, *The Brazilian Monarchy and the South American Republics, 1822–1831: Diplomacy and State Building* (Baton Rouge, La., 1984), is an excellent study that places Brazil's diplomacy in its regional and international context. The important theme of Anglo-American rivalry in nineteenth-century Brazil is examined in Alan K. Manchester, *British Preeminence in Brazil: Its Rise and Decline* (Chapel Hill, N.C., 1933), Richard Graham, *Britain and the Onset of Modernization in Brazil, 1850–1914* (Cambridge, England, 1968), and Antonia Fernanda Pacca de Almeida Wright, *Desafio americano à preponderância britânica no Brasil, 1808–1850* (São Paulo, 1978). These studies, however, emphasize the much more significant role of Great Britain in terms of political, economic, and cultural influence.

Few Americans traveled to Brazil during the nineteenth century. Among the best-known accounts are Daniel P. Kidder and James C. Fletcher, *Brazil and Brazilians Portrayed in Historical and Descriptive Sketches* (Philadelphia, 1857), Professor and Mrs. Louis Agassiz, *A Journey in Brazil* (Boston, 1868), and Thomas Ewbank, *Life in Brazil* (New York, 1856). William Clark Griggs, *The Elusive Eden: Frank McMullan's Confederate Colony in Brazil* (Austin, Tex., 1987), and Cyrus B. Dawsey and James M. Dawsey, eds., *The Confederados: Old South Immigrants in Brazil* (Tuscaloosa, Ala., 1995), recount the many difficulties that ex-Confederates found in trying to establish settlements. Views of American travelers on slavery in Brazil are collected in Manoel Cardozo, "Slavery in Brazil as Described by

Americans, 1822–1888," *Americas* 17 (1961): 241–60. The celebrated work comparing the history of race relations in the United States and Brazil is Carl N. Degler, *Neither Black nor White: Slavery and Race Relations in Brazil and the United States* (New York, 1971). Another excellent study that analyzes Brazilian views on race is Thomas E. Skidmore, *Black into White: Race and Nationality in Brazilian Thought* (New York, 1974). Gerald Horne, *The Deepest South: The United States, Brazil, and the African Slave Trade* (New York, 2007), reveals the participation of Americans in the operation of the Atlantic slave trade. The diplomatic controversy over suppressing the trade is examined in Hugh G. Soulsby, *The Right of Search and the Slave Trade in Anglo-American Relations, 1814–1862* (Baltimore, 1933).

A readable account of Dom Pedro's visit to the United States in 1876 is John H. Williams, "Brazil's Most Curious Monarch," *Americas* 36 (1984): 20–29. On diplomatic relations between the United States and the "Old" Republic see Joseph Smith, *Unequal Giants: Diplomatic Relations between the United States and Brazil, 1889–1930* (Pittsburgh, 1991). Steven C. Topik, *Trade and Gunboats: The United States and Brazil in the Age of Empire* (Stanford, Calif., 1996) and Joseph Smith, "Limits of Diplomatic Influence: Brazil versus Britain and the United States, 1886–1894," *History* 92 (2007): 472–95, are the latest works to cover the diplomatic issues of the 1890s involving recognition of the republic, reciprocity treaties, and the Naval Revolt. Walter LaFeber, "United States Depression Diplomacy and the Brazilian Revolution, 1893–1894," *Hispanic American Historical Review* 40 (1960): 107–18, stresses the importance of economic factors. For the views of Brazilian scholars on the Naval Revolt see Sergio Corrêa da Costa, *A diplomacia do marechal: Intervenção estrangeira na revolta da armada* (Rio, 1979), and Clodoaldo Bueno, "A diplomacia da 'Consolidação': A intervenção estrangeira na revolta da armada (1893/94)," *História* 3 (1984): 33–52. Salvador de Mendonça's diplomatic activities are outlined in Carlos Süssekind de Mendonça, *Salvador de Mendonça: Democrata do Império e da República* (Rio, 1960), and José Afonso Mendonça Azevedo, *Vida e obra de Salvador de Mendonça* (Rio, 1971).

The diplomacy of Rio Branco has deservedly attracted great interest. E. Bradford Burns, *The Unwritten Alliance: Rio-Branco and Brazilian American Relations* (New York, 1966) is the standard work on the baron and the policy of seeking approximation with the United States. Rubens Ricupero, *Rio Branco: O Brasil no mundo* (Rio, 2000), highlights the baron's diplomatic legacy. Based on a conference celebrating the centenary of Rio Branco assuming the office of foreign minister, *Rio Branco, a America do Sul e a modernização do Brasil*, ed. Carlos Henrique Cardim and João Almino (Brasília, 2002), contains a wide-ranging collection of articles on the baron's diplomacy, including Steven C. Topik, "O Barão do Rio Branco e a aliança com os Estados Unidos," pp. 407–33. Clodoaldo Bueno, *Política externa da primeira república: Os anos de apogeu — de 1902 a 1918* (São Paulo, 2003), is an excellent analysis of the diplomacy of the period. Useful information on the Acre question is found in Lewis A. Tambs, "Rubber, Rebels, and Rio Branco," *Hispanic American Historical Review* 66 (1966): 254–73, and Frederic W. Ganzert, "The Boundary Controversy in the Upper Amazon between Brazil, Bolivia, and Peru, 1903–1909," *Hispanic American Historical Review* 14 (1934): 427–49. A. Curtis Wilgus, "The Third International American Conference at Rio de Janeiro, 1906," *Hispanic American Historical Review* 12 (1932): 420–56, considers the high point of approximation and is informative but dated. On Joaquim Nabuco see Carolina Nabuco, *The Life of Joaquim Nabuco*, trans. Ronald Hilton (Stanford, Calif., 1950), and João Frank da Costa, *Joaquim Nabuco e a política exterior do Brasil* (Rio, 1968). Thomas H. Holloway, *The Brazilian Coffee Valorization of 1906* (Madison, Wis., 1975), explains the reasons for the policy of valorization, while Leon F. Sensabaugh, "The Coffee-Trust Question in United States-Brazilian Relations: 1912–1913," *Hispanic American Historical Review* 26 (1946): 480–96, competently examines the dispute.

For Brazilian diplomacy toward World War I see the chapter titled "Brazil and the War" in Percy A. Martin, *Latin America and the War* (Baltimore, 1925), pp. 30–106, and Francisco Luiz Teixeira Vinhosa, *O Brasil e a primeira guerra mundial* (Rio, 1990). The change in U.S. attitudes toward Brazil and its role in World War I is explained in David Healy, "Admiral William B. Caperton and United States Naval Diplomacy in South America, 1917–1919," *Journal of Latin American Studies* 8 (1976): 297–323. Joseph Smith, "American Diplomacy and the Naval Mission to Brazil, 1917–30," *Inter-American Economic Affairs* 35 (1981): 73–91, considers the advance of U.S. naval influence that resulted in the winning of the contract to supply a postwar naval mission. Another example of the displacement of Great Britain's formerly pre-eminent influence during the early twentieth century was the rise of U.S. trade and investment, a development covered in Emily S. Rosenberg, "Anglo-American Economic Rivalry in Brazil during World War I," *Diplomatic History* 2 (1978): 131–52; Richard Downes, "Autos over Rails: How US Business Supplanted the British in Brazil, 1910–28," *Journal of Latin American Studies* 24 (1992); and Victor V. Valla, *A penetracão norte-americana na economia brasileira, 1898–1928* (Rio, 1978). Joseph S. Tulchin, *The Aftermath of War: World War I and U.S. Policy toward Latin America* (New York, 1971), includes Brazil but deals more broadly with U.S. economic foreign policy. Greg Grandin, *Fordlandia: The Rise and Fall of*

Henry Ford's Forgotten Jungle City (New York, 2009), tells the story of the disastrous American enterprise, while Warren Dean, *Brazil and the Struggle for Rubber: A Study in Environmental History* (New York, 1997), deals more broadly with the history of the rubber industry. Micol Seigel, *Uneven Encounters: Making Race and Nation in Brazil and the United States* (Durham, N.C., 2009), discusses Hoover and the valorization dispute and provides a fascinating study of U.S.-Brazilian cultural attitudes during the 1920s and 1930s. Brazil's diplomatic relations with the United States during the 1920s are examined in Smith, *Unequal Giants*, pp. 134–82, and are mentioned in Stanley E. Hilton, "Brazil and the Post-Versailles World: Elite Images and Foreign Policy Strategy, 1919–1929," *Journal of Latin American Studies* 12 (1980): 341–64, and Eugênio Vargas Garcia, "Antirevolutionary Diplomacy in Oligarchic Brazil, 1919–30," *Journal of Latin American Studies* 36 (2004): 771–96. The best account of Brazil's imbroglio with the League of Nations is Eugênio Vargas Garcia, *O Brasil e a Liga das Nações (1919–1926)* (Porto Alegre, 2000).

Relations during the period after the 1930 Revolution have attracted a good deal of attention from historians. An outstanding work on Brazil's diplomatic relations with the United States during the 1930s and how they were affected by the challenge posed by Germany is Stanley E. Hilton, *Brazil and the Great Powers, 1930–1939: The Politics of Trade Rivalry* (Austin, Tex., 1975). Allen F. Repko, "The Failure of Reciprocal Trade: United States–Germany Commercial Rivalry in Brazil, 1934–1940," *Mid-America* 60 (1978): 3–20, argues that U.S. policy was not successful in halting the German trade offensive. The pragmatic approach of Getúlio Vargas in exploiting the rivalry of the great powers for Brazil's benefit is perceptively analyzed in Gerson Moura, *Autonomia na dependencia: A política externa brasileira de 1935 a 1942* (Rio, 1980); Roberto Gambini, *O duplo jogo de Getúlio Vargas: Influência americana e alemão no Estado Novo* (São Paulo, 1977); and John D. Wirth, *The Politics of Brazilian Development, 1930–1954* (Stanford, Calif., 1970). For a lucid account of diplomatic events during World War II see the chapter "Brazil at War" in R. A. Humphreys, *Latin America and the Second World War, 1942–1945* (London, 1982), pp. 59–85. Frank D. McCann, *The Brazilian-American Alliance, 1937–1945* (Princeton, N.J., 1973), is an excellent study of U.S.-Brazilian wartime collaboration. The argument that Brazil's passivity resulted in a disadvantageous relationship with the United States is further amplified in Frank D. McCann, "Brazil, the United States, and World War II: A Commentary," *Diplomatic History* 3 (1979): 59–76, and is criticized in Stanley E. Hilton, "Brazilian Diplomacy and the Washington–Rio de Janeiro 'Axis' during the World War II Era," *Hispanic American Historical Review* 59 (1979): 201–31, with a "Critique" from McCann on pp. 692–701. Gary Frank,

Struggle for Hegemony in South America: Argentina, Brazil and the United States during the Second World War (Coral Gables, Fla., 1979), is a short study that underscores the significance of the triangular diplomatic relationship between Brazil, the United States, and Argentina. Stanley E. Hilton, "The Argentine Factor in Twentieth-Century Brazilian Foreign Policy Strategy," *Political Science Quarterly* 100 (1985): 27–51, and Rubens Ricupero, "O Brasil, a América Latina e os EUA desde 1930: 60 anos de uma relação triangular," in *Sessenta anos de política externa brasileira (1930–1990)*, ed. José Augusto Guilhon Albuquerque (São Paulo, 1996), 37–60, explore this theme in a wider historical context. The political and cultural impact of the United States on Brazil is examined in Gerson Moura, *Tio Sam chega ao Brasil: A penetração cultural americana* (São Paulo, 1985); Antonio Pedro Tota, *O imperialismo sedutor: A americanização do Brasil na época do segunda guerra* (São Paulo, 2000); and Sergio Miceli, *A desilusão americana: Relações acadêmicas entre Brasil e Estados Unidos* (São Paulo, 1990). For contemporary American views on Brazil in the early 1940s see Morris L. Cooke, *Brazil on the March: A Study in International Cooperation* (New York, 1944), which is the report of the U.S. Technical Mission that visited Brazil in 1942.

In the period immediately following World War II, Gerald K. Haines, *The Americanization of Brazil: A Study of U.S. Cold War Diplomacy in the Third World, 1945–1954* (Wilmington, Del., 1989), contends that U.S. policy sought to "Americanize" Brazil, while Elizabeth A. Cobbs, *The Rich Neighbor Policy: Rockefeller and Kaiser in Brazil* (New Haven, Conn., 1992), provides an illuminating study showing the growing impact of U.S. private investment as exemplified by Nelson Rockefeller and Henry Kaiser. Stanley E. Hilton, "The United States, Brazil, and the Cold War, 1945–1960: End of the Special Relationship," *Journal of American History* 68 (1981): 599–624, effectively argues that U.S. neglect and lack of sympathy for Brazil's economic problems brought about a steady decline of the close relationship that had been a feature of World War II. Contemporary criticism of Washington's misguided attitude on the merits of giving financial aid is contained in Simon G. Hanson, "Brazilian-American Relations: Case Study in American Foreign Policy," *Inter-American Economic Affairs* 5 (1952): 3–35. Sonny B. Davis, *A Brotherhood of Arms: Brazil-United States Military Relations, 1945–1977* (Niwot, Colo., 1996), points out that Brazil was disappointed at the lack of U.S. military assistance but that close ties were established between Brazilian and U.S. military personnel. On the role of the Brazilian military see Alfred Stepan, *The Military in Politics: Changing Patterns in Brazil* (Princeton, N.J., 1971). The constraints and tensions in Brazilian foreign policy are described in Mônica Hirst, *O pragmatismo impossível: A política externa do segundo governo Vargas (1951–1954)* (Rio, 1990), and Alexandra de Mello e Silva, *A política externa de JK: A Operação Pan-Americana* (Rio, 1992). Jânio Quadros, "Brazil's New Foreign Policy," *Foreign Affairs* 40 (1961): 19–27, gives an explanation of the "independent foreign policy" undertaken by his administration.

The theme of growing Brazilian disillusionment at the lack of U.S. diplomatic attention and financial assistance and its damaging effect on bilateral relations is lucidly explained in W. Michael Weis, *Cold Warriors and Coups D'État: Brazilian-American Relations, 1945–1964* (Albuquerque, N.M., 1993). Peter D. Bell, "Brazilian-American relations," in *Brazil in the Sixties*, ed. Riordan Roett (Nashville, Tenn., 1972), pp. 77–101, is a sound overview of the main issues in U.S.-Brazilian diplomatic relations during the 1960s. The growing U.S. interest in Brazilian affairs dating from the end of the Eisenhower administration is described in Stephen M. Streeter, "Campaigning against Latin American Nationalism: U.S. Ambassador John Moors Cabot in Brazil, 1959–1961," *Americas* 51 (1994): 193–218; and Ruth Leacock, "JFK, Business, and Brazil," *Hispanic American Historical Review* 59 (1979): 636–73. Riordan Roett, *The Politics of Foreign Aid in the Brazilian Northeast* (Nashville, Tenn., 1972), highlights not only the significance attached by Washington to the vulnerability of the northeastern region to Communist influence but also the practical difficulties of implementing aid programs. On the impact of the Alliance for Progress in Brazil see W. Michael Weis, "The Twilight of Pan-Americanism: The Alliance for Progress, Neo-Colonialism, and Non-Alignment in Brazil, 1961–1964," *International History Review* 23 (2001): 322–44, and the chapter "Brazil and the Alliance for Progress" in Jeffrey F. Taffet, *Foreign Aid as Foreign Policy: The Alliance for Progress in Latin America* (New York, 2007), pp. 95–122. Stephen G. Rabe, *The Most Dangerous Area in the World: John F. Kennedy Confronts Communist Revolution in Latin America* (Chapel Hill, N.C., 1999) shows that Washington identified Brazil as a key element in the Alliance for Progress. On Brazilian diplomacy and the Cuban Missile Crisis see James G. Hershberg, "The United States, Brazil, and the Cuban Missile Crisis, 1962 (Parts 1 and 2)," *Journal of Cold War Studies* 6, no. 2 (2004): 3–20, and 6, no. 3 (2004): 5–67.

The declassification of U.S. archival materials, especially in presidential libraries, has led to considerable historical research and writing on the degree of U.S. involvement in the 1964 coup. The existence of a covert U.S. role including contingency planning for "Operation Brother Sam" is affirmed in Phyllis R. Parker, *Brazil and the Quiet Intervention, 1964* (Austin, Tex., 1979); Ruth Leacock, *Requiem for Revolution: The United States and Brazil, 1961–1969* (Kent, Ohio, 1990); and Jan

Knippers Black, *United States Penetration of Brazil* (Philadelphia, 1977). The prominence of U.S. Ambassador Lincoln Gordon in both formulating and executing U.S. policy in Brazil is highlighted in Jan Knippers Black, "Lincoln Gordon and Brazil's Military Counterrevolution" in *Ambassadors in Foreign Policy: The Influence of Individuals on U.S. Latin American Policy*, ed. C. Neale Ronning and Albert P. Vannucci (New York, 1987), pp. 95–113. Lincoln Gordon, "U.S.-Brazilian Reprise," *Journal of Inter-American Studies and World Affairs* 32 (1990): 165–78, uses the opportunity to write a book review of Leacock's *Requiem for Revolution* to mount a robust defense of his ambassadorial record. Supportive comments are made in Vernon A. Walters, *Silent Missions* (Garden City, N.Y., 1978), which acknowledges the author's close personal ties with Brazilian military leaders but vigorously denies any active involvement in the execution of the coup.

W. Michael Weis, "Government News Management, Bias and Distortion in American Press Coverage of the Brazilian Coup of 1964," *Social Science Journal* 34 (1997): 35–55, reveals that U.S. officials were able to influence the U.S. media to interpret the 1964 coup as a signal victory for democracy in the Cold War. Andrew J. Kirkendall, "Kennedy Men and the Fate of the Alliance for Progress in LBJ Era Brazil and Chile," *Diplomacy and Statecraft* 18 (2007): 745–72, discusses Ambassador Lincoln Gordon's relations with the military government of Castelo Branco. The reasons for Brazil's participation in the Inter-American Peace Force that was sent to the Dominican Republic in 1965 are assessed in Ralph G. Santos, "Brazilian Foreign Policy and the Dominican Crisis: The Impact of History and Events," *Americas* 29 (1972): 62–77. On the "nationalist" foreign policy of the military governments see Paulo F. Vizentini, *A política externa do regime military brasileiro* (Porto Alegre, 1998); and Thomas E. Skidmore, *The Politics of Military Rule in Brazil, 1964–85* (New York, 1988). Albert Fishlow, "Flying Down to Rio: Perspectives on U.S.-Brazil Relations," *Foreign Affairs* 57 (1978/79): 388–405, considers the close relationship between the United States and the military government of Castelo Branco and how this had been damaged by U.S. neglect and misunderstanding. The controversy over nuclear proliferation is examined in William W. Lowrance, "Nuclear Futures for Sale: To Brazil from West Germany, 1975," *International Security* 1 (1976): 147–66; and Norman Gall, "Atoms for Brazil, Dangers for All," *Foreign Policy* 23 (1976): 155–201. James N. Green, "Clerics, Exiles, and Academics: Opposition to the Brazilian Military Dictatorship in the United States," *Latin American Politics and Society* 45 (2003): 87–117, shows that the military governments attracted growing criticism and condemnation in the United States as a result of revelations about the systematic use of torture. The role of

U.S. officials in training the torturers is exposed in Martha K. Huggins, *Political Policing: The United States and Latin America* (Durham, N.C., 1998).

For studies of U.S. relations with the New Republic, see the excellent analysis in Hirst, *The United States and Brazil.* Eul-Soo Pang, "Brazil and the United States," in *United States Policy in Latin America: A Decade of Crisis and Challenge,* ed. John D. Martz (Lincoln, Neb., 1995), pp. 144–83, deals specifically with the 1980s and how relations were affected by the Debt Crisis and controversy over trade issues. A sympathetic assessment of Brazil's plight is contained in Riordan Roett, "Brazil and the United States: Beyond the Debt Crisis," *Journal of Inter-American Studies and World Affairs* 27 (1985): 1–15. The chapter "Brazil: Ally or Rival?" in Russell C. Crandall, *The United States and Latin America: After the Cold War* (New York, 2008), pp. 145–61, is balanced and informative. Susan Kaufman Purcell, "The New U.S.-Brazil Relationship" in *Brazil under Cardoso,* ed. Susan Kaufman Purcell and Riordan Roett (Boulder, Colo., 1997), pp.89–102, sees an improvement in relations based on a convergence of U.S.-Brazilian interests as a result of the end of the Cold War. An alternative interpretation stressing the dangers of U.S. hegemony is Luiz Alberto Moniz Bandeira, *As Relações Perigosas: Brasil-Estados Unidos (De Collor à Lula, 1990–2004)* (Rio, 2004). For the views of leading Brazilian officials on their country's foreign policy see Amaury de Souza, *A agenda internacional do Brasil: A política externa brasileira de FHC a Lula* (São Paulo, 2009).

Index

CPSIA information can be obtained at www.ICGtesting.com
Printed in the USA
LVOW110823051111

253614LV00001B/63/P